FATHERS,

SONS,

AND DAUGHTERS

This *New Consciousness Reader*
is part of a new series of original
and classic writing by renowned experts on
leading-edge concepts in personal development,
psychology, spiritual growth, and healing.

Other books in this series include:

Dreamtime and Dreamwork
EDITED BY STANLEY KRIPPNER, PH.D.

Healers on Healing
EDITED BY RICHARD CARLSON, PH.D., AND BENJAMIN SHIELD

Meeting the Shadow
EDITED BY CONNIE ZWEIG
AND JEREMIAH ABRAMS

Mirrors of the Self
EDITED BY CHRISTINE DOWNING

Reclaiming the Inner Child
EDITED BY JEREMIAH ABRAMS

Spiritual Emergency
EDITED BY STANISLAV GROF, M.D., AND CHRISTINA GROF

To Be a Man
EDITED BY KEITH THOMPSON

To Be a Woman
EDITED BY CONNIE ZWEIG

What Survives?
EDITED BY GARY DOORE, PH.D.

SERIES EDITOR: CONNIE ZWEIG

FATHERS,

SONS,

AND DAUGHTERS

Exploring Fatherhood, Renewing the Bond

EDITED BY

CHARLES S. SCULL, Ph.D.

JEREMY P. TARCHER, INC.
Los Angeles

Library of Congress Cataloging in Publication Data

Fathers, sons, and daughters: exploring fatherhood, renewing the bond
/ edited by Charles S. Scull.
p.   cm.
ISBN 0-87477-681-3
1. Fatherhood. 2. Fathers and sons. 3. Fathers and daughters. I. Scull,
Charles S. (Charles Sohngew)
HQ756.F387   1992
306.874 ' 2—dc20   91-45075
                                                          CIP

Jeremy P. Tarcher, Inc.
5858 Wilshire Blvd., Suite 200
Los Angeles, CA 90036

Manufactured in the United States of America
10   9   8   7   6   5   4   3   2   1
First Edition

I dedicate this anthology to my two children:
my son, Alexander,
whose birth two years ago
initiated and gave substance to this project;
and my daughter, Siri,
who has blessed my fatherhood
with immeasurable beauty and happiness.

Contents

Acknowledgments

I wish to acknowledge those unheralded fathers who are doing the work every day. I feel gratitude not only to the contributors in this volume but also to those authors whose work has expanded our knowledge of the father but could not be included.

Special thanks to my wife, Julia, for tending the family garden in my absence, and for her heartfelt support of this project. I also wish to acknowledge my father. I hope he will retain enough sight to read this book once it is printed. If not, I'll read it to you, Pop.

I extend warmhearted gratitude to fellow anthologist Keith Thompson for his generosity in sharing with me some of the findings of his detective work. And particular thanks to Jeremiah Abrams for encouraging me to embark on this project, for his advice during our lunches overlooking Tomales Bay, and for setting a standard of excellence.

Thanks to literary agent Peter Beren for his assistance and confidence during the proposal stage.

I wish to acknowledge two editors at Jeremy P. Tarcher, Inc.: Rick Benzel, for his organizational assistance and his efforts in getting me to write more simply, and Connie Zweig, for her embodiment of the "conscious feminine," and for her invaluable midwifery prior to my submitting the final manuscript.

To others who touched me with their interest and helpfulness: I thank Gordon Clay, Martin Greenberg, David Giveans, Covey Cowan, Sanh Tolbert, Jay Gaynor, Brent MacKinnon, Henry Iasiello, and Jason.

I am grateful to Robert Bly, Robert Moore, and Michael Meade, whose work with men has been so inspirational.

Charles Scull

Prologue

Recently I stopped by a friend's house before he came home from work, and I couldn't keep myself from reading a note his wife had left on the kitchen counter. In her organized exit at dawn, she wrote: "Left early. Pick up Jake on your way home, help with his math, warm up the casserole, the washer is still leaking. I'll be home by eight. Is your men's group on for tomorrow night? Call me at work."

In a few simple words, this woman's note captured the changing image of fatherhood. Father the provider and father the fixer are familiar roles in our culture, so timeless that they seem carved in stone. But fathers leaving work early to transport and help sons with homework, fathers warming up dinner, attending a men's group, calling *her* at the office—these novel roles add up to a substantial shift from the stereotypical 1950s image of the father who "knows best," but is relatively uninvolved in family life.

Fathers reside near the core of human experience, yet they remain elusive. The father lacks the mother's bodily ties to birth and nursing. His role is more culturally than biologically determined, so it is more difficult to define.

Until fairly recently, most social scientists assumed that fathers were unimportant in child rearing. Many fathers themselves accepted this idea and remained in the background of their children's lives. In addition, because of this widespread belief, fathers rarely gain custody of children after divorce.

More than ever today, with the proliferation of changing roles, many fathers struggle to find new identities, to be present for their children, and to deepen their family ties, yet not lose track of themselves. Fatherhood is a noble and humbling task that demands a warrior's commitment and courage as well as a lover's vulnerability and capacity for surrender. Especially today, fatherhood calls upon men to develop all of themselves—a kingly command, a boyish playfulness, a businessman's acumen, an artist's sensitivity. Ultimately, fathers have a sacred opportunity to break through our cultural trance and to authentically communicate to their children what has heart and meaning.

It is difficult to generalize about where fatherhood stands today in the fast-moving crosscurrents of society. Clearly the family, which has been long identified as a conservative force in culture, is undergoing radical shifts. Fathers are moving both toward and away from the home. Some fathers are choosing more family involvement and active parenting, taking on tasks that were formerly reserved for mothers, such as changing diapers, cooking, housekeeping, and teaching children. Others spend less and less time with their children, entrenched at the office, disinterested in family affiars, or absent altogether.

These opposing trends also parallel the collective psychological climate. On one hand, there is continuing widespread denial of the epidemic of family dysfunction associated with divorce, adultery, alcoholism, battering, child abuse, and neglect. Any of these can leave children feeling betrayed by their fathers (or mothers) and deeply wounded. On the other hand, there is a rising awareness, due to the popularity of psychotherapy and twelve-step recovery programs, of the depth of suffering inside most American families.

Several trends create the backdrop for the dramatically changing roles of fathers, sons, and daughters:

A rising divorce rate. With the shift toward freedom in personal relationships in the 1960s and the introduction of no-fault divorce, the divorce rate soared in the last quarter century, fragmenting nuclear and extended families, leaving in its wake single-parent households and stepfamilies.

Changing work patterns. During the same period, millions of women entered the work force, creating upheaval in male/female roles, parents living apart, and extended child care. At the same time, a growing number of men and women are relocating their offices into the home. Facilitated by such communication capabilities as fax transmission, this countertrend is a response to frustrations with time-consuming commuting.

As more and more families become dual-income households, men are called on to play a more active role in the home, although many still feel pressure to put in more hours at work as their economic needs increase. This conflict between work and family is intensifying for men and women alike.

Daniel J. Levinson, psychology professor at Yale University, says that family is the force for stability in our society, and work is the force for change. But the conflict between the two is becoming more pronounced as fathers spend about 40 percent less time with their children than they did in 1965, whether by choice or economic necessity.

Unchanging business patterns. Although family patterns have changed, in general corporate patterns have not. By asking men to work more than fifty hours a week and by failing to grant paternal leave or provide adequate day care, our corporations' message to men is clear: Work comes before family.

This work ethic has undermined the foundation of the father in the home. Most men are exhausted by a competitive working environment, then return home with nothing left to share. When asked to switch channels and participate in the emotional life of the family, many fail, unable to leave behind at the office the warrior mode of "getting it done."

The men's movement. As men's support groups proliferate and seminars to explore masculinity touch tens of thousands of men, those who are fathers return home deeply changed, more willing to shed old patterns of loving and working. In groups men see themselves mirrored in many different styles and temperaments, and thereby discover that there are many ways to be masculine: the instinctive wild man; the ritual elder; the nurturing father; the earth father—these archetypes offer alternatives to traditional roles and inspiration for personal change.

The men's movement also encourages people to explore the shadow side of masculinity. What I hear from many male friends and fathers in my groups is that they are hurting. They feel separate from other men, from their families, from themselves. They have created identities based on achievement, often at the expense of soul. Many suffer from addictions, and all feel a lack of intimacy with their fathers. As a result, the father as a role, a symbol, and a joyful commitment has been belittled for many men.

Today, fathers are on the run, but many lack direction. I believe all of us, women and men, need to slow down and explore what is essential about our fathers, about ourselves, and about our children. When more than 90 percent of 7,000 men in the Shere Hite survey, which reported on male sexuality, say they are not close to their fathers, something is seriously amiss. The computer does not have the answer, nor do the media heroes. Fathers need to journey inside themselves, feel what is there, and then make a declaration as to how to come home to their fathers and to themselves.

Men have a tendency to busy themselves with mechanics, the business of the workplace, the news of the world. Fatherhood asks men to put down the newspaper and join family life. By seeing their reflection in the mirrors of their family members, fathers can emerge from their isolation and self-centeredness.

Literally and metaphorically, fatherhood brings men back home in a humbling and liberating manner. It allows them to work with their perceived shortcomings and vulnerabilities and ultimately to find the ground of their humanity. In the process fathers feed body and soul with a mysterious but altogether necessary substance, which Robert Bly calls "father water."

Fathering may be a man's most challenging role. It can lead him to deal with the wounds he received from his own father. It can force him to lose his primary bond with his wife, as she turns to the needs of a child. It can help him to relinquish his authoritarian role, or his indifferent mask, or his workaholism, and lead him to offer support in the spirit of cooperation. Given the obstacles, duration, and sacrifices fatherhood calls for, it has been said that it's amazing anyone chooses to do it at all.

I believe that good fathering requires more than getting the task done with a focus on the rightness. Fatherhood is about being who you are and revealing that to those you love. When I contemplate the relationships between fathers, sons, and daughters, the words of the twelfth-century Sufi poet Rumi come to mind: "Out beyond rightdoing and wrongdoing, there is a field. I'll meet you there."

Fatherhood is a gift. To receive this gift is to step into a different order of commitment. To deny this gift is to cut oneself off from a father's essential qualities of generativity, order, calmness, and a deep sense of protection. Fathers can choose whether this commitment is borne with resignation or cherished as an invitation to share the most precious human bonds.

My Own Story

Two years ago, at forty-five, with my second marriage just under way, I was unexpectedly blessed with a son. I had thought diapers and interrupted sleep would remain a distant memory. I now find myself positioned between a father who is losing bladder control and an infant son who is finding it.

The birth coincided with my launching a new career direction, in addition to moving from city to countryside. I found myself living in what Thoreau called quiet desperation. I felt that I was running to catch up with my life's changes. So, rather than immerse myself in work that comfortably took me away from domestic demands and my role as father to a newborn, I decided to embrace my fatherhood by exploring this topic in a home office. This anthology is the fruit of my efforts.

With my shifting to a home office, I needed to delineate a new set of boundaries in order to protect my work as well as my family. In becoming more accessible to my family, I noticed how often I use the expression, "I need to work now." When I stand up in the family room, my son prepares himself for my leaving and utters, "Daddy go work." There is a touch of irony and sadness in working on a book about positive fathering while I perceive my family suffering from my relative unavailability. But the project is nearing completion. I am on my way home to living fatherhood, rather than researching it.

I hope that this anthology presents an informed view of the father, while honoring the initiatory mystery that surrounds fatherhood. Some of the chapters are intimate family stories. Other selections should help you to identify and possibly overcome your confusion, to name your pain and move through it. Still other pieces offer a more universal or archetypal perspective on the father/child relationship, presenting a broader vision of the possibilities.

This book is divided into five parts. Part I explores the evolving father, who is circling the perimeter of the family, seeking to come back in but not quite knowing how. It speaks to the need in each of us for a father's presence and the varied ways in which men currently are transforming this role. It offers a glimpse of possibilities, such as parenting as a spiritual practice, the joys of fatherhood, and the vision of a healthy father.

Part II focuses on the father-son relationship. Through personal tales, it explores the wounds that result from feeling isolated, failed communication, and an absence of initiation. Because every son has a father who lives forever in his soul, these tales are unending, and reconciliation is a lifelong story.

Part III examines the father-daughter relationship, its wounds of betrayal and addiction and its gifts of support and guidance. You will read moving stories from the daughter's point of view, as well as insightful pieces from fathers of daughters.

Part IV describes the challenges and opportunities involved in the new images of fatherhood: the stepfather, the expectant father, the gay father, the single parent who has or does not have custody, and the grandfather.

Part V emphasizes reconciliation with our actual fathers and healing those inner images of father that live in our hearts and minds. Through digging in the dirt, we may uncover the gold of forgiveness.

There are as many ways of fathering as there are fathers. There are as many ways of being a loving son or daughter as there are people. I invite you to share the wisdom of this book with your loved ones and, perhaps, as a result, to care for each other more deeply.

I

The Evolving
Father:
From Absence
to Presence

The father is the most powerful incarnation
of the archetypal masculine.

CARL JUNG

Whether he knows it or not, and no matter
what his position in society, the father is the
initiating priest through whom the young
being passes into the larger world.

JOSEPH CAMPBELL

The missing father is not your or my
personal father. He is the absent father in our
culture, the viable senex who provides not
daily bread but spirit through meaning and
order. The missing father is the dead God
who offered a focus for spiritual things.

JAMES HILLMAN

The absent father, by his very absence,
fathers creative work in others.

ALIX PIRANI

You have to dig deep to bury your father.

GYPSY PROVERB

Introduction

The father is a lonely figure walking the perimeter of the family circle. His peripheral location, however, facilitates contact between his family and the outer world. As a representative of the world at large, he can introduce, initiate, and prepare his children as they venture forth.

But the periphery is a dangerous location in terms of his own isolation, lack of intimacy, and difficulty of communication with others. It is one step away from absence, from abandonment. In relation to the center of the home, it is like the garage or basement, often detached and dark. From the garage, it's just a turn of the key and father is long gone.

In past times, when the father was more available, the garage was one place where he and his son or daughter stood together and made something, where he taught them about tools and ingenuity, where he was finally free to putter, whistle, sculpt something, and to tell his children about a special moment he had shared with his own father. Today fathers, like garages, have lost much of their character and size, and the whole family has suffered.

MOVING FROM ABSENCE TO PRESENCE

The term "absent father" brings up feelings of longing, distance, loss, remoteness, abandonment, and neglect. Absence can be physical or psychological—such as the absence of fathers who seldom inhabit the home, and those who are physically present but emotionally and energetically unavailable.

On the other hand, we experience presence through love, care, attention, close relationship, and availability in the moment. Rather than being a condition per se, presence is revealed in our willingness to engage with ourselves and others. Father who can surrender their

3

rigid notions of control are better able to access their active and receptive capacity for really being available for another person. Presence involves giving and receiving at a human level. We know presence when we experience it.

In Chapter 5, Jack Kornfield describes parental presence in this way: "Having a child came from a deep desire to keep my heart open. . . . There is a tremendous amount of surrender to parenting and a kind of love that people rarely touch in their lives." David Riley, in Chapter 7, describes the presence of his child: ". . . there's a freshness about the way this little boy meets every morning that lifts up our lives. It's like the freshness of early morning sun sparkling off the dew on the grass. It's the same sun and the same grass every morning, but it still makes your heart stop and take notice."

Being present for our fathers, whom we will survive, and for our children, who will survive us, holds special meaning. Fathers and fathering enrich our current experience because they provide us with a link to the past and to the future.

In a changing world, fatherhood gives us some measure of continuity, a thread that runs through us, connecting us with our ancestors and our offspring. Our lives assume more context, more meaning when we follow someone in name and in blood, and someone follows us. As Fred Gustafson comments in Chapter 10, "A young man needs to look imaginatively into the face of his father and see his sacred ancestors living there."

In order to better understand the absent-present theme, let's explore two perspectives on the father—the cultural and the archetypal.

THE CULTURAL PERSPECTIVE

In this line of reasoning, fatherhood is largely a social acquisition. According to John Miller in *Biblical Faith and Fathering,* "there is no biological compelling reason for the father to have anything to do with the child he may have engendered." Because the father's role is not as biologically necessary as the mother's, by implication it is more abstract, psychological, and strongly influenced by prevailing cultural mores. Men aren't equipped for gestating a fetus, giving birth, and nursing. Therefore, they must exercise more intentionality about their commitment because they are free from the biological constraints.

In addition, fathers are necessarily physically absent while they pursue activities outside the home. At various times in history, men have hunted in the woods, labored in the factories, and commuted to "Silicon" valleys. It is a fact, not a judgment, that most of a father's waking time is spent away from the home. By protecting and providing for his family, he has played two traditional but essential roles, particularly in times when survival was a primary issue.

The cultural focus on the breadwinning role over more nurturing activities appeals to men's heroic aspirations. Most men are led to believe, primarily through the media, that it is more exciting and manly to seek self-fulfillment outside the home. So they regard the choice between work and home in terms of identity and self-esteem.

Beyond physical absence there is among fathers what British psychotherapist Alix Pirani calls pathological absence, the failure to bring home something of value other than a paycheck. If, on the other hand, the father's absence results in such intangible gifts as inspiration, guidance, and kindness when he returns home, then his absence or detachment might be viewed as less pathological. According to Pirani in *The Absent Father: Crisis and Creativity,* the father's absence, whether physical or simply emotional, may lead to his being scapegoated by other family members when the responsibility for his absence resides with the whole family and the wider social context. Pirani suggests that in the culture at large, male elders could potentially, through ritual and guidance, encourage the father to focus more on inner values, which keep him connected to home and family.

When our culture emphasizes breadwinning and individual success for men at the expense of caregiving, the welfare of the children and the marriage is at risk. Research has shown that the father's absence influences the son and daughter's development of social skills, self-esteem, and attitudes toward achievement. A crippled understanding of masculinity contributes to various forms of maladjustment, such as lack of impulse control, incompetence, dependence, and irresponsibility. The son of an absent father experiences a weakened identification with maleness, and the daughter experiences a weakened relationship to the masculine.

An absent father means an absent husband, which usually spells disaster for the marriage. In the name of family financial and psychological welfare, our divorce courts reinforce the preeminence of the father's job, and therefore his absence, and award child custody to the mother nine times out of ten. When the prevailing societal attitudes are unsupportive of the father's active involvement in the family, then we see the fragmentation of the family that is so common today.

THE ARCHETYPAL PERSPECTIVE

The archetypal perspective from Jungian psychology helps us to more fully grasp the meaning of absent fathers. Jung proposed that the collective unconscious contains primary psychic forms or blueprints called archetypes. An archetype is a preexistent universal pattern, yet is experienced in a personalized way by each of us. In the words of Jung: "The personal father inevitably embodies the archetype, which is what endows his figure with its fascinating power. The archetype acts as an amplifier, enhancing beyond measure in the effects that proceed from the father, so far as these conform to the inherited pattern."

The personal father is often associated with and confused with the archetypal qualities of kings or of God the Father. Jungian analyst Robert Moore and poet Robert Bly have spoken compellingly about the necessity to withdraw the unconscious archetypal projection of the omnipotent king from our biological fathers and instead to reown our own kingly qualities, such as authority, order, centeredness, calmness, generosity, blessing, and life potency. A father's job is to satisfactorily model these qualities for his sons and daughters and to help them cultivate them.

The task for all of us is to develop a conscious relationship to archetypes, or they will control us. The more mature we become, the more we are able to develop our inner relationship with these kingly qualities and then to express them in our outer lives.

As our patriarchal gods have fallen or been pulled down from their pedestals, there has been a simultaneous loss of authority and power invested in the personal father. Without their affiliation with the patriarchal gods, fathers have been left isolated and adrift, unable to carry the magnitude of archetypal projections. Both Bly and Moore believe that contemporary fathers are unempowered because they have lost their connection with these mythic father figures. Because archetypal energies must manifest somewhere, the father is still a viable recipient of kingly projections by young and uninitiated boys and girls. Through awareness, sons and daughters

eventually withdraw those attributes that don't fit a personal father when he inevitably fails to measure up to their naive idealiza-
tions.

If fathering is to be a continuous and rewarding process, certain
conditions must affirm the father's presence. Cultural and environ-
mental support are certainly helpful. But fathers also need to learn
to carry the fatherly projections in a manner that psychologists call
"good enough." Part of this task can be accomplished by fathers understanding the difference between the personal father and the
archetypal father. Without this understanding, overidentification
with the archetypal energies is as much a danger as is a lack of vi-
talizing connection with them.

OVERVIEW

We begin with a history of fatherhood since the Industrial Revolution by David Giveans and Michael Robinson, educators in men's
issues. Giveans, a writer and lecturer, and Robinson, a counselor
and former "house-husband," describe the emerging role of the father as reflecting economic and social changes. In this essay from the
anthology *Dimensions of Fatherhood,* the more nurturing and compassionate qualities of recent fathers are portrayed as adding to their
masculinity rather than being devalued as feminine.

Andrew Merton identifies the physical and psychological dynamics that create "father shortage" and "father hunger." His prem-
ise is that men's inability to form intimate relationships "may be
traced to flawed relationships with their own fathers." He proposes
that the cycle of father hunger breaks when men come to terms with
their own feelings about their fathers. This energetic excerpt from
an article that appeared in *New Age Journal* offers a brief historical
review of fatherhood since 1900 and humorous perspective on the
similarity between the "macho" and the "wimp." Merton is director of the journalism program at the University of New Hampshire.

Jungian analyst Anthony Stevens skillfully summarizes research studies confirming that the father has the potential for early
positive influence over the development of autonomy and gender
identity in his children. In this excerpt from *Archetypes: A Natural
History of The Self,* Stevens observes that a father's style of love is

more conditional on behavior and performance than a mother's, thus a father's love has to be earned.

Drawing on her life experience, writer Sara Maitland effectively distinguishes between the archetypal and personal fathers, a task difficult for her precisely because her father was very "Father-like, one of the old gods . . . powerful." An expanded version of this article first appeared in *Fathers: Reflections by Daughters.*

Chapters 5 through 8 are personal and positive in their portrayal of real fathers. Chapters 5 and 7 are written from the perspective of the author's own fatherhood. These authors affirm that the quality of presence in fathering translates as a felt experience.

Jack Kornfield, a Buddhist teacher of insight meditation and a psychologist, shares his personal choice to live more fully as a father and husband. In "Parenting as Spiritual Practice," he describes how the basic tenets of Buddhist practice are precisely what is required to survive the trials of fatherhood. With humility and humor, he illustrates how parenting presents infinite obstacles and opportunities for mindfulness and spiritual evolution.

A mother of four children, Karen Anton appreciates the bountiful love expressed through the effort and attention of her own full-time father. Her father was the grandson of a slave, past fifty when his wife was committed to a mental hospital and he was left to care for three infant children. "Remembering a Father Who Mothered" first appeared in *Being a Father: Family, Work and Self.*

In "The Joys of Fatherhood," David Riley offers an unequivocal yes to the question as to whether fatherhood feeds the soul. Riley describes the joy and gratitude derived from engaging with his child as "an unfinished sculpture creating itself." He feels privileged to receive the gifts of humor, freshness, hope, and wisdom that come from his son. Riley is an activist living in Washington, D.C., with his wife and three children.

In a selection from Loren Pedersen's book *Dark Hearts: The Unconscious Forces That Shape Men's Lives,* this Jungian analyst presents us with a positive picture of a healthy father. It's a concise and comprehensive affirmation of what it could mean to be a father.

When Jack Kornfield observes that parenting is "a tremendous field in which to cultivate giving and surrender and patience and loving," his words *cultivate* and *field* conjure up for me the image of a father/farmer who is connected to the earth in a nurturing way. A provider, yes, but also a steward and protector of what is growing and precious. While the farmer may be a vanishing breed, his legacy provides fertile roots for the evolving father to renew his ties to both earth and family. So when Robert Bly stands before five hundred men and asks Antonio Machado's poetic question, "What have you done with the garden that was entrusted to you?"—the poignant silence in the hall speaks many truths.

CHAPTER ONE

David Giveans and Michael Robinson

Old and New Images of Fatherhood

The traditional definition of fatherhood conforms to the social ideas and realities of the 1940s through the early 1960s, with the exception being during World War II when men were drafted into the armed forces and women assumed traditional masculine occupations in civil and defense work. During the war preschool children were cared for in public school child-care facilities and some industry-sponsored facilities such as the Kaiser Shipbuilding Company.[1] After World War II, mothers were once more relegated to the kitchen and caring for their children while fathers returned to the work force.

Fathers expressed care for their families by successfully participating in the marketplace. Their role at home was limited to providing for the family so that mothers would be free to devote themselves to the care of the children. Men were seen as responsible for the family's relationship with the outside world (primarily the world of work) whereas women were the primary givers of love at home.

The father's role in the traditional home environment was extremely limited. The major image of father in the traditional perspective is of the aloof breadwinner. In times past, so much time and energy were used in his role that at home he was thought of as reserved and firm, yet kindly. Typically, a father was respected although feared by his children, and the two never learned to know each other very well. The traditional nuclear father's interaction with his children was restricted to a brief interaction at bedtime, typically masculine work activities in the home on the weekends, Sunday outings in the family car, and the annual summer two-week vacation.[2]

Prior to the 1960s, most social scientists had mistakenly assumed that fathers were unimportant in child rearing.[3] However, a more modern definition of father has since evolved in which the importance of the fathering role is recognized. Now, a father's role in the home reflects the economics of the decade, the egalitarian approach to parenting, the increased influence of single fathers and househusbands, and a tentative societal awareness and acceptance of men in nurturing roles. Today's father is apt to be as comfortable pushing his child in the supermarket as he is seeking success for himself in the job market. He shares his parental concern not only with his wife but also with other fathers as he strives to be a positive influence in his child's life. Many are cognizant of their fathers' lack of involvement and nurturance and are seeking to dispel previously accepted myths of how fathers are supposed to interact with their children. No longer is the father assuming the posture of an autocrat but he is now embracing a more human identity. He is recognizing that by adopting a more gentle, compassionate approach to his role he is adding to his masculinity rather than detracting from it. The father, in his more human role, is developing an awareness that he can learn from his children and that they can help him clarify his values and priorities. The marketplace is no longer the salient guideline for his life. He is now learning to attach a new importance to the domestic environment by contributing to it as a respectful husband, a loving and compassionate father, and a contributing member of the community. Fathering has come to express a caring human being who nurtures the love of life, the preservation of humane values, and is warm, loving, and worthy of a child's trust.[4]

An extension of the present-day image of a father takes the form of the psychological father. The psychological father is a person who responds to and is a significant influence in forming a child's future. Psychological fathers include friends of the nuclear and binuclear (single-parent) family, men participating in organized groups for children such as PAL, Big Brothers, and foster grandparent programs, and male teachers. The male teacher, of young children in particular, provides a balancing role model in the home as well as providing a comparative role model to children who lack a constant male model to children from nuclear family homes. As

Dr. Benjamin Spock states, "Children know that they need a father figure and will create one out of whatever materials are at hand."[5]

Any attempt to explain or describe the dimensions of fathering in the United States would be out of focus without a clear awareness of the historical and social context of the father role. Historically men and women shared the responsibilities for family economic support and child rearing. It was not until the transition in this country from a subsistence to a market (money) economy that the role of the father as the *good provider* came into being.[6] The Industrial Revolution firmly entrenched the breadwinning role of father and relegated child rearing and household maintenance to the mother. With the factory now taking over work formerly done in the home, a separation of work based on the sex of the worker was fully established. Women, because they bore and fed children, performed the necessary labor of child rearing and homemaking. Men, because work at home could no longer support the family, left home in search of paid employment in order to provide real goods for their families.

Toward the end of the nineteenth century, as new advances in industrialization and production resulted in higher wages, more and more families found it possible to achieve what had formerly been a special status afforded by the wealthy: the full-time, at-home housewife. "No wife of mine will ever have to work" became the signifying phrase of the successful man of the twentieth century. It also signified the beginning of the end of active, involved, participatory fathering.[7]

Socialization practices in our society have resulted in the provider role being firmly embedded in the male psyche. The goal of socialization in any society is to insure that each newly arrived individual will act and believe in much the same manner as other individuals already present. Society's institutions—family, church, school, marketplace—demand and reinforce properly socialized behavior corresponding to traditional sex role stereotypes of "feminine" and "masculine."

It is within these societal demands that boys learned sanctioned notions of what it means to be a male and manly. It makes little difference that a young boy may not understand the demands being placed upon him. What is important is that he learns, and learns quickly, the dangers of deviating from them.[8]

Although the provider role is primarily fulfilled through the father's occupational endeavors, there are additional expectations inherent in the role. Society also requires that a father be instrumental in affecting reproduction, material support, survival skills, and crisis handling and cooperation with others outside the family.[9] As such, male norms stress values such as courage, inner-directedness, certain forms of aggression, autonomy, mastery, technological skills, group solidarity, adventure, and toughness in mind and body.[10] Thus, the gentleness, nurturing, and emotionality associated with child rearing has come to be believed as foreign and incompatible to most men's priorities, experiences, and abilities.

As the father became less and less involved and, in fact, less and less visible in the home, he came to be replaced by what has been referred to as the TV model male.[11] This depiction presents males as adventurous, active, always right and seductive toward females. Accordingly, the father was typically depicted in such programs as "The Donna Reed Show," "Father Knows Best," and "Ozzie and Harriet." Beginning in the early 1970s, the father was increasingly viewed as a more gentle, loving person with interests expanded beyond traditionally accepted and prescribed masculine pursuits—more closely associating himself with the rearing of his child in various parenting situations. Programming such as "Scenes from a Marriage" and "An American Family" presented a more accurate view of the realities of family life. By the end of the decade even Archie Bunker and George Jefferson had mellowed and were not quite the same men they were a few TV seasons before.

In the movies of the late 1950s and the early 1960s, the father was portrayed as a friendly but incompetent buffoon steered through the daily routines of family life by a thoroughly involved, highly skilled, full-time wife and mother.[12] It is noteworthy and encouraging, therefore, to recognize that Hollywood—long the bastion and perpetrator of the male macho image—singled out *Kramer vs. Kramer* to receive its highest honor, the 1980 Academy Award for the best picture of the year, and continues to produce films depicting competent, nurturing fathers.

THE EMERGING PERSPECTIVE OF FATHER

The 1960s and 1970s were decades of social upheaval in America. The Civil Rights Movement, Vietnam, the Women's Liberation Movement, and Watergate were events that stretched the moral fiber of our society and challenged the very nature of our American way of life. Important as each of these events was, it was the Women's Liberation Movement that created the greatest change in men's lives.

Sex roles being reciprocal,[13] the changes and redefinition of self and situations that women have experienced necessarily affect how men view and define themselves. As women declared housework and child care oppressive and fought for entry into the male dominated work world, men were forced to take stock of their heretofore unquestioned and unchallenged family role as the distant breadwinner. The growing literature on men is a direct result of and response to the cultural upheaval initiated by the Women's Liberation Movement.

In terms of men's family roles, current literature indicates that there is a new, emergent perspective on fathering that states that "men are psychologically able to participate in a full range of parenting behaviors and, furthermore, that it may be good for both parents and children that men take active roles in child care and child rearing."[14] This new perspective on fathering is but one segment of a growing Men's Liberation Movement across the nation. The movement—although not as well-organized, accepted, or mainstreamed into the average male's consciousness (or, for that matter, society's)—is nonetheless affecting significant social change relevant to the lives of fathers, thereby increasingly reinforcing Hugo's statement that "there is nothing so powerful as an idea whose time has come." Betty Friedan describes the Men's Movement as "a quiet movement, a shifting in direction, the saying of no to old patterns, a searching for new values, a struggling with basic questions that each man seems to be going through alone."[15]

Although still in its embryonic stage, the movement is typified by a new breed of fathers who are sharing the emotional as well as the physical experiences of pregnancy. It is today commonplace for new fathers to participate in childbirth classes, simultaneously bond with the newborn at birth, and actively participate in the subjective stages of their children's development. Though less common, yet still significant, the involvement of many fathers seems so involved that they experience physical symptoms (couvade)[16] during their wives' pregnancy and postpartum depression after delivery. In short, fathers are becoming "hooked" on their children, thereby modeling a more humane parenting style for subsequent generations to emulate.

In addition, based on the authors' observations at educational and family conferences, men are no longer merely accompanying their wives to such gatherings. Rather, they are in their own right actively participating in male caucuses, organizing workshops focusing on their roles as fathers, and enthusiastically attending parenting meetings as well as participating in their children's early childhood learning environments. Such behavior changes in men indicate a more caring and nurturing fathering image that may, as Margaret Mead stated toward the end of her career, "be the only development that can save our nuclear family."[17]

Research literature clearly indicates an almost total lack of societal support for men who want to take a increased role in the raising of their children. This attitude is evidenced by rigid work schedules, lack of parental leave policies, the unavailability of good part-time work, and unavailable or inadequate day care. The issue for men is clearly not one of capability but rather whether society and its institutions will encourage men to pursue fathering as a legitimate, rewarding, and respected activity.

The authors offer the following quotations to reinforce the essence of the material discussed—the usually missing, yet critical human side of the fathering issue as described by Farrell; and the optimistic, foreseeable future presented by Eichenbaum and Orbach:

> The father's presence should transmit a *new masculine identity* based on the type of human values likely to be found in a man who cares enough to be a parent to his children. The man with a human identity—the basis of the new masculine identity—is as free to choose to be home with his children while his wife works as vice versa. He is free to choose a job which is really forty hours a week— not sixty. He is not manipulated by his job striving, leadership striving, or physical strength. This freedom is an obvious prerequisite to his being home more frequently. When he is home, his sons and daughters are seeing a new image of masculinity—*a father who shows respect for the domestic setting by participating in it*—within a society which offers approval for that image.[18]

> A new balance must be created in which both women and men participate in the world outside of the home as well as the world inside of the home. . . . Men no longer will be cut off from their own offspring. Men will no longer be forced to be out in a world of competition, only to return home for a few hours each evening. Men no longer will enter their children's psychologies through their absence.[19]

CHAPTER TWO

Andrew Merton

Father Hunger

I am going to tell you a secret about men. But first let me remind you of something you already know, although if you are a woman, part of you keeps denying it—the part that takes over late at night as you are drifting off to sleep, alone, and whispers things like, *How come I never have any luck with men? How come the only guys I meet are insensitive louts or oversensitive wimps or both rolled into one?* The implication being that everyone else is meeting men who are wonderful.

Here is the good news: There is nothing wrong with *you*.

The bad news (and this is what you already knew) is that the kind of man you want—one who is strong yet sensitive, virile yet faithful, decisive yet considerate—really *is* in short supply. When it comes to intimacy—sustained, egalitarian intimacy—men are incompetent.

Maybe not all men. But a lot of them. Probably most of them. And (this may or may not comfort you) this condition is not confined to available men. A lot of married men are afflicted as well. Unfortunately, the same problems that prevent them from becoming truly intimate with their wives also frustrate their attempts to establish close relationships with their children—and this is true even if men intend to take active roles in child rearing.

Now, here is the secret. It has two parts. Part one is dark, so dark that a lot of tough guys—men with well-developed pectorals and lots of notches on their bedposts—will go to great lengths to deny it, but it is true nonetheless: In terms of psychological development, there isn't much difference between a macho and a wimp.

Oh, I know. On the surface they are opposites. Sylvester Stallone and Woody Allen. One uses force to achieve his goals, while the other manipulates through weakness. The wimp may be harder to spot, because he does seem genuinely concerned about *you*; only later do you realize that when he asks about your feelings, it's a cue to answer quickly and then ask him about *his*.

They have this in common: Both are incapable of dealing with a woman as an equal. Therefore, neither is able to enter into an intimate, stable partnership with a woman.

Experts have been telling us about men's inability to connect with women for a while now. In *The Seasons of a Man's Life*, psychologist Daniel J. Levinson warns, "Most men in their twenties are not ready to make an enduring inner commitment to wife and family, and they are not capable of a highly loving, sexually free, and emotionally intimate relationship." His studies show that, in this regard, a lot of men never leave their twenties. In her book *In a Different Voice*, psychologist Carol Gilligan pinpoints the different qualities men and women value in relationships: "Male and female voices typically speak of the importance of different truths, the former of the role of separation as it defines and empowers the self, the latter of the ongoing process of attachment that creates and sustains the human community." Levinson, Gilligan, and others point out that from the day he is born a boy is conditioned to be strong, stoic, and independent. Little in the culture at large tells him he should value intimacy or nurturing. The male cartoon heroes on television are lone warriors. (Voltron? He-Man? Tom Selleck? You might as well share your feelings with a B-52.) Girl's and women's magazines are full of articles about relationships. But you will not find articles on "How to Make This Relationship Last" in *Playboy*.

But here is something that, from experience, you may have trouble believing: A lot of men, deep down, want intimacy as much as women do. The trouble is, they don't know how to go about achieving it. And while the culture around them has a lot to do with this, some researchers are concluding that for an enormous number of men the inability to form intimate relationships may be traced to flawed relationships with their own fathers.

Which brings us to the second part of the secret: It is likely that both wimp and macho behavior are different manifestations of the same underlying psychological problem—the yearning for a father who never was.

Harvard University psychoanalyst James Herzog invented the

term *father hunger* to describe the psychological state of young children who had been deprived of their fathers through separation, divorce, or death. In his study, "On Father Hunger," published in *Father and Child,* he found that children thus affected—particularly boys—tended to have trouble controlling their aggressive impulses. He speculated that on a long-term basis "father hunger appears to be a critical motivational variable in matters as diverse as caretaking, sexual orientation, oral development, and achievement."

In that study Herzog applied the term *father hunger* to men whose fathers had been physically absent. But based on recent work by psychologist John Munder Ross and psychologist Samuel Osherson, as well as on my own interviews of fifty men, the term can be expanded to include the offspring of fathers who were physically present, but psychologically absent or inadequate. We can define *father hunger* as a subconscious yearning for an ideal father that results in behavior ranging from self-pity to hypermasculinity and frustrates attempts to achieve intimacy.

If a father is bad enough, he can short-circuit his daughter's capacity for intimacy as well. But that's another story. And while inadequate fathering may do damage to a daughter, it is more likely to wound a son—and the wound is likely to be deeper and longer lasting.

And this is for the simple reason that a daughter can identify with her mother, while a son, at least beyond the age of two, can't. For it is at that age a boy begins to understand that he cannot be a woman. That is to say, he learns he cannot satisfy his creative and nurturing instincts directly by bearing a child. He must separate his own identity from that of his mother. He needs someone else to identify with.

According to John Ross of Cornell Medical College, the boy lucky enough to have a good father will develop a broad and flexible concept of what being a man is all about—a concept that includes tenderness, vulnerability, and open displays of feeling, alongside strength and fortitude. He will be secure enough to "expand and deepen his concept of manhood to encompass a variety of affects and activities that might otherwise become associated with the mother's exclusive province, with being womanly."

But chances are that if you are an adult between twenty and fifty-five your father was not a big part of your childhood, or big only in a negative way: remote, angry, repressed, vindictive.

A boy with an inflexible, authoritarian father might go one of two ways: He might rebel against his father with such rage that, in his rebelling, he becomes just as macho as the father. Or he might succumb to his father's bullying, take shelter with his mother, and perpetually seek women who will mother him.

A boy with a father who is not a strong presence in the home is likely to have a dominant, if not domineering, mother. He, too, can go one of two ways: If he is strong, he will strive to become the man his father is not and, in doing so, become overly aggressive, macho. Or he can succumb to his mother's will and perpetually seek women who will give him direction.

Father hunger tends to be passed from generation to generation—the son of a father-hungry father will be father hungry himself. For a man who fails to develop an intimate relationship with his wife has an extremely poor chance of doing so with his children. James Herzog is certain that, with men (but not necessarily with women), "adult-adult interaction predicts adult-child interaction"— that is, if a man is in touch with his own feelings and those of his wife, he is likely to be attuned to his children as well, but if his relationship with his wife is poor to begin with, the odds of his becoming a good father are long. Which is why the idea of having a baby to solidify a relationship is almost always a bad one. Even for a well-adjusted man, the transition from husband to husband-and-father, starting with pregnancy, can be daunting. Suddenly he is no longer the center of his wife's attention. He has fulfilled his biological function in reproduction and is reduced to a supporting role. His wife may become moody. Lovemaking is likely to become less frequent. "There's just some existential pain in becoming a father," Samuel Osherson says. "You're a deeply feeling person who is on the periphery."

Herzog studied a group of men whose wives had recently given birth and found that those who had been the most supportive of their wives during pregnancy tended to be able to come to terms with their feelings about their own fathers (living or dead), while men who had never resolved these feelings "seemed to become progressively less able to participate in their expectant fatherhood." During the third trimester, many of these men, he says "seemed . . . to make a career of the pursuit of . . . maleness." And he stresses again "that the male's caretaking line of development is fatefully affected by the presence of a good-enough male mentor-father, who helps the boy grieve the loss of his earlier identification [with his mother] and helps him see what a man is and what a man does."

Once the child is born, the problems are likely to intensify. The father, already insecure, feels displaced by the child. Ed Wyzanski, a computer technician in his late thirties, said his relationship with his wife deteriorated dangerously following the birth of their first child: "I remember being very angry at times. Holding the baby, trying to get him to stop crying, bouncing him, being so mad I wanted to do something violent. That was scary. I had never seen that in myself. I'd swing him around in desperation, slam him back into the crib."

"I saw him as a rival for my wife's affections. Here was someone else getting the affection I had gotten. . . . I pushed myself on her sexually shortly after birth. I regret that."

Wyzanski, who is in therapy, describes his own father as an insecure manipulator and misogynist. "If my mother was saying something he didn't like, he would glare and purse his lips. 'Shut up.' It was a very destructive relationship. I learned insecurity from him."

In his book, *Finding Our Fathers,* Samuel Osherson sums up persuasive evidence of the psychological gap between men and their fathers:

> Shere Hite's survey of 7,239 men revealed that "almost no men said they had been or were close to their fathers." Judith Arcana writes that in interviews for her book on mothers and sons only "about 1 percent of the sons had good relations with their fathers."
>
> Psychologist Jack Sternbach examined the father-son relationship in seventy-one of his male clients. He found fathers were physically absent for 23 percent of the men; 29 percent had psychologically absent fathers who were austere, moralistic, and emotionally uninvolved; and 15 percent had fathers who were dangerous, frightening their sons, and seemingly out of control. Only 15 percent of Sternbach's cases showed evidence of fathers appropriately involved with their sons, with a history of nurturance and trustworthy warmth and connection.

Osherson adds that his own interviews with men in their thirties and forties convinced him "that the psychological or physical absence of fathers from their families is one of the great underestimated tragedies of our times."

The American man who grew up with a father who was affectionate, strong, and significantly involved in the upbringing of his children is so rare he is a curiosity. It has not always been this way. At the turn of the century the average family included a father who, whether affectionate or not, at least provided a concrete role model for his sons. Typically he worked on a farm or ran a store or business near home; typically, as a matter of course, he included his sons in his affairs. They went to work with him and were expected to follow in his footsteps or urged to do better.

But a series of historical events beginning with World War I altered this state of affairs dramatically. Beginning in 1917 and again in 1941, millions of United States men went off to war, leaving their families for as long as four years. They came home to sons who had grown up in their absence. And they came home to a changed society.

For a sizable portion of American men, the nature of work itself changed drastically after 1946. The ideal living situation was no longer an apartment next to the store but a house in the suburbs. In addition to spending eight or more hours away from his family at work, a man now spent an additional two, three, or even four hours commuting to and from his job. He came home to sleep. And on weekends he went bowling or golfing with his buddies. To his family he was a phantom.

And the nature of his job had changed from something that his son could identify with to something rendering the father even more remote, mysterious, and abstract than he already was. No longer could a boy say with confidence that his father was a cobbler or a merchant; now he might scratch his head and say, "Well, he deals in futures," or "He's a consultant," with no understanding of what that meant. In his 1968 book, *Fatherhood: A Sociological Perspective,* Leonard Benson declared the separation of the father from the rest of the family complete and self-perpetuating:

> Mother is the primary parent. She is first by popular acclaim, in actual household practice, and in the minds of students of family life. . . . The fact that the father is assigned the role of breadwinner rather than that of caring for the children guarantees that boys will not develop and cultivate skills appropriate to child care. The primary skills of fathers are often beyond the understanding or even appreciation of contemporary children, and their style in social relations is usually conditioned by the demanding singularly adult world of "work."

Today's adult males grew to maturity under those conditions. But Benson was wrong to predict that the situation would remain unchanged forever, because even when a man is pigeonholed as the worker, the achiever, the distant voice of authority, he has creative and nurturing instincts; to the extent that they are suppressed in the service of a macho image, he is not whole. All it takes are the right conditions to bring these instincts to the surface. And those conditions now exist.

The women's movement was in its infancy when Benson wrote his book. Women were only beginning to discover that they were not whole, that they too possessed traits encouraged only in men: assertiveness, independence, aptitudes for an enormous variety of occupations outside the home. During the intervening eighteen years they have done something about it—in schools, in consciousness-raising groups, in therapy. In unprecedented numbers women have tapped these previously latent reserves, have made themselves whole. And men in large numbers are beginning to understand: Whole women want whole men. Macho men and wimps need not apply.

Despite Rambo, values are changing. In 1970 only 30 percent of Americans believed that it was important for fathers to spend as much time with their children as mothers do. In 1986 the figure was 91 percent, according to the Ethan Allen Report on the Status of the American Family. Another recent study by *USA Today* found that 65 percent of men think they are closer to their kids than their fathers were. Within the past fifteen years scholars and the media have pronounced men's private and family lives fit subjects for investigation. The pressure is on for men to change. And men who grew up in the '60s and '70s have a hunger to *be* the father they never had. Were it not for this pressure, father hunger as a concept probably would not exist.

Fortunately, once a man discovers that his unresolved frustrations about his father are causing some of his distress, he is in a position to change. By coming to terms with their feelings about their fathers, men are becoming better fathers themselves. And in doing so, they are breaking the cycle of father hunger.

CHAPTER THREE

Anthony Stevens

The Father Archetype

While a vast literature has grown up in recent decades on the significance of the mother–child bond, fathers have been relatively neglected. This is, perhaps, only to be expected as our culture continues to recoil from the "patrism" of the nineteenth-century life toward the "matrism" of the present time. However, it is surely going too far to assert, as some social scientists and women's liberationists have done, that fathers are largely irrelevant to the well-being of their progeny, that their sex is immaterial, and that their sole useful contribution to child rearing is to function from time to time as breastless mother-substitutes. Such a degree of contempt for the paternal virtues would contrast sharply with the clinical experience of psychiatrists and the personal experience of most of us that fathers do indeed have great influence on the lives of their sons and daughters. Fortunately, this dissonance between theory and fact has led to some interesting research in recent years, the implications of which we shall be examining in this chapter. Broadly speaking, the findings are in keeping with Jung's belief that the father plays a crucial psychological role in "the destiny of the individual."

In his 1909 paper Jung first stated his opinion that the seemingly "magical" hold and influence that parents have over their children was not merely a function of their individual personalities, or of the child's relative helplessness, but was primarily due to the numinosity of the parental archetypes activated by them in the child's psyche. "The personal father inevitably embodies the archetype, which is what endows this figure with its fascinating power. The archetype acts as an amplifier, so far as these conform to the inherited pattern."[1]

In myth, legend, and dreams, the father archetype personifies as the Elder, the King, the Father in Heaven. As Lawgiver he speaks with the voice of collective authority and is the living embodiment of the *Logos* principle: his word is law. As Defender of the Faith and of the Realm he is guardian of the status quo and bastion against all enemies. His attributes are activity and penetration, differentiation and judgment, fecundity and destruction. His symbols are heaven and the sun, lightning and wind, the phallus and the weapon. Heaven symbolizes the spiritual aspirations of the masculine principle, of which the father is the prime carrier, but in nearly all religions and mythologies heaven is by no means the realm of universal Good: it is also the origin of natural disasters and human catastrophes, the seat from which the godhead passes judgment and from which he punishes with thunderbolts and rewards with boons; it is the throne room of the primordial patriarch, where he freely exercises his powers of life and death over his wives and children. For like the Mother, the Father has a terrible side: he possesses the dual aspect of Jehovah and of the fecundating and destructive Hindu god, Shiva. He is Kronos who prevents his sons from replacing him by eating them alive.

As far as the growing child is concerned, Jungians all agree that the father archetype is activated later in the ontological sequence than the mother archetype, though rather vague opinions are expressed about when this may be said to occur. Jung was of the opinion that the father archetype showed little sign of activity until about the fifth year, but thereafter it assumed greater influence over the developing personality than the mother archetype and that this influence persisted well into puberty. As we shall see, however, there is good reason for supposing that the father becomes of considerable importance much earlier than Jung believed.

Clearly, the first archetypal constellation through which the Self gropes its way out of the uroborus into conscious reality is the Mother, but it seems probable that the post-uroboric 'Mother' is, in fact, still at the stage of the (undifferentiated) 'parent': only later, with the emergence of ego-consciousness and the formation of attachment bonds with both parents, is it likely that 'separation of the parents' occurs, the parental archetype becoming differentiated into its maternal and paternal poles.

That this process of parental distinction is already started by the second year, and is well advanced by the fourth, is indicated by a number of studies. For example, H. Biller has consistently found that paternal deprivation beginning before the age of four has a more disruptive effect on a child's development than father absence commencing at a later date.[2] In a study by M. Leichty college men whose fathers were at home during their childhood were compared with a group whose fathers were away in the Army when they were between three and five years old. These 'paternally deprived' men had considerable difficulty in adjusting to the return of their father, some finding it impossible to identify with them or to accept them as a masculine ideal.[3] R. Burton studied the effects of father absence on the development of gender identity in children in Barbados and found that the presence of the father during the first two years of childhood was critical if the development of feminine orientation in boys was avoided.[4] Moreover, J. Money and A. Erhardt and others have assembled evidence which strongly suggests that gender identity has usually been accomplished by *eighteen months*.[5] Attempts to correct a wrong gender attribution after this age gave rise to impressive difficulties. It is clear, therefore, that the father is much more to the child than an occasional mother-substitute and that the father archetype becomes both differentiated and active at an earlier age than Jung supposed.

But where Jung was not mistaken was in his view of the contribution that the father makes to psychogenesis: it is through the father-child relationship that gender consciousness emerges. Slowly the boy comes to recognize that his bond to his father is based on *identity* ('I and the father are one'), while the girl comes to appreciate that it is based on *difference* (i.e. the father constitutes, both spiritually and sexually, her first profound experience of the essential 'otherness' of the male). Jung believed that the father's presence was crucial if the boy was to actualize in consciousness and in behavior his own masculine potential. Since formation of the mother bond predates the onset of gender consciousness, it is based on mother-identity for the boy no less than for the girl. The girl, therefore, has to make no readjustment to her original sense of identity with mother, while the boy has to undergo the revolutionary transformation from mother-identity to identification-with-father. Lack of a father makes this transition hard, and sometimes impossible, to achieve. Many studies confirm the high incidence of sex-role confusion in boys who grow up without fathers, and the relative absence of such confusion in fatherless girls.

However, there is little doubt that fathers do influence in significant degree the manner in which their daughters *experience* their feminity vis-à-vis the man. His loving affirmation can greatly assist her to happy acceptance of her female role, while his rejection or mockery can cause deep injury which may never heal. Girls who grow to maturity without fathers may have few doubts that they are women, but when it comes to living with men as their partners they can feel hopelessly lost and unprepared.

The father's influence over the development of his children extends far beyond the question of sexual identity and relationships, however. In the great majority of patrilineal societies, he acts as the bridge between family life and the life of the society at large. This is what Talcott Parsons calls the father's *instrumental* role, which he distinguishes from the mother's *expressive* role.[6] Almost universally, the father possesses a centrifugal orientation (i.e. towards society and the outside world) in contrast to the mother's centripetal concern (i.e. with home and family), and our culture is no exception, despite attempts in some quarters to change it. By representing society to the family and his family to the society, the father facilitates the transition of the child from home to the world at large. He encourages the development of skills necessary for successful adult adaptation, while at the same time communicating to the child the values and mores prevailing in the social system. That he performs this function is no mere accident of culture: it rests on an archetypal foundation. "Whereas mother in her eternal aspect represents the earth that does not change, the transpersonal [i.e. archetypal] father represents consciousness as it moves and changes. In this sense father is subject to time, subject to aging and death; his image changes with the culture he represents."[7] The mother is outside time and dominates the realm of feelings, instincts, and the unconscious; the father is concerned with events occurring in the tangible world in the context of space and time—events which are approached, controlled and modified through consciousness and the use of will. It is not just that a father's attitudes to work, social achievement, politics and the law condition the developing attitudes of his children, but that he constellates for them the whole extraverted potential of the world as place-to-be-known-and-lived-in. In as much as he succeeds in this role, he sets them free from their involvement with mother and fosters the necessary autonomy (ego-Self axis) for effective living. For her part, the mother's *expressive* function continues to provide the emotional support and security enabling them to go out and meet the world's challenges.

That the fathers and mothers are constitutionally geared to their respective social and personal roles does not, of course, deny the existence of 'instrumental' capacities in the mother or of 'expressive' ones in the father. What we are discussing are those typical dispositions and modes of functioning which are the hallmarks of archetypal expression. Certainly, men can function in the same roles as women, and vice versa, but that is not what they are best equipped for. When it comes to the expression of Eros, for example, the archetype is characteristically actualized differently by men and women in relation to their children. It is as if, as Wolfgang Lederer says, fathers and mothers stand for two different modes of loving: for the mother it is usually sufficient that her child *exists*—her love is absolute and largely unconditional; a father's love, however, is more demanding—it is *contingent* love, love which is conditional upon performance in the world.[8] Thus, Eros is actualized by the mother directly through her expressive role; while in the father it is inextricably linked to this instrumental function. Mother-love is *a priori* precondition of the bond to her child; father-love is something that has to be won through achievement. And since the father's love has to be earned, it is an incentive to the development of autonomy, and an affirmation of that autonomy once it is attained. Growth of the ego-Self axis, therefore, which begins through the relationship to mother, is consolidated and confirmed through the bond to father.

CHAPTER FOUR

Sara Maitland

Two for the Price of One

I have two fathers.

I have a material, biological father. His name was Adam Maitland; he was born in 1913. His earliest memory was of waiting on a station platform for his father (a serving officer) to come home on leave. He had an odd, unlovely childhood. He went to Cambridge, served in the war; in 1948 he married my mother. It was a very strong and happy marriage. He had six children. At the age of fifty he retired from his job as managing director of a large London printing press and went home to southwest Scotland to manage his inherited acres. In March 1982, in his own home, after "a long illness bravely borne," as they say, he died of cancer.

I have another father. This one is alive and well and rampaging inside me. He never goes away, although sometimes he is silent; he is never ill, never weakened, never leaves me alone. He lurks about under other names—God, Husband, Companion—and all those relationships are made possible (which is nice) and impossibly difficult and conflicting because of the father who is in and under and through them all. In my late teens I fled my father's house; it has taken me a long time to realize that I carried with me the Father from whom I could not escape by escaping childhood, from whom I have not yet escaped, and from whom I have had, and still have, to wrest my loves, my voice, my feminism, and my freedom. It is this Father that I have hated loving and loved hating. It is this Father that I want to kill, and dare not.

In the eighteen months between the diagnosis of my father's

cancer and his death, it became vital for me to separate the two fathers, because—of course—I did not want to kill my father. I really did not want to; because in the last ten years or so of his life I had come to respect this person who happened to be my father—an unusual, distinguished, and in many ways admirable man. I liked him. And with his death, his absence was going to mean that I could no longer use the childish device of blaming him for everything difficult in my life. The years of evasion and projecting were coming to an end, the dark Father in my head was coming into consciousness, was putting on the pressure. I did not know how to use that Father. I wanted him out. I did not want to kill my father, but my guilt rose up and indicted me: at one point I actually believed that his cancer had developed because I had started seeing a therapist in a new attempt to subdue and vanquish the wild Father inside my own self.

I wanted to separate the fathers not just to allay my own guilt, but because I honestly learned that they were not the same person. When he became ill, my brothers and sisters and I talked of him in a new way, recalling him through memories and anecdotes and stories, shoring up his presence. I noticed something odd: what I had thought of as literal chronological memories were either so absent from their heads that they could not believe that the episodes I remembered had ever happened (and vice versa); or they did recall the incidents, but flavored with such different emotions and meanings as to render them almost unrecognizable. I had to see that we, who shared the same historical father, all had different fathers inside our heads. Between the six of us we had seven fathers.

Quite soon before he died I realized that I had a special bequest from him. He gave us many gifts, and among them he gave me a real knowledge and deep love for mythology. I started with his classical pantheon and with the tales from the Old Testament, and these have been tools of my thinking and working ever since. In Jane Lazarre's book *On Loving Men* I read that in classical mythology, that bloody and treacherous web of connections and hatreds, there is no story in which the daughter kills the father. I was taken aback. I searched high and low. I sifted through the equally blood-strewn corpus of the Bible. I extended my research into other mythologies. I thought to myself, "Aha, here is male dominance at work, this is one tale they cannot afford to know." Then I started looking at the historical murders, the ones that make it to the sleazy annals of crime literature. Women, I discovered, after traveling in some pretty gruesome places, do not murder their fathers. Or do so very seldom, and under some pretty bizarre circumstances. It is an extremely rare crime. Women murder men—their lovers, their employers, their children, their rapists, their ancient uncles, and the victims of stray meeting on the street. Clytemnestra drowned Menelaus in the bath; Jael made a bloody mess of Sisera; Myra Hindley mutilated children. Nothing can be claimed about women's gentleness, their lack of violence, their tender, loving hearts; but they don't kill their fathers. If we don't kill our fathers, then I could not have killed mine. Why did he, who taught me so many things, never teach me that my anger would not kill him? Or me? Or our love?

I think of this little fact as a gift because it set me free of some fears and helped me begin to separate the fathers. But it is not easy, and learning to separate them means also learning how they are joined. They grow from one root and it cannot be severed. To canonize my biological father at the expense of my mythic Father, to absolve my physical father by projecting onto the interior Father every dark thing that father means in a sexist society, will bring me no nearer to the truth—about myself, or him, or fathers, or daughters.

I am my father's daughter. I cannot love myself unless I love him.

I am a woman. I cannot be free while I am a daughter possessed by the Father Inside My Head.

He was just a man, I tell myself. He was a man whom I loved, as it happens. He was my father; he was the most influential person in my life. He was a man who introduced me into a male-dominated world. One of my problems with my father is that he really did correspond to the archetype of the Father. Many women grow out of their father when they discover that he is not really like what fathers are supposed, imaginatively, mythologically, to be: he is weak, or a failure, or dishonest, or uninterested, or goes away. My father was not a perfect person, but he was very Fatherlike.

He was one of the old gods—Zeus, Yahweh, Odin. The medieval Christian God-the-Father was distant and unapproachable, above and beyond emotions. The Oriental god is pure impersonal spirit-in-the-cosmos. The modern god suffers humbly with his poor (and may even be imaged as female). But the old gods were in there with their people: emotional, excitable, passionate, the administrators of a deeply partial justice, jealous of their prerogatives, zealously prejudiced in favor of their own, vengeful and dangerous when crossed, and delightedly generous when pleased by services rendered. They were powerful, and willing to use that power.

That might be a thumbnail sketch of my father.

Of course his power was partly social. On grounds of class and wealth he had a simple confidence about who he was, where he came from, and his ability to give his children what he wanted. It was physical—he was strong and very good-looking; he could not tolerate physical weakness, his own or other people's. It was personal, too; he had presence, a sort of shining inflexibility which, while it could and did infuriate people, also commanded respect.

He was not a distant father. He cared. His energy was directed at us in flood waves. He held a responsible and demanding job; he was an intelligent man and friends with influential and powerful people; he was actively interested in politics (Conservative), philanthropy, and, with limitations, culture. But we came first. He came home from the office every day and ate high tea with his family. He bathed his babies, climbed trees, kicked footballs, hugged, kissed, and played with his children. Above all he *taught* us, but not from far away. It started at dawn; whichever of us was at that stage of education went to get dressed in his dressing room. While he shaved he taught us our times tables, his face visible only in the mirror registering pleasure or irritation at our answers. When we knew our times tables impeccably, and the boys went off to prep school, he turned his attention to me and to wider fields of knowledge. With him, at seven-thirty in the morning, I learned by heart irregular Latin verbs, the dates of the kings of England and Scotland, and—along with quantities of other Victorian verse—the whole of "How Horatius Kept the Bridge in the Brave Days of Old" from Macaulay's *Lays of Ancient Rome.* When I was in interminable labor with my first child, I found myself muttering, "And how can man die better/than by facing, fearful odds/for the ashes of his fathers/and the temples of his Gods." There are seventy verses. I found I still knew them all and was comforted. He was a master pedagogue, full of zeal, enthusiasm, and the expectation and demand that we would perform well. We did.

He really came into his own when we went to live in Scotland. There the split between business and family, work and play, inside and outside disappeared. We were organized, energized, empowered by him, with scarcely a moment's break. I can easily understand how the ancient Hebrews did not believe in an individual soul, but only in the spirit of the community—Yahweh and my father seem to have had a lot in common, and the driving force was "the tribe in activity." Now we were communally involved in high-energy activities as much of the time as possible: gardening, planting trees, playing tennis, playing bridge, climbing hills, rowing boats, dancing reels, entertaining visitors, shooting, fishing, fighting, laughing, teasing. (He encouraged us, and joined us almost to the point of brutality in the permitted ranges of teasing—so long as it was witty it was fine. Simple rude abuse was not allowed, but to be funny at someone else's expense was "good for them." How long you could stand it without bursting into tears and rushing from the dining room was a measure of merit.) He was the direct force. Because the boys went away to school, and because too of a natural affinity of mind, there was at least a time when I was the central recipient of his energetic love.

He was partial. There was nothing cold about either his justice or his loyalty, nor about what he expected in return. He had an extraordinary sense of family, not particularly snobbish, but he lived in the home of his ancestors and saw himself—and all other members of his brood—in a curiously tribal way; simply one link in a chain that should not be broken. He handed on to us what he had received from them: education, pride, class privileges and class responsibility, a wealth of belonging as much as of belongings. He delighted to see that continue; he certainly deprived himself and my mother of many material luxuries (and some basic comforts) in order to hand on intact a promise of a future for the family estate. His grandchildren gave him special joy. In the last days of his life when speech had become impossible and when a great weariness seemed his main emotion, he still wanted to have the babies—mine and my sister's smallest children were then only months old—on the bed with him or playing on the floor around him.

CHAPTER FIVE

Jack Kornfield

Parenting as Spiritual Practice

Parenting is one of the most rewarding and demanding practices that one will undertake in this life. It makes a very demanding guru seem like a piece of cake. If your guru or teacher says to you, "Get up at three in the morning and do your bhajans, prayers, or zazen," you usually get up. But if you don't feel well you can sleep in and say you're sick. After all, what is he or she going to say? You can get away with it. But when your child wakes up in the middle of the night, sick and throwing up, you have to get up and care for her. It doesn't matter if you're exhausted from a very full week, or are sick yourself, or were up all day taking care of your other child.

I have looked into my heart to figure out why I became a parent. I was successful as a teacher and certainly living a wonderful life. Being a dharma teacher is a great job to have because you get to meet really nice people who are on their best behavior in beautiful places and circumstances, and talk about love and things that are basically noble and profound. You feel like you are doing something valuable (whether it's true or not is another question).

But before becoming a parent there was some sense of a lack in my own personal life. I felt that if I continued to teach and travel, that something else would get dry in me. This may not be so for other people, but I sensed that while I would continue to develop skills as a teacher, I would also lose contact with something that's more alive within, something that has to do with heart. So having a child came from a deep desire to keep my heart open. Certainly, being a parent is a very hot fire a lot of the time. Also, I think I became a parent because I like challenges.

Yet, I don't want to make this decision sound too thoughtful and conscious. It wasn't. It really came from the guts and the heart. It came from being in love with someone and saying, "Well let's try this one." But it's really a big ride. When you take the ticket you go for twenty years. Older friends say the problem is not the "empty nest syndrome," it's the "empty the nest out and they come in the back door" and want to live with you a little longer and get you to support them into their thirties.

Somehow, consciously chosen or not, having a child is mostly an expression of love. It has continued to deepen the intimacy and connection in my marriage. For me, it was pretty amazing because I never had a sexual life where we tried to do what sex is actually connected with—making babies. It was really powerful to make love and have the intention be to have a child, really quite extraordinary, mysterious, and wonderful.

When the baby was born it was awesome. You cannot be at a birth and not have your heart touched in some way. The pain and the beauty is amazing. At Caroline's birth I was exhausted because it was a three-day labor for my wife and I tried to stay fully with her. There was this glow as the baby was born, but at the same time I was checking her out and saying, "Are you the right one?" "Is this my child?" For anyone who has had children, it's very clear that they are not blank slates. A baby has her own personality, agenda and karma from the very beginning.

As your baby grows, as she walks, looks around or just smiles, you experience a sense of wanting to take care of her. It is so ingrained in us it must be cellular. Who can see a baby crying or some child that's hurt and not want to respond? In some ways it speaks to the innate goodness in all beings that there's that kind of response to children. The natural response of our hearts is to care for someone that's hurting or in need.

There is a mixture of pleasure and pain as you look at a baby and say, "I don't want her to suffer." Caroline's just learning about "hot." The other day she went over to a candle and said "hot," and when she went to touch the flame, we pulled her hand away and said "No, no, hot." She put her hand in anyway and it burned her fingers—not badly—just a little bit. She cried. Then her face changed to outrage. Why should it hurt? If it's not the candle or the stove it will be the heater. Yet what can a parent do? Life is pleasant and painful. From the beginning you realize that you can't fully protect anybody. You can love them, but you can't protect them. Eventually, everyone has to openly engage in the world that is light and dark, up and down, sweet and sour, and pleasant and painful.

In the beginning of parenting there is a tremendous sense of surrender. Once I lived with a woman who had two children. I got really jealous of the children. I wanted to be with her and have her attention. The children were jealous of me too. After a day in pre-school they wanted mommy's attention and kept pulling on her. "Stay here, read to us, play with us." It was a real struggle for a number of weeks over why we couldn't go out. I said, "Let's get more baby-sitters. Why do they have to get up so early and then bounce on the bed at six in the morning?" In the end there was no contest: I finally just gave up and raised the white flag of "I surrender." They came first. There was no question about it. I was defeated. It wasn't that I didn't want what I wanted. But it was really clear who came first. There is a tremendous amount of surrender to parenting and a kind of love that people otherwise rarely touch in their lives.

A good friend of mine had four daughters and a son. Her youngest daughter had a brain tumor when she was thirteen years old and needed an operation. She came out of her operation as if she had had a really bad stroke: unable to walk, unable to speak, unable to feed herself. Her mother was a Hawaiian and grew up in an Asian culture where, when someone's in the hospital, you go and camp out in the hospital with them. She camped in the hospital for three months with her daughter, until she could bring her home. She said, "I spent every waking hour for two and a half years bringing her back so she could walk and speak and eat and read. I knew somewhere in my heart that she hadn't died, that she was still in there and could be brought out. I would pick up her hand and put it down, pick it up again until she could speak, and help her walk." You couldn't pay somebody for that. This tremendous capacity we have to love another person is evoked by having children.

We also have a tremendous capacity to hate, or feel frustration. Already I have a very deep understanding about why child abuse happens. Here Caroline was a wanted baby and I consider myself someone who's got a decent amount of equanimity and awareness and still when the baby is colicky and crying, and just won't stop, what am I going to do? It's not just one night but nights and nights.

And then you think of people in a poor apartment where it's cold, not so comfortable, there are five kids and the latest one is just crying and screaming for two months and is colicky and won't stop.

I remember teaching at a conference one day with a whole roomful of people. In the room there was a young child that was really fussy. He started to scream and throw a tantrum. Finally the child was quieted and taken out and then one of the women in the room (obviously a professional mother) said, "Don't you remember the time when you just wanted to take them and throw them out the window and it didn't matter how many floors down it was?" And every mother in that room laughed. Every mother in the room laughed because they all knew that somehow their children had taken them to their very edge of sanity.

Parenting is a place of tremendous surrender and giving. You just give. You get back sometimes. Sometimes you don't get anything. Then they become teenagers and they don't seem to care about you at all. All they seem to want to do is be free and leave. "But I raised you and I did this and I gave you that." And they say "See ya, so long." If you're lucky, they say "See ya," before they disappear. What did I get from my giving? What you get is what you gave.

When you look at the path of perfections in Buddhism, generosity, patience, surrender, virtue, attention, and equanimity are all major components in the practice. For a start, parenting is a tremendous field in which to cultivate giving and surrender and patience and loving. It is really a practice if you can do it in even a somewhat mindful way. Perhaps those of us who are involved in becoming more aware are also relearning certain things that are known in simpler cultures, but have been forgotten in the busyness and ambition of our Western society. We're trying to relearn what it means to be part of a village or a sangha or a community and to raise our children in a way that's more caring and less ambitious, more patient and less greedy. Still it's hard. You give up a lot of yourself. If you think that sitting in meditation comes first, you really have to re-orient. There's a lovely book by Zen master Thich Nhat Hanh called the *Miracle of Mindfulness* and this is the first question he addresses, speaking to the parents who say they never have enough time for themselves. Until you make a shift and see that your time with another person is also time for yourself, you will be frustrated. Somehow you must learn to take that time with another person as your practice, as your own place of opening. Otherwise you will be frustrated all the time.

So in parenting there's *dana,* which means giving, patience and surrender. Next there's *sila,* the step in practice which means virtue. As a parent there are all kinds of ways to work with virtue. In the beginning it's simply learning how to say no to somebody and setting appropriate boundaries, saying no an awful lot of times and learning that it's really important that you're able to say no. People don't like to say no. I feel uncomfortable saying no to anybody. It really becomes very obvious with a child. You don't have to think about it . . . "No, cut that out . . . Stop it . . . Don't go in the street . . ." Of course you can find skillful ways to do it which don't undermine your child's exploration and self-esteem but still it must be said. Your whole sense of self changes as a guardian, a caretaker for another person, as a parent. So, at first, there's a kind of *sila* of setting of boundaries.

But, in a much deeper way, as the children grow older, life makes you have to look at your own values. What are you going to teach them? You're a daddy or you're a mommy. Are you going to teach them to play football or knit or whatever your image of what a young man or young woman is supposed to learn? You look at those parts of your values. Even more, it makes you question what kind of school they're going to, what they are going to learn. You see the blessings of our culture: its variety, its choices, its richness that your children will inherit. And you see as well the curses, the difficulties, the consumerism, the kind of superficiality, the shallowness. Just turn on the TV. Have your children watch TV for a while. Do you want to do that for some young person? . . . have them watch TV? So what do you teach kids? And how do you educate them? Raising children really makes you look at your values.

And, of course, every step of the way is compromise. There's no perfection in this game whatsoever. If you're a bad parent, then they will probably go to therapy and work it out. If you're too good, then they go to the therapist because they're unable to separate; they're too connected with you. There is no way you can win at the game. And in a way that's perfect. Because the perfection is that you realize that the child's not supposed to be a certain way or that you're not supposed to be a certain way. You give what you can give and maybe learn not to judge yourself so much.

I remember Kalu Rimpoche, an old Tibetan Llama, coming to

visit friends of mine with a two-year-old. They asked him, "Would you please tell me how to raise him so he will be spiritual and wise, a compassionate child, and a fine person?" And this eighty-year-old Tibetan Llama just shook his head and said, "No no . . . You have the wrong idea." He said, "He will be whoever he's going to be. If you want to raise somebody properly, raise yourself. You can do your own practice with a sincere heart and let him feel that from you."

Somebody said that parenting is one of the few things that's left in the world for amateurs. We get training to become drivers. We get training to be teachers. We get training to be counselors. Then there's this basically impossible task of trying to be kind and wise and helpful, set limits and teach your child how to be a fine human being and we get zero training for that. We're really amateurs. If you can keep a beginner's mind, wisdom can truly grow. You don't know what your child will be like when he is born. You just get him. And you don't know what he's going to be like as a grown-up. You have a fifteen-year-old and you don't know what career she will take. You have a twenty-year-old and you don't know what mischief she will get into. It's really a process of learning how to deal with the unknown, holding your breath, waiting and seeing what happens.

Caroline, who likes to eat Cheerios for breakfast, can really teach me how to live in the moment. She can sit down with her Cheerios, and line them up or put them on top of one another or spear one with her little finger or look around . . . put it in her mouth . . . chew it . . . take it out and see what happened to it . . . then stick it in my mouth to see if I like it . . . then pull it out again and spend twenty minutes experimenting with all the properties of a Cheerio. Then she'll put it down and experiment with the spoon. This tremendous capacity to be in the present moment reevokes that spirit of the child in ourselves. I love going out with Caroline and looking at a tree, introducing her to it, "Wow, that's a tree. Look, it has leaves and moves in the wind and there's lots of them all around, different kinds. They smell different." But we adults forget. We take trees for granted. When I walk down the street with Caroline, I remember. "Oh look. There's dry leaves. They crumble and crunch." We forget that the world is tremendously interesting. We lose a certain mystery. Maybe that's the best thing about children. They keep us awake, seeing the world in a fresh way.

Not only do you learn the samadhi of being very present with your attention, but you also learn the other special practice called in

Sanskrit *sampajanna,* which means to be able to do many things mindfully at once: like change a diaper, hold the child still and get some clothes or take care of two or three children, one who's pouring things on the floor, and one who's running around, and the other who needs to be fed and all at the same time, while you're also trying to answer the phone that's ringing. For me it's been a very different kind of meditation, that of walk when you walk, eat when you eat. Kids know how to do that. Eat when you eat and play with your Cheerios when you play with your Cheerios. But being a parent is more like the Korean Zen master Seung Sahn, who was sitting at the table at the Zen center one morning eating his breakfast and reading the morning paper. A student came up to him very upset and said, "How can you do this, Roshi. Here you teach us to just eat when you eat, walk when you walk and sit when you sit and now you're eating and also reading. What kind of example is that?" He looked up and laughed, "When you eat and read, just eat and read." Keep it simple.

A friend of mine, a poet and a faculty member at Naropa Institute, is a wonderful teacher and a successful business woman, having started a company that makes millions of dollars. She also spent many years in India. Right before our baby was born, I asked her, "What do you think about having children and a family?" And she said, "You know, it is the one thing in my life I really don't regret doing at all. It brought me the most satisfaction, the most happiness and the most joy."

Being a parent connects us with the earth. It brings us back to the trees and to biology and to our bodies and to our hearts. I think of what Mother Teresa said when I interviewed her: "If the world is to end nuclear war, if we're to stop the arms race and its madness that we find around us, it's not just the politicians who must do it, but it's each person in their own family in their own neighborhood. If you can't learn to love your own children, and your neighbors, the people who live next door to you, how do you expect the world to change in any way that will bring peace for us?"

CHAPTER SIX

Karen Hill Anton

Remembering a Father Who Mothered

She was eighteen when they married, he was fifty. My brother was born in March 1944, I in April 1945, my sister in April 1946. My mother didn't make it. She disappeared when my sister was a few months old. (Was it for two weeks, a month? I never knew exactly how long, but it was long enough for handbills to be passed out giving a description of what she was "last seen wearing.") When found, she was committed to a state mental hospital, diagnosed as having amnesia. Though I knew what that word meant, it wasn't until much later that I could understand how much my mother must have wanted to forget.

"Put them in foster homes or an orphanage," my father was urged. "A man, especially a man of your age, can't possibly raise three young children."

The grandson of a slave, my father certainly never expected that life would be easy. Born in Mississippi in 1893, he was one of many blacks who went north in the early years of this century not only in search of the "promised land" but also to escape the constant threat of the lyncher's noose.

Although he managed to get an education, even graduating from Hampton Institute, it was clear to me as a young child that he thought himself fortunate to have any job at all. When he could find employment, it was often as a presser in a cleaning shop. I lied and told my friends he was a tailor, because even at that age, I appreciated the perceived difference between a professional and a laborer.

The cleaning shops he worked in were often local ones (so he could "keep an eye on us" while he worked). We would sometimes stop by to wave at him through a tiny window or go to the steamy back of the shop, knowing that no matter how busy he was, he would be glad to see us. The sweat poured off him as he stood over the large presser in the sleeveless undershirt he always worked in. "Daddy, can we have a nickel for a cream soda?" we'd ask.

The first word I knew how to spell was *Mississippi*—forward, backward, and fast. My father's education did not get him a job, but he passed on what he knew to his children. Gathering not only us but the neighbors' kids as well, he taught us our "sums," penmanship, and spelling. He knew American history thoroughly, especially that of the Civil War and the period of Reconstruction. "Please, Mr. Hill, tell us about the time . . ." sounded the pleas of the children as he told tales of the old South; and if he told a ghost story, you really got scared!

I knew my father had the only typewriter in the neighborhood—an old heavy, black Royal—and probably the only set of encyclopedias. He was openly looked on as a resource and was often called on to draw up a petition, write a eulogy, chair the PTA or the community league, or lead a rent strike. When he wrote in his "fine hand," you could hear his pen scratching across vellum and bond; you could hear the pauses when he dipped the point into blue-black ink. His personal letters were treasures of wit, wisdom, and penmanship. The typed ones, to editors and congressmen, were fiery expressions of right and responsibility.

My oldest memory of anything is of my father coming back from work one day, and me running down our long hall (how long was that hall, I wonder now?) to meet him. He hunched down to half his size to give me a kiss and a hug, and I could see the top of his head and smell the pomade on his slicked-black hair. I must have been about four.

I remember, too, the time I accidentally ate the "dead man's meat," or gills of a crab. All of my friends said it would kill me, and I accepted their word, because we all knew you were never supposed to eat that part. I was afraid to sleep that night, knowing death would claim me as soon as I closed my eyes. But then I realized that if I slept with Daddy I couldn't possibly die. So I crept into his bed and fell asleep with my head nestled on his chest and in the soft hair of his underarm. Surely death would not snatch me from the safety of my father—and it didn't.

"He does everything a woman would do for those kids."

Didn't he do everything a man would do? In any case, he did what had to be done. So, of course, it never occurred to me that a man couldn't do what I'd seen my father do daily. Although the women's movement informed me that most men didn't do these things, I certainly knew they could. Friends joked that my husband would have a "hard act to follow."

When I was growing up, we didn't have a washing machine. I don't think anyone in our neighborhood had one. My father spent Saturday mornings scrubbing on a washboard in the bathtub with a large bar of brown laundry soap. I would trail after him as he took the enameled basin filled with well-wrung-out clothes and a paper bag of wooden clothespins up to the clothesline on the roof. Even after laundromats came into use, it took John Hill a long time to accept them.

All clothes were cotton then (remember?), and my father spent his Saturday nights ironing our dresses and pinafores with their wide sashes. ("Oh, he ties those girls' sashes as well as any woman.") At that time no one even considered letting his or her hair go its own natural way, so he would spend hours straightening, braiding, and curling our hair so we could look "just as nice as the other little girls"—the girls who had mothers.

He could really "put the pots on," as I loved to brag to my friends, and make tasty soups and stews from just the bare essentials. He never had a cookbook; he never looked at a recipe; we didn't even have a measuring cup and spoons. We never canned or froze anything. Sometimes our cupboard was truly bare, and there was "nothing in the icebox," but when I was a child I assumed everyone was hungry some of the time and that they were as happy as we were on the days when Daddy came home with heavy shopping bags.

Years later, when I was pregnant with my first child in Spain, I so longed for my father's cooking that I drew up a list of the things he made that I loved in an effort (not an entirely futile one, either) to assuage my cravings: stuffing for turkey, okra gumbo, black-eyed peas and rice, corn bread, biscuits, collard greens, mustard greens, baked beans. Later, when I wrote from Denmark of Nanao's birth, he promptly answered, "Now, Karen, you must begin to cultivate patience," and I wondered, how did he know? Nursing her, I found myself singing a song my father had sung to us at bedtime when we were very little. I hadn't heard that song for twenty years, and I'd never heard anyone other than my father sing it, but it seemed to be waiting in my throat for my baby.

Nothing was easy about not having a mother. It wasn't easy having to tell my father when I began menstruating or having to ask for the money to buy my first bra. It used to hurt like hell when some well-meaning person would say, "Your father is a wonderful and exceptional man," because it underscored the fact that we had no mother. I didn't like to be told that I, much more than my sister and brother, looked like and had the temperament of my father. But now there is pride in all that, and gratitude.

CHAPTER SEVEN

David Riley

The Joys of Fatherhood

From the moment he was born, I was smitten with Jake, more, I think, than even my wife dared to hope. I never knew how much you could get by giving. Jake takes a lot of time, but he gives back a dimension to my life that I cherish, and I've come to think that the world might be a very different place if its workaholics had more of this dimension in their lives.

I've always known that it's nice to be needed, but there's something so refreshingly simple and fundamental about the way Jake needs me: without words, without convoluted feelings to be sorted out, without mixed messages. He often needs simply to be held— nothing more—just loving, physical contact, accompanied by a soothing voice perhaps.

At certain predictable times, such as when he wakes up, Jake needs attention, no matter what our mood. Sometimes it's an interruption, and I don't like being interrupted. But I've come to look at it another way, too. If my work is going badly and I'm depressed about it, Jake still needs breakfast in the morning, and I know I can still make it for him and meet his need, which suggests that after breakfast I can still do my work, too, and meet some of my needs. There's comfort in the continuity of the routine; nurturing Jake has become a way of nurturing myself.

Jake makes my intellect take time off, which allows my senses and feelings to be more active. Raising a child requires plenty of intellect, certainly, but not in the same way writing does, at least not at his age. There's a refreshing difference between meticulously struggling to find the right phrase and instinctively knowing the right time to plant kisses on a soft cheek.

I get an atavistic joy out of listening to Jake's sounds. It's like watching a wildflower unfold. In the absence of words, he bursts out screams of excitement. He gestures with his voice, gurgling forth fresh, delightfully garbled notes that must sound like words to him. He is like an unfinished sculpture creating himself.

Nights are another new experience. How often do we enjoy the simplicity of total darkness? I'm much too busy (or self-important) to do so on my own accord. Only mystics soothe their souls with the experience of nothingness. And fathers and mothers walking infants at night. Normally, if I can't sleep, I read. Now, even when I sleep, I sometimes treat myself to the mystic's pleasures, or watch moonlight glisten off the stone wall outside our living room, punctuated by Jake's rhythmic breath warming the hollow of my shoulder.

Why do people glow so at the sight of babies? A month after Jake was born, we spent a weekend in New York at Christmastime. He won over the city for us. You might have thought we were carrying the deity for all the goodwill we encountered on the streets of this city where murderers and rapists prowl.

I used to resent the extra attention babies get. It seemed unfair to the rest of us. I understand it better now. There's a special charm in the way small children go about discovering the world. The slightest thing, like a piece of dust on a rug, brings squeals of delight. What an elixir for sadness! Infants delight adults by bringing them out of their frame of reference, out from under the weight of the world that hangs over them. It's hard to stay grumpy in the face of such innocent joy.

Humor often grows out of incongruity, and the sight of Jake parodying us, like a miniature adult, doubles the laughter in my life. I think of him walking around tapping a soup ladle on the floor like a cane, or looking in the mirror on the closet door, then peering behind it to see if he's there.

I don't mean to suggest, of course, that everything is easy. Jake's lack of language may be charming, but it's also frustrating and sometimes exhausting. So are the endless diaper changes and washings, the boundless energy, the constant picking up after him, the lack of sleep, the early morning risings, the arranging of baby-sitters and coordinating various siblings' needs, the car pooling, and so on.

But there's a freshness about the way this little boy meets every morning that lifts up our lives. It's like the freshness of early morning sun sparkling off the dew on the grass. It's the same sun and the same grass every morning, but it still makes your heart stop and take notice.

I've learned that having a child doesn't have to turn you inward away from concern for the world. On the contrary. One evening my wife Martha and I watched the film, *War without Winners;* in it people were interviewed on the streets of New York and Moscow, speaking from their hearts, all saying the same thing: nuclear war would be unspeakably horrible, and it must never happen. The film also included interviews with government officials spouting nationalistic bravado, and interviews with retired officials saying that such talk is crazy. As I watched and held Jake—hovering in the hollow of my shoulder, wispy hair bobbing, dark eyes peering out, a soft ear against my cheek—I couldn't stop crying.

I was crying because Jake is so innocent and sweet and vulnerable, and we have brought him into a world being paved over with arms. Jake's being—his size, his soul, his natural openness to the world—cuts through all the rationales that keep us from building more arms for more people to use for killing even more people. Watching that movie with Jake, we knew that we would have to make room in our lives for disarmament in order for our lives to make any sense.

Children remind us of our common humanity. Sometimes when I hold Jake at night, one arm resting against my chest, the other on my shoulder, I think of the picture I saw in a magazine of a Russian father holding his young son in a car on the Trans-Siberian Railway. I see the twinkle in that boy's eye, much like Jake's when he gets the idea that we'll chase him. I think of that little Russian boy staggering across the floor, as Jake does, arms careening in all directions until he collapses in a pool of belly laughs when his parents capture him.

I don't read as many books as I used to because of the time I spend with Jake. I don't know as much about the sociology of that Russian father's life as I might if I had more time to read. But through Jake I make other connections—to myself and the world around me. When I'm sad, Jake's eyes still shine. He greets me as if I were shining. He greets the world as if it were shining, and before long it shines again for me, too. In an era that reveres intellectual and physical power, I learn from this little being, just to my knees, whose power lies not in his body or his mind but in his soul. Through him I learn about my connection to that Russian father. It helps to believe—I guess I have to believe—that through such connections the world will somehow make its way toward peace.

CHAPTER EIGHT

Loren Pedersen

The Healthy Father

A man who wishes to be a healthy father might begin by making a conscious decision to accept the responsibilities of parenthood. He could accept that his future son has a right to be born into a family where he will be cared for within the best psychological and emotional environment that can be provided for him. He could accept the significance of his role as a father, even during pregnancy. He could participate in the delivery process as much as possible and be there to support his wife and to greet his son at birth. His emotional commitment to his son could continue until his son has reached a sufficient level of emotional and physical maturity to adequately care for himself.

Above all, the healthy father possesses self-awareness. He is emotionally and intellectually open, and he is honest enough to be able to reflect on his own attitudes, feelings and behavior. He doesn't take for granted that he is always right, but he is willing to examine himself and, if need be, come to a more appropriate way of feeling and acting without being coerced to change by outside forces. In fact, he sees change as representing a healthy continuation of growth within the family structure. He is not emotionally invested in an exaggerated sense of masculine identification. He also accepts traits within himself that are traditionally considered to be feminine or even maternal—that is, he accepts his anima. A father who accepts his own contrapsychological qualities provides a model that will allow his son to be more accepting of his own feminine qualities and consequently more accepting of women.

If the father accepts his sensuality and sexuality as an integral part of his nature, his son is likely to do the same. This enables them to talk about the positive and negative aspects of sexuality as an important part of their manhood without diminishing or denigrating women.

The healthy father is also aware that he is not perfect, and that there will always be qualities in himself that he needs to work on to improve. He accepts these "darker" aspects of himself as part of who he is. By accepting his *shadow,* he spares his son the burden of having to unconsciously carry it for him. He also accepts his son's shortcomings as part of his personality, without assuming the right to impose his values on his son. He accepts his son's reasonable disappointments in him as a healthy expression of their differences. He introduces his son to the outside world in a way that helps him to develop a respect for the natural social and moral boundaries between himself and others.

The healthy father realizes the importance of developing honest communication skills with his son and ensures that he has time to do this. He is able to see his son as an individual and not as an extension of himself, even though he realizes his son will use him for a model well into his adolescent years. He sees some disagreements as his son's way of testing his perception of his father as all-powerful and invulnerable.

He allows his son to begin to break his dependence on him when the son begins to strike out in his own direction; he sees a certain degree of healthy rebellion as his son's way of experimenting with being his own person. He is able to understand and accept that his son may increasingly see him as less than perfect. But the flaws his son sees allow the son to resist placing unrealistic demands upon himself. They allow him to see his own limits of physical and intellectual performance. Through this, he can develop a stable concept of what it means to apply himself fully to his tasks in life, as well as to know what "good enough" means for him.

In early adulthood, the son may turn away from the father to another mentor, often an older man in an area of mutual interest or profession—a transitional figure whom the son may idealize in place of his father. The healthy father may view this as a loss but he also understands it as his son's way of starting to let go of the idealization of his father. In later adult life the son stops idealizing his mentor as well; while he may retain respect for him, he increasingly turns to himself as the ultimate validator of his life.

In old age, the father comes to portray the spiritual values developed over a lifetime of experience. By demonstrating them, rather than espousing values that have been mindlessly borrowed from a dogmatic theory or belief system, he continues to be a source of inspiration for his son. At the same time, the healthy father continues to encourage his son to explore and find his own values.

The healthy father-son relationship allows the son to increasingly see his father's humanness and natural vulnerability, as well as his own strength. It also eventually allows him to separate his projections of the archetypal father from his own father, the man.

II

Father and Son: The Search

Father and son form the most dangerous and critical animal relationship on earth, and to suppose otherwise is to invite catastrophe.

WESTON LABARRE

I am that father whom your boyhood lacked and suffered pain for the lack of.

HOMER

Father! Father! Where are you going? Oh do not walk so fast. Speak, father, speak to your little boy or else I shall be lost.

WILLIAM BLAKE

If you don't understand my silence, you'll never understand what I say.

ANONYMOUS

Introduction

Our fathers profoundly influence us, more than most of us care to acknowledge. I have noticed that when middle-aged sons speak of their fathers (dead or alive), there is often hesitancy in their voices, a telling silence full of muted emotion. Sons spend a large portion of their lives idealizing, separating from, and reconciling themselves with their personal fathers, along with integrating inner, more universal fatherly qualities. Wives, lovers, friends, and careers may come and go, but a son remains a son—even if he is a father himself.

In Part I, we discussed how paternal absence and ambiguity stimulated an appetite for more presence from the father. We will continue that exploration in this part with the son looking up to his father, then individuating from his father, and finally bridging the distance between himself and his father. Opportunities for connection thrive in the spacious gap between father and son. When sons work at getting close to their fathers, they often find that a doorway opens to the love they seek.

But first let's review some thematic steps leading toward the reconciliation and forgiveness that we'll encounter in the concluding part of this anthology. This journey to find the father can be simply described as a search for (1) a boyhood hero in the father; (2) autonomy, independence from the father; and (3) reunion with the father.

THE SEARCH FOR A BOYHOOD HERO

We all know that fathers loom larger than life for children. Kids naturally tend to idealize and project all kinds of inflated images on to their dads. Young boys expect too much from their fathers, especially in light of the decline in extended family and community participation. A son wanting more from a father is native to the father-son territory.

Sometimes this desire for closeness gets reinforced by family members as well as the culture, and then carried into adult life. It is typified in expressions like: "follow in his footsteps"; "filling his shoes"; "like father, like son"; "a chip off the old block." Note the potential for both overidentification and competition in these comparative expressions.

When the son substitutes is own inflated heroic image for his real and unheroic father, he feels betrayed. Inevitably, the father is not who the son thought he was. The son may reject the father then, cutting him out of his life, or he may accommodate a more realistic view of him. James Hillman has written that whenever the son idealizes the father, he remains in sonship, in the false security of a good ideal, and by implication, the son invites betrayal. Betrayal in this sense serves the growth process if it forces a son's awareness toward what is real.

THE SEARCH FOR INDEPENDENCE

We move away from our fathers to explore our own paths, learning to stand as separate but equal persons. Whether we regard a father as a positive or negative role model, separating from him is a healthy and necessary part of growing up. Separation from a father brings a bird's-eye, more objective view of him, which serves as a preamble to a more empathetic reunion later on.

Traditionally, the father moderates independence and freedom. If the father dispenses too much freedom too soon, the son may trash such symbols as the family car. If he doesn't permit enough freedom, the son may fall into a deadening submission that often carries an underlying resentment or, at the other extreme, open rebellion. In either case, more than the family car is at risk. A father needs to closely monitor the amount of age-appropriate latitude he gives his son.

A father who is a negative role model also serves his son's independence, for he teaches him how not to live. If a son learns from his father's mistakes, he can break the endless chain of dysfunction passed down through the generations. However, the space between father and son can seem like an endless minefield. Here are a few of the inflammatory issues that can either derail or vitalize a later reunion between father and son.

Obstacles and Catalysts for the Son's Independence

A father can stand in the way of a son's search for independence. Often what may be camouflaged as care and concern is really the father fueling his own ego and ambition at the expense of letting the son make his own way. The father may relish the son's accomplishments, which reflect back on the father, or he may parasitically attach himself to the son in an attempt to realize his own dreams. An insecure father may use his son in an attempt to heal his own sense of shame handed to him by his father. The son in turn often picks up the father's shadow, the excess baggage and failed dreams, and carries them on his back.

A father's expectations of a son commonly surface around sports, educational achievement, career choices, friends, and choice of wife. This well-wishing goes so deep that the father may disregard his son's individuality, projecting his own fantasies without awareness of the younger man's wishes. His aspirations for his son may be a cover for his own unfulfilled needs.

A son's confrontation with a father is part of the larger process leading to final reconciliation, but in the short run it is an attempt to claim power, independence, and declare his own values. Confrontation has a way of escalating toward open conflict when it is not contained by trust. In the *Star Wars* movies, the hero Luke Skywalker challenges the corrupt values of his powerful, dark father, Darth Vader. It is a battle not only for his life; it echoes a universal tension between good and evil.

The father does not need to be powerful for confrontations to occur. Willy Loman in Arthur Miller's play *Death of a Salesman* is a beaten man, yet his son Biff beseeches him to discard his phony dreams for Biff's instant success. He wants his father to let him live his own life, to discover who he is on his own. Here, the father-son conflict turns when the son asks the perennial question, "Why am I trying to become what I don't want to be?"

Father-son competition is undeniably present in areas of work, women, and sports. I recall a number of men commenting to me how important it was when they first made more money than their fathers did. Robert Bly writes convincingly about the father and son competing for attention from the same woman—the wife/mother. I'll never forget the father-son basketball scene in the movie *The Great Santini*. The father, played by Robert Duvall, can't accept losing to his son in a one-on-one competition.

Michael McGill, in *The McGill Report on Male Intimacy,* calls fathers and sons "the intimate adversaries." He found that competition between father and son was both the primary vehicle for and obstacle to intimacy. Competition brings them closer together "while the very structure of competition constrains the development of intimacy."

The Son's Initiation by Fathers and by War

Initiation is much more than a buzz word of the men's movement and Jungian psychology. It is the ritual road to individuation and marks the times when we make significant shifts in self-development. At best, initiations are intentional, ordered, and contained processes whereby elders honor a rite of passage. At worst, they are unconscious, traumatic processes, such as gang wars or violent near-death experiences, which destructure the psyche and leave us crippled in our attempts to integrate anything of value. Since there is so little purposeful initiation in our culture, the father is cast with the difficult role of initiating boys into a reality that includes pain and limitation. The father initiates the son so that the son won't step into the world outside the home with naïveté.

An element of mystery surrounds a father initiating a son into manhood. The induction has a numinous quality and a strong energetic presence. Sherwood Anderson's silent initiation by his father one stormy night (Chapter 12) radically changed their relationship and clarified the young man's destiny to be a writer.

For centuries both fatherhood and war have been primary initiations for boys into the brotherhood of men. Having personally gone to war and subsequently fathered children, I believe fatherhood is a more life-affirming initiation than war. It upholds a deeper meaning for the concept of protecting the species than do most acts in war. Yet both fatherhood and war can be a painful replay of wounds passed down through the generations.

While I was researching trauma among Vietnam veterans, a link between fathers and war became apparent to me. I was surprised when the majority of participants spontaneously and emotionally referred to their fathers within the first three minutes of an open-ended interview. Their intense feelings of anger, betrayal, abandonment, and sadness were connected with losing rapport with their fathers after coming home from the war.

Their fathers were instrumental, for the most part unconsciously, in their choice to volunteer for war. Several themes were involved in choosing to volunteer: Often the son had a utopian picture of the father's World War II combat experience and was trying to prove himself to his father. Or he was trying to get away from his father or punish him. After the war, most veterans felt their fathers were not interested in hearing about what they had endured. An illegitimate war, coupled with a severed relationship between father and son, left a wake of tragedy across America from which we are still recovering.

The fathers in my study were perceived by the sons as remiss in protecting them from unnecessary suffering, and they neglected to accompany their sons during their healing from the war. The fathers had denied their own pain, and they had failed to teach their sons about the harsh realities of war and life. Thus the cycle was perpetuated, and the sons went to war to receive a seemingly more brutal than necessary initiation.

THE SEARCH FOR REUNION

The journey home to rediscover our fathers is a sacred undertaking that touches the soul. It is replete with power and feeling. The biological connection, the shared history, the generational differences combine, elevating this personal journey to one of universal dimensions. Sons return to the homes of their fathers to bless and be blessed and to hear the declaration that every son wants to hear: "You are my son, and I am well pleased."

When a man earns his independence and feels that his cup is full enough, then he can raise it to toast his father. In this special moment the cup figuratively becomes a chalice. Often the father is not alive to receive his son's gift. It comes as some kind of a eulogy after the father's death. The eulogy ranges from a recognition of karmic connection and indebtedness to an irreverent tinge of "good riddance."

Reunion with the father involves working through feelings of shame, blame, judgment, and resentment before real forgiveness can occur. Developing empathy and understanding of our fathers is a prerequisite for reunion. Empathy means expressing interest in and finding compassion for our fathers' lives. In a culture that places a premium on independence and individual achievement, sons are all too likely to resist this final step of returning home.

OVERVIEW

In Part II we will explore issues of initiation, potent silence, confrontation, and some passages in which fathers and sons have found a bond that connected them to each other.

In a poignant excerpt from his bestseller *Iron John: A Book about Men,* celebrated poet Robert Bly reveals the roots of the individual and cultural wounds that damage a son's attitude toward older men. Isolated from genuine values, many of today's fathers feed their sons' disappointment and distrust by passing on their moods rather than their teaching. Bly observes how many sons today attempt to redeem the dark father by ascending above him rather than through the kind of confrontation that occurred in recent generations.

In Chapter 10, Jungian analyst Fred Gustafson explores how woundedness in the father-son relationship results in a crippled sense of masculinity. He passionately calls for fathers to initiate sons into the masculine mysteries through deep, honest communication about their life philosophies. This selection is composed of excerpts from his book *Fathers, Sons and Brotherhood;* the excerpts appeared in *Betwixt & Between: Patterns of Masculine and Feminine Initiation.*

Archetypal psychologist James Hillman brings us a stimulating excerpt from *A Blue Fire,* a compilation of his writings. He contends that even the terrible traits of the father facilitate initiation because they kill idealization, initiate the son into the hard lines of his own shadow, and create a countereducation.

Shifting gears, the next four selections are stories by sons who find both their fathers and themselves. They are tales of honor, initiation, and compassion.

Themes of silence, mystery, and initiation are beautifully described in a classic excerpt by author Sherwood Anderson (1876–1941). He tells of his initiation by his father while swimming naked during a nighttime thunderstorm.

In "Of Lineage and Love," professor Stephen T. Butterfield discovers that he belongs to a line of Butterfields, a thread of continuity that holds his family together. Ironically, it is the author's oldest son who brings him back in touch with the family's genealogy. It's a moving portrait of this author understanding his father's anger and wounded pride and appreciating his father for the teacher and nurturer that he was. This article appeared in an expanded form in *The Sun*.

Based on a lecture later published in *The Only Dance There Is,* Ram Dass (Dr. Richard Alpert) brings home from India to his father's kitchen table a message of "being-love." It's an amusing and very real example from his early 1970s "here and now" philosophy. Ram Dass is a prolific writer and lecturer.

The quest for the father, the search for a sense of home and center, is the material from which mythology is made. Framed between birth and death, there is ample plot and duration. We may long for, abandon, rediscover, and finally forgive our fathers.

Seeking and finding links between fathers, sons, and ancestors brings sons a feeling of fullness and connection. This feeling provides a container that enables sons to trust that their appetites for more father can be fed. When sons begin to feel their own inner sense of masculinity, then they can become the fathers they were seeking.

CHAPTER NINE

Robert Bly

The Hunger for the King in a Time with No Father

DISTURBANCES IN SONHOOD

As I've participated in men's gatherings since the early 1980s, I've heard one statement over and over from American males, which has been phrased in a hundred different ways: "There is not enough father." The sentence implies that father is a substance like salt, which in earlier times was occasionally in short supply, or like groundwater, which in some areas now has simply disappeared.

Geoffrey Gorer remarked in his book *The American People* that for a boy to become a man in the United States in 1940 only one thing was required: namely, that he reject his father.[1] He noticed, moreover, that American fathers expect to be rejected. Young men in Europe, by contrast, have traditionally imagined the father to be a demonic being whom they must wrestle with (and the son in Kafka's "The Judgment" does wrestle his father to the death and loses). Many sons in the United States, however, visualize the father as a simple object of ridicule to be made fun of, as, in fact, he is so often in comic strips and television commercials. One young man summed it up: "A father is a person who rustles newspapers in the living room."

Clearly, "father water" in the home has sunk below the reach of most wells.

TOO LITTLE FATHER

When the father water-table, the groundwater, drops, so to speak, and there is too little father, instead of too much father, the sons find themselves in a new situation. What do they do: drill for new father water, ration the father water, hoard it, distill mother water into father water?

Traditional cultures still in existence seem to have plenty of father. In so-called traditional cultures, many substitute fathers work with the young man. Uncles loosen the son up, or tell him about women. Grandfathers give him stories. Warrior types teach weaponry and discipline, old men teach ritual and soul—all of them honorary fathers.

Bruno Bettelheim noticed, too, that in most traditional cultures Freud's version of father-son hatred doesn't hold. The wordless tension between fathers and sons in Vienna, which he assumed to be universal and based on sexual jealousy, was, in Bettelheim's opinion, true mostly in Vienna in the late nineteenth century.[2]

Fathers and sons in most tribal cultures live in an amused tolerance of each other. The son has a lot to learn, and so the father and son spend hours trying and failing together to make arrowheads or to repair a spear or track a clever animal. When a father and son do spend long hours together, which some fathers and sons still do, we could say that a substance almost like food passes from the older body to the younger.

The contemporary mind might want to describe the exchange between father and son as a likening of attitude, a miming, but I think a physical exchange takes place, as if some substance was passing directly to the cells. The son's body—not his mind—receives and the father gives this food at a level far below consciousness. The son does not receive a hands-on healing, but a body-on healing. His cells receive some knowledge of what frequency the masculine body is. The younger body learns at what frequency the masculine body vibrates. It begins to grasp the song that the adult male cells sing, and how the charming, elegant, lonely, courageous, half-shamed male molecules dance.

During the long months the son spent in the mother's body, his body got well tuned to female frequencies: it learned how a woman's cells broadcast, who bows to whom in that resonant field, what animals run across the grassy clearing, what the body listens for at night, what the upper and lower fears are. How firmly the son's body becomes, before birth and after, a good receiver for the upper and lower frequencies of the mother's voice! The son either tunes to that frequency or he dies.

Now, standing next to the father, as they repair arrowheads, or repair plows, or wash pistons in gasoline, or care for birthing animals, the son's body has a chance to retune. Slowly, over months or years, that son's body-strings begin to resonate to the harsh, sometimes demanding, testily humorous, irrelevant, impatient, opinionated, forward-driving, silence-loving older masculine body. Both male and female cells carry marvelous music, but the son needs to resonate to the masculine frequency as well as to the female frequency.

Sons who have not received this retuning will have father hunger all their lives. I think calling the longing "hunger" is accurate: the young man's body lacks salt, water, or protein, just as a starving person's body and lower digestive tract lack protein. If it finds none, the stomach will eventually eat up the muscles themselves. Such hungry sons hang around older men like the homeless do around a soup kitchen. Like the homeless, they feel shame over their condition, and it is the nameless, bitter, unexpungable shame.

Women cannot, no matter how much they sympathize with their starving sons, replace that particular missing substance. The son later may try to get it from a woman his own age, but that doesn't work either.

Distrust of Older Men

Only one hundred and forty years have passed since factory work began in the West, and we see in each generation poorer bonding between father and son, with catastrophic results. A close study of the Enclosure Act of England shows that the English government, toward the end of that long legislative process, denied the landless father access to free pasture and common land with the precise aim of forcing him, with or without his family, to travel to the factory. The South Africans still do that to black fathers today.

By the middle of the twentieth century in Europe and North America a massive change had taken place: the father was working but the son could not see him working.

Throughout the ancient hunter societies, which apparently lasted thousands of years—perhaps hundreds of thousands—and throughout the hunter-gatherer societies that followed them, and the subsequent agricultural and craft societies, fathers and sons worked and lived together. As late as 1900 in the United States about 90 percent of fathers were engaged in agriculture. In all these societies the son characteristically saw his father working at all times of the day and all seasons of the year.

When the son no longer sees that, what happens? After thirty years of working with young German men, as fatherless in their industrial society as young American men today, Alexander Mitscherlich developed a metaphor: a hole appears in the son's psyche. When the son does not see his father's workplace, or what he produces, does he imagine his father to be a hero, a fighter for good, a saint, or a white knight? Mitscherlich's answer is sad: demons move into that empty place—demons of suspicion.[3]

The demons, invisible but talkative, encourage suspicion of all older men. Such suspicion effects a breaking of the community of old and young men. One could feel this distrust deepen in the sixties: "Never trust anyone over thirty."

The older men in the American military establishment and government did betray the younger men in Vietnam, lying about the nature of the war, remaining in safe places themselves, after having asked the young men to be warriors and then in effect sending them out to be ordinary murderers. And so the demons have had a lot to work with in recent American history. The demons urge all men to see *Lawrence of Arabia* and *Dead Poets Society* because they remind us how corrupt all men in authority are and how thoroughly they betray the young male idealist. Mentorship becomes difficult to sustain; initiation is rejected.

Anthropologists affected by those demons suggest that elders in primitive cultures always perform sadistic and humiliating acts on young men under the cover of initiatory ritual. A young architect controlled by the demons secretly rejoices when a Louis Sullivan building gets knocked down; and the rock musician plays with a touch of malice the music that his grandfather could never understand.

This distrust is not good for the son's stability either. The son, having used up much of his critical, cynical energy suspecting old men, may compensate by being naive about women—or men—his own age. A contemporary man often assumes that a woman knows more about a relationship than he does, allows a woman's moods to run the house, assumes that when she attacks him, she is doing it "for his own good." Many marriages are lost that way. He may be unsuspecting in business also: he may allow a man his own age to steal all his money, or he may accept humiliation from another man under cover of friendship or teaching. Having all the suspicion in one place—toward older men—often leads to disaster in relationships and great isolation in spirit and soul.

In the next decade we can expect these demons of suspicion to cause more and more damage to men's vision of what a man is, or what the masculine is. Between 20 and 30 percent of American boys now live in a house with no father present, and the demons there have full permission to rage.

It seems possible, too, that as more and more mothers work out of the house, and cannot show their daughters what they produce, similar emotions may develop in the daughter's psyche, with a consequent suspicion of grown women. But that remains to be seen.

Temperament without Teaching

When a father, absent during the day, returns home at six, his children receive only his temperament, and not his teaching. If the father is working for a corporation, what is there to teach? He is reluctant to tell his son what is really going on. The fragmentation of decision making in corporate life, the massive effort that produces the corporate willingness to destroy the environment for the sake of profit, the prudence, even cowardice, that one learns in bureaucracy—who wants to teach that?

We know of rare cases in which the father takes the sons or daughters into his factory, judge's chambers, used-car lot, or insurance building, and these efforts at teaching do reap some of the rewards of teaching in craft cultures. But in most families today, the sons and daughters receive, when father returns home at six, only his disposition or his temperament, which is usually irritable and remote.

What the father usually brings home today is a touchy mood, springing from powerlessness and despair mingled with longstanding shame and the numbness peculiar to those who hate their jobs. Fathers in earlier times could often break through their own humanly inadequate temperaments by teaching rope-making, fishing, posthole digging, grain cutting, drumming, harness making, animal care, and even singing and storytelling. That teaching sweetened the effect of the temperament.

The longing for the father's blessing through teaching is still present, if a little fossilized; but the children do not receive that blessing. The son particularly receives instead the nonblesser, the threatened, jealous "Nobodaddy," as Blake calls him: "No One's father"—the male principle that lives in the Kingdom of Jealousy.

A father's remoteness may severely damage the daughter's ability to participate good-heartedly in later relationships with men. Much of the rage that some women direct to the patriarchy stems from a vast disappointment over this lack of teaching from their own fathers.

We have said that the father as a living force in the home disappeared when those forces demanding industry sent him on various railroads out of various villages.

No historical models prepare us for the contemporary son's psychic condition. To understand the son's psyche we have to imagine new furniture, new psychic figures, new demon possessions, new terrors, new incapacities, new flights.

Enormous changes have appeared at the last minute; few of us—fathers or sons—are prepared for such vast changes. I have mentioned so far the young men's father hunger and the starving bodies of the sons; also the demons of suspicion who have invaded the psyches of young men; and the son's dissatisfaction when he receives only temperament and no teaching. We might look now at the disappearance of positive kings.

THE DARKENED FATHER

The patriarchy is a complicated structure. Mythologically, it is matriarchal on the inside, and a matriarchy is equally complicated, being patriarchal on the inside. The political structure has to resemble our interior structure. And we know each man has a woman inside him, and each woman has a man inside her.

The genuine patriarchy brings down the sun through the Sacred King, into every man and woman in the culture; and the genuine matriarchy brings down the moon, through the Sacred Queen, to every woman and every man in the culture. The death of the Sacred

King and Queen means that we live now in a system of industrial domination, which is not patriarchy. The system we live in gives no honor to the male mode of feeling nor to the female mode of feeling. The system of industrial domination determines how things go with us in the world of resources, values, and allegiances; what animals live and what animals die; how children are treated. And in the mode of industrial domination there is neither king nor queen.

The death of the Sacred King, and the disappearance of the group King, means that the father shortage becomes still more acute. When a father now sits down at the table, he seems weak and insignificant, and we all sense that fathers no longer fill as large a space in the room as nineteenth-century fathers did. Some welcome this, but without understanding all its implications.

These events have worked to hedge the father around with his own paltriness. D. H. Lawrence said: "Men have been depressed now for many years in their male and resplendent selves, depressed into dejection and almost abdication. Is that not evil?"[4]

As the father seems more and more enfeebled, dejected, paltry, he also appears to be the tool of dark forces. We remember that in *Star Wars* we are given the image of "Darth Vader," a pun on dark father. He is wholeheartedly on the side of the dark forces. As political and mythological kings die, the father loses the radiance he once absorbed from the sun, or from the hierarchy of solar beings; he strikes society as being endarkened.

The demons who have set up a propaganda shop in the son's psyche convince him that his father's darkness is deeper than the son ever imagined. What can be done about that? The son finds out early that his mother cannot redeem his father; moreover, in most cases, she doesn't want to. The only other one to do it is the son.

As long as the political kings remained strong, the father picked up the radiance from above; and the son tried to emulate the father, to become as bright as he is, to reach his height. The son perceives the father as bright. Though this may not have been true in reality, we notice that literature as late as the eighteenth century is full of this sort of deference, this reverence for the father, and emulation.

In our time, when the father shows up as an object of ridicule (as he does, as we've noted, on television), or a fit field for suspicion (as he does in *Star Wars*), or a bad-tempered fool (when he comes home from the office with no teaching), or a weak puddle of indecision (as he stops inheriting kingly radiance), the son has a problem. How does he imagine his own life as a man?

Some sons fall into a secret despair. They have probably adopted, by the time they are six, their mother's view of their father, and by twenty will have adopted society's cortical view of fathers, which amounts to a dismissal. What can they do but ask women for help?

That request is not all bad. But even the best-intentioned women cannot give what is needed. Some father-hungry sons embody a secret despair they do not even mention to women. Without actually investigating their own personal father and why he is as he is, they fall into fearful hopelessness, having fully accepted the generic, diminished idea of father. "I am the son of defective material, and I'll probably be the same as he is." Then, with this secret they give up, collapse, live with a numb place inside, feel compelled to be dark because the father is dark. They lose the vigorous participation in political battles, so characteristic of nineteenth-century men in the United States, feel their opinions do not matter, become secret underground people, and sometimes drown themselves in alcohol while living in a burrow under the earth.

Other sons respond by leaping up and flying in the air. The deeper the father sinks in their view, the longer their flights become. More and more evidence comes out in the newspapers and books each day about sexual abuse perpetuated by fathers, inability of fathers to relate in a human way, the rigid promilitary stance of many fathers, the workaholism of fathers, their alcoholism, wife-beating and abandonment. All of this news intensifies the brightness that some sons feel compelled to achieve because the father is dark.

We can sense in this situation one answer to the question "Why are there more and more naive men in the world?" Whether the fathers are actually darker than they were in the past, they are perceived so, and a son assigns himself the task of redeeming the dark father.

We can look once more at the phenomenon we talked of earlier, the phenomenon of the ascending son, the "eternal boy," the moth mad for the light, the "puer," or "constant boy," as some people call him. Marie-Louise von Franz, in *Puer Aeternus,* understands his flight upward as a revolt against the earthly, conservative, possessive, clinging part of the maternal feminine.[5]

James Hillman in his essay "The Great Mother, Her Son, Her Hero, and the Puer" sees it all differently. He relates the phenomenon to the father.[6] It is characteristic of contemporary psychology that it has so far related everything to the mother. Both Freud and Jung were mothers' men, and our psychology comes out of them.

We have suggested that a young man in our times may sense that his father is somehow immersed in demonic darkness, the sort of darkness suggested by the words workaholism, weakness, submission, isolation, alcoholism, addiction, abusiveness, evasion, or cowardice.

Many contemporary sons, then, do not fight the father as in earlier eras, or figure out strategies to defeat him, but ascend above him, beyond him. We have Transcendental Psychology, the psychology of men like Thoreau determined to have a higher consciousness than their fathers. That is not wrong at all; but it is flying.

I count myself among the sons who have endured years of deprivation, disconnection from earth, thin air, the loneliness of the long-distance runner, in order to go high in the air and be seen. Such a son attempts to redeem the "endarkened father" by becoming "enlightened."

This is not entirely new; it is new only in degree. James Hillman has suggested that we can find a model for the redeeming in the Egyptian god Horus, the son of Osiris. He is a hawk and falcon god, and magnificent statues have survived, depicting him in his falcon form with his far-seeing eyes.

We all remember Osiris went into darkness. His brother Set tricked him into lying in a coffin; the lid was nailed down, and the coffin was thrown into the Nile. There, enclosed in darkness, Osiris eventually drifted across the Mediterranean to Byblos, where he became incorporated into a second darkness inside a tree trunk. Osiris remained so endarkened for years. The soaring of Horus' falcon can be thought of as a response to the father's imprisonment.

Horus says of himself that he intends to fly farther than any of the other gods. One script says:

> Horus soars up into the sky beyond the flight of the original god's soul, and beyond the divinities of former times . . . I have gone beyond the bounds of Set. I am unique in my flight.

We can do a great deal with this image. We have mentioned that the son, flying toward the sun, will not see his own shadow, for his shadow falls behind him as he flies. He has seen his father's shadow, but his own remains hidden.

Flying of that sort does not rescue the father either. The ascensionist son is flying away from the father, not toward him. The son, by ascending into the light, rising higher on the corporate ladder and achieving enlightenment, to some extent redeems the father's name.

This explanation for the drive for ascension moves me, because it suggests that not all this labor gets done out of fear of the possessive mother, but that some of it gets done out of love of the endarkened father.

Some sons have always been ascenders, but never so many as now. A man may of course pursue spirituality too early in his life. The ascension, then, I add to our list of imbalances brought about by the diminishment and belittlement of the father.

Society without the father produces these birdlike men, so intense, so charming, so open to addiction, so sincere, as those great bays of the Hellespont produced the cranes Homer noticed that flew in millions toward the sun.

THE MALE AS A SET-APART BEING

We know that each child begins in the womb as a female, and the fetus chosen to be male goes through hundreds of changes before he is born. John Layard reports that one old tradition holds that a stone, while still attached to the mountainside or the bedrock, is female. It becomes a male stone when it is moved away from its quarry place and set up by itself.[7] The Easter Island stones, then, are male, and the Stonehenge rocks also.

We conclude, then, that every father is set apart. He stands alone, not only apart from his wife, but from his children. Sitting on the western cliff of the main Aran Island, I wrote of my father:

> *Aren't you farther out from the mainland*
> *even than these granite cliffs?*
> *perhaps I want you*
> *to be still farther from land*
> *than these Aran Islands, to be at the edge*
> *of all human feeling.*

Most of us want our father to be close, and at the same time, we want him to be "at the edge of all human feeling," where he already is.

69

Mythology is full of stories of the bad father, the son-swallower, the remote adventurer, the possessive and jealous giant. Good fathering of the kind each of us wants is rare in fairy tales or in mythology. There are no good fathers in the major stories of Greek mythology—a shocking fact; and very few in the Old Testament. Uranus, Cronos, and Zeus exhibit three styles of horrendous fatherhood. Abraham, a famous Old Testament father, was perfectly willing to sacrifice Isaac; and his grandson Jacob was good to Joseph, but apparently not to his other eleven sons, and he certainly didn't protect Joseph from his brothers' rage.

It is interesting that we find very few examples of close or chummy father-son relationships in mythological literature. King Arthur radiates generosity, but as uncle, as initiator and guide of young men, not as father.

It is possible that we will never have the closeness we want from our fathers. "Male," John Layard says, "symbolizes that which is 'set apart.'"

I say this to speak to many young men who want from the father a repetition of the mother's affection, or a female nurturing they haven't gotten enough of. Whatever the father gives us, it will not be the same kind of closeness that our mother offered. And some men have to be satisfied with a relationship to their father that is not close. In many traditional cultures the men older than the father give and teach nurturing. The old man's power to nurture began with the foundation given by female nurturing, the mother's warmth, love, singing. Later the boy transfers to the earth as teacher; this is the time of the hunt, the cold, the wind, the weather. When the foundation of mother nurturing and earth companionship is in place, then the old men can move in and bring nurturing and its vision.

Men seem apart at birth; but we know a woman experiences set-apartness also, particularly when as an adult she begins to develop her masculine side.

The father's birth gift, then, is one thing, and the old men's gift another. The father gives with his sperm a black overcoat around the soul, invisible in our black nights. He gave, and gives, a sheathing, or envelope, or coating around the soul made of intensity, shrewdness, desire to penetrate, liveliness, impulse, daring. The father's birth gift cannot be quantified. His gift contributes to the love of knowledge, love of action, and ways to honor the world of things. It seems particularly important these days to name some of the father's gifts.

We recognize that we have hit something hard here. The sons and daughters in the United States still feel "too little father," and that is probably not going to get better. Fathers themselves have not changed so much; it is, rather, that they seem to us smaller, because we do not see behind them or through them the Blessed or Destructive King. The father seems opaque; the Sacred King seems farther away, and our eyesight is not too good.

When the mythological layer collapses, and the political kings fall, then the patriarchy, as a positive force, is over. The sun and moon energies can no longer get down to earth. Ancient Celtic mythology has an image for the end of the patriarchy, and it is this:

Eagles sit on the top branches of the sacred tree, with dead animals underneath their claws. Rotting bits of flesh fall down through the branches to the ground beneath, where the swine eat them.

We are the swine. When all the meat that comes down from above is rotten, then neither the sons nor daughters receive the true meat. Women have been and still are right in their complaints about the food they find on the earth, but men are not well fed either. Naturally, everyone is dissatisfied, for neither men nor women are receiving the true meat.

That doesn't imply that we need to build up the patriarchy again, but that we need to understand that we are starving. The more difficult it is to visit the King, the more hungry everyone is. The perceived absence of the father is actually the absence of the King. Addiction does not have to do with Columbian drug lords, but with the absence of the King.

Men and women have been separated from the King before; this separation has happened many times in past centuries.

CHAPTER TEN

Fred Gustafson

Fathers, Sons and Brotherhood

In today's culture, the father-son relationship is in terrible condition. It is both wounded and wounding. It is armored with a rage that rarely gets defined and tightly conceals a pain and a sadness that, once touched, usually brings tears or uncontrolled weeping. When the father-son bond is not intact in a way that nourishes the son's growth, and when the father does not act as a vehicle for transmitting some of the masculine mysteries to the son, that child will grow up with a limited and crippling sense of his masculinity. Several impediments to masculine individuation can transpire:

1. The son may get caught living out his father's unlived shadow side or be pressured to duplicate the father's way of doing things. His individual male identity will then be too limited and confined by reactions to the father. This can lead to feelings of emptiness, depression, or open rebellion.

2. Without a healthy masculine identity, the son's anima is likely to dominate the empty spaces created by weakly defined male ego. This leaves a man feeling driven by and infatuated with self-importance, or depleted of energy and creativity. Without a solid father figure to relate to, the son's anima, like any woman he might meet, will "lose respect" for him and will counter him with ridicule, provocation, seduction, and insatiable demands.

3. The son will often be controlled by women through guilt or a sense of duty. The power to impose such guilt is one of the strongest weapons a woman (or a man) has, whether she realizes it or not. This power can be unwittingly bestowed on her by the immature male through his projection of the mother complex onto her. This complex escalates on the absence of a "good enough" father bond.

4. If the father's influence is weak, the son may get caught up in the force field of the mother's animus, especially if the mother-son bond is strong (as it so often is). The mother will unconsciously project her own animus into the son. He will feel responsible for living out her animus drive—pushed to achieving, perhaps successfully, in any given field. But he will never quite be fulfilled because the animus is the woman's inner male image whose superman nature may be debilitating and impossible to live up to.

In the modern male psyche, the mother must be "defused" and the father "infused" with a nurturing authority. This has become increasingly possible in a contemporary society where women are gaining a greater sense of themselves and are not resigned to living out their lives through their children. Women are helping men to be more conscious of their needs as father to nurture their children. And though women are generally far ahead in realizing the importance of fathers in parenting, men are also beginning to discover this and to make attempts to relate more closely to their children. Some fathers, if they hug at all, find it much easier to hug their daughters than their sons. In the privacy of a consulting room, many fathers will declare that they just do not hug their sons or even put an arm around their shoulders, and that their fathers never did that to them. But the absence of the father's touch creates a hunger among men for other men, even though there may be little consciousness of it. How important it is that the father start early expressing his affection for his children instead of being so often "absent" even when he is physically present!

THE INITIATION OF THE SON

Today, initiations into manhood are conducted, if at all, in a limited fashion, and often in an unconscious manner. Young men unthinkingly try to initiate themselves by the way they drive, drink, rebel against their parents or society, or treat women. Others "get initiated" after a thorough round with alcoholism, divorce, critical accident, or a crippling depression at midlife. These are like initiatory experiences in that they bring a man to his knees and leave him feeling helpless, broken, and dead. Life crises become the critical and necessary wounds that are essential for psychic transformation. For males so afflicted, such wounds hold the promise of renewal through the birth of a more humane and sensitive view toward themselves and the world around them.

It seems that the male psyche begins to require initiations for itself in the preadolescent and early adolescent years. At this time, parents should begin to assume that their boys can take care of themselves. If they do not assume this, their sons will continue to allow themselves to be cared for. This means the boys must learn how to make their own beds, do their own laundry and ironing, cook, and pick up after themselves. If the parent imagines the son can only carry five logs to the fireplace, he/she might add a sixth one. If the parent thinks that making him clean the garage is about as much as can be expected, he/she might have him clean the basement also. In the previous years there was parental need to protect the young child, but now conscientious effort should be given to counter the inertial force of the childhood years.

The parents' "letting go" of the need to protect their son means that they must become attuned to his need to be severed. They must follow the ancient custom of allowing their son to be forcibly ripped away from the parental home as it exists with the boy himself. For the young man, the process of severance from his boyhood years takes two forms: the mother's role diminishes and the father's role becomes very important.

Now the father must move toward a level of honesty and open discussion with his son as never before. The time has come for the revelation of the masculine mysteries in an unabashed, straightforward manner. It is important that the father actually take his son aside more than once as the boy moves into these later years, and share his thoughts and feelings about his view of himself, his experiences with life, his religious views, his attitudes about women and sexuality, and his relationships to family, work, and friends. Now he can nonjudgmentally share his perception of his son's strengths and weaknesses, share his memories of the past, and encourage his son to envision possibilities for his future. In every possible way he must pass on the power he possesses to his son, allowing the son to become strong and psychologically to step beyond him without counterattack, when the time is right. In the end, the family will bequeath a paternal blessing that the son will remember decades after the fact. To fail to do this is tantamount to pronouncing a paternal curse. On the other hand, to succeed in breaking the old and forging these new parental bonds is to duplicate as closely as he can these ancient initiatory rites that proved so effective for our ancestors.

It is quite possible that initiation rites can be restyled and enacted by modern fathers. One man told me he is thinking that when the time is right he will take his son on a two-week wilderness outing away from everyone and tell him as much as he knows about life. Another man suggested that since his son and mine are about the same age, we could switch sons for a month and instruct each other's sons on growing into manhood. Such a proposal reflects the primitive practice of not allowing the father to be the principal initiator of his son. However a modern initiation might be performed, intentionality and originality are needed to make this rite a viable process for channeling the archetypal energy behind it. Its power would be enhanced if the boy himself helped to plan it.

A young man needs to look imaginatively into the face of his father and see his sacred ancestors living there. "Old Men" need to appear in his life as reminders of the elderly character of the masculine archetype as a mature and refined source of wisdom. He also must be able to look forward through his own sons and the sons around him and at all that is new and possible in him whether he sires a child or not. This new consciousness, which is part of the initiation process, is essential for a view of what, in the profoundest sense, the "masculine" is.

FATHERS, SONS AND BROTHERHOOD

There are many stories from the past that capture the drama between fathers and sons and the need for connection with the brotherhood of men. Take, for example, the Old Testament saga of the patriarch Isaac and his two sons, Jacob and Esau. Jacob betrayed his blind and dying father by stealing the birthright of the first-born brother, hairy Esau. Fleeing for his life, Jacob went to the land of his uncle, Laban, and lived there for twenty years. Finally, in the time of his greatest prosperity, he knew he must return to the land of his father, meet his brother, and effect a reconciliation. Like Jacob, the modern male feels deeply within himself a need for reunion with his twin—the wild, hairy, instinctual side of himself—and yet he is at a great distance from the psychic ground of his fathers and the brotherhood. He must return to his own country and be reconciled in brotherly love with his wild twin, as did Jacob, and realize the fruits of that union.[1]

Nevertheless, it is not always possible for a man to physically connect with his actual father. He then faces the awesome but not impossible task of becoming the father to his own neglected inner boy and healing himself. He begins by encouraging an imaginal relationship between himself and his inner child. Can he envision himself sitting next to or walking with the little boy he once was and has long neglected? What would he say to this boy? What would he do? What would be the boy's response?

Because every man has a father and a son within himself, he is a member of a great brotherhood of ancestors, grandfathers, fathers, sons, uncles, brothers, and nephews who all possess the same inner knowing. Though today the concept of "brotherhood" is all too often limited to the local bowling team or to the guys in the office or shop, the concept itself is still powerful enough to collectively support the masculine archetype in any individual man. Brotherhood enables men to see a bit of their own masculine identity in every male they see or experience. When they fail to recognize themselves in other men, they project their own incompleteness on other men, and turn brother against brother. A woman active in the feminist movement told me she works hard to remind women not to despise one another, for they are all sisters and must work for mutual growth and liberation. In the same way, all men need to risk opening themselves and to assist one another in the expansion of their understanding of what being male actually means. No one man can do this comprehensively himself.

I believe that men are hungry for intimate, brotherly connections with other men, even as now they are becoming more aware than ever of their inward weeping for the fathers they hardly knew. It has become quite clear to me why I have such an intense need to strengthen my bonds with my older relatives and to connect my young son with his father's ancestry. I am seeking to understand in the deepest sense what it is to be a man.

CHAPTER ELEVEN

James Hillman

Fathers and Sons

[The] desire in the father to kill the child we ignore to our peril, especially since psychoanalysis descends from fathers. If this myth is foundational to depth psychology, then infanticide is basic to our practice and our thought. Our practice and our thought recognize infanticide in the archetypal mother, its desire to smother, dissolve, mourn, bewitch, poison and petrify. We are aware that inherent to mothering is "bad" mothering. Fathering too is impelled by its archetypal necessity to isolate, ignore, neglect, abandon, expose, disavow, devour, enslave, sell, maim, betray the son—motives we find in biblical and Hellenic myths as well as folklore, fairy tales and cultural history. The murderous father is essential to fathering, as Adolf Guggenbuhl has written. The cry to be fathered so common in psychological practice, as well as the resentment against the cruel or insufficient father so common in feminism—whether as cruel or insufficient ruler, teacher, analyst, institution, program, corporation, patriarchy, or God—idealize the archetype. The cry and the resentment fail to recognize that these shadow traits against which one so protests are precisely those that initiate fathering.

This because: first, they kill idealization. The destructive father destroys the idealized image of himself. He smashes the son's idolatry. Whenever, wherever we idealize the father, we remain in sonship, in the false security of a good ideal. A good model, whether kind analyst, wise guru, generous teacher, honest chief, holds these virtues of kindness, wisdom, generosity, and honesty fixed in another, projected outside. Then, instead of initiation, imitation. Then the son remains tied to the person of the idealized figure.

Second, the terrible traits in the father also initiate the son into the hard lines of his own shadow. The pain of his father's failings teaches him that failing belongs to fathering. The very failure fathers the son's failings. The son does not have to hide his share of darkness. He grows up under a broken roof which nonetheless shelters his own failings, inviting him, forcing him, to be dark himself in order to survive. The commonality—and commonness—of shared shadow can bond father and son in dark and silent empathy as deep as any idealized companionship.

Third, the terrible traits in the father provide a countereducation. How better bring home a true appreciation of decency, loyalty, generosity, succor, and straightness of heart than by their absence or perversion? How more effectively awaken moral resolve than by provoking moral outrage at the father's bad example?

CHAPTER TWELVE

Sherwood Anderson

The Night I Became the Son of My Father

There came a certain night. Mother was away from home when Father came in and he was alone. He'd been off for two or three weeks.

He came silently into the house. It was raining outside. It may be there was church that night and Mother had gone there. I had a book before me and was sitting alone in the house, reading by the kitchen table.

Father had been walking in the rain and was very wet. He sat and looked at me. I was startled, for on that night there was on his face the saddest look I have ever seen on a human face. For a long time he sat looking at me, not saying a word.

He was sad and looking at him made me sad. He sat for a time, saying nothing, his clothes dripping. He must have been walking for a long time in the rain. He got up out of his chair.

"You come on, you come with me," he said.

I was filled with wonder but, although he had suddenly become like a stranger to me, I wasn't afraid. We went along a street and out of the town.

Finally we came to a pond. We stood at the edge. We had come in silence. It was still raining hard and there were flashes of lightning followed by thunder. My father spoke, and in the darkness and rain his voice sounded strange. It was the only time after we had left the house that he did speak to me.

"Take off your clothes," he said. Still filled with wonder, I began to undress. There was a flash of lightning. I saw that he was already naked.

And so naked we went into the pond. He did not speak or explain. Taking my hand, he led me down to the pond's edge and pulled me in. It may be that I was too frightened, too full of a feeling of strangeness to speak. Before that night my father had never seemed to pay attention to me.

And what is he up to now? I kept asking myself. It was as though the man, my father I had not wanted as father, had got suddenly some kind of power over me.

I was afraid and then right away, I wasn't afraid. It was a large pond and I didn't swim very well but he had put my hand on his shoulder. Still he did not speak but struck out at once onto the darkness.

He was a man with very big shoulder muscles and was a powerful swimmer. In the darkness I could feel the movement of his muscles. The rain poured down on us. The wind blew. There were flashes of lightning followed by the peals of thunder.

And so we swam, I will never know for how long. It seemed hours to me. There was rain on our faces. Sometimes my father turned and swam on his back; and when he did, he took my hand in his large powerful one and moved it over so that it rested always on his shoulder. I could look into his face. There would be a flash of lightning, and I could see his face clearly.

It was as it was when he had come earlier into the kitchen where I sat reading the book. It was a face filled with sadness. In me there was a feeling I had never known before that night. It was a feeling of closeness. It was something strange. It was as though I had been jerked suddenly out of myself, out of a world of a school boy, out of a place where I had been judging my father.

He had become blood of my blood. He the stronger swimmer and I the boy clinging to him in the darkness. We went back along the road to the town and our house.

It had become a strange house to me. There was the little porch at the front where on so many nights my father had sat with the men. There was the tree by the spring and the shed at the back. There was a lamp in the kitchen and when we came in, the water dripping from us, there was my mother. She smiled at us. I remember that she called us "boys." "What have you boys been up to?" she asked, but my father did not answer. As he had begun the evening's experience with me in silence, so he ended it. He turned and looked at me, and then he went, I thought, with a new and strange dignity out of the room.

He went upstairs to his room to get out of his wet clothes, and I climbed the stairs to my own room. I undressed in the darkness and got into bed. I was still in the grip of the feeling of strangeness that had taken possession of me in the darkness of the pond. I couldn't sleep and did not want to sleep. For the first time I had come to know that I was the son of my father and that I would be a story-teller like himself. There in the darkness of my bed in the room I knew that I would never again be wanting of another father.

CHAPTER THIRTEEN

Stephen T. Butterfield

Of Lineage
and Love

My father was a machinist. He took me to work and introduced me to everybody as "Number Two Son." When a machine was down, a light flashed on a board in his tiny office, and he went forth with his tool kit to find the problem. One of his tools was a piece of coat hanger.

He often worked in the backyard on summer weekends, wearing light blue denim U.S. Navy shirts and a white sailor's hat with the brim pulled down. He carried a folding measuring rule in his pant pocket. I thought he could fix anything.

Confronted by a huge boulder that he wanted out of our cellar, he gazed thoughtfully at the stairs.

I said, "You'll never move that rock by yourself."

"I'll have it out by supper time," he said.

He was right. "How did you do it?" I asked.

He smiled. "I used my head."

My mother wanted more counter space in the kitchen. There seemed no way to accomplish this goal and still leave room for the washer and dryer. My father built a counter top that anyone could quickly disassemble in case the appliances had to be serviced.

"There are three ways to do a job," he said. "The right way, the wrong way, and the Navy way."

His arms were hairy. He rolled his sleeves up past his bulging muscles. My mother said he stank. I liked the way he smelled, except when he was glaring down at me, threatening, "You better straighten out and fly right or I'll blister your ass—"which he would sometimes do. At those times I wanted to punch his false teeth down his throat.

He saw this in my eyes and smiled. "You can think anything you want, as long as you keep your trap shut."

Instead of punching him, I learned how to beat him at chess. I won my first authentic victory at the age of fourteen. After a battle of seven hours, as the dawn grayed the windows, he acknowledged that he had lost. He was too good a sport to chicken out by insisting it was past my bedtime. We laughed together and cooked bacon and eggs.

"Don't get too big for your britches," he warned. "The old man can still teach you a thing or two." By age twenty, I beat him so consistently that he stopped playing with me.

Bitten by the American Dream right after he got out of the Navy, my father was determined to become a millionaire. He set up a printing business on the GI Bill and went bankrupt within two years. It was a devastating collapse that wiped out everything he had.

His dream of making a fortune shattered, his third child born dead, and his credit ruined, he went to work fixing linotypes for a newspaper. Then he began telling his sons the stories of his boyhood.

"When I was sixteen," he said, "I tracked a buck in the snow for a whole day. I followed his tracks right out into the middle of an open field . . . and they disappeared! Jesus, I thought, did he take off and fly? Sonobitchin' deer—he walked backward, in his own tracks, until he came to a thicket, and then jumped sideways, fifteen feet on the other side of that thicket, where you couldn't see his tracks, and took off. He didn't miss a single hoof print. You could walk up and down his trail a dozen times and never figure it out—unless you know deer. Dad found the new tracks for me the next day. He laughed at me over that one for years."

My father taught us to shoot, fish, fight, snowshoe, tap maple trees, cut wood with a bucksaw, and make our own Christmas presents. His mother had knitted afghans and sweaters, braided rugs from old clothes, and made shelf knickknacks out of twigs and thread spools. "We never had any money," he said. "To get a jackknife for Christmas, that was a major gift."

Having been defeated in business, and knowing he would be poor for a long time, he moved us to a place that resembled the woods and villages where he had been raised; then he drew from his past the stories, memories, myths, and customs that enabled him to keep his sense of humor and self-respect.

His stories gave me a sense that I, too, belonged to a family lineage, a tradition. I began building toy villages and forts to reenact the frontier life of colonial Massachusetts, without realizing how deeply personal was the meaning of this play. The great swamp that extended from our backyard was the ground where I explored the myth of the wilderness. He had forbidden me to hike there alone, and this transformed my explorations into a rite of passage.

"When you walk on the ice," he said, "if it starts to crack, lie down and spread your weight."

The following winter, lost in the woods, I started across a frozen river and heard it crack. I lay down at once to spread my weight; it saved my life.

Whatever his failures as a husband, he spent a great deal of time teaching and nurturing his sons. We took in children from the state, whom he helped to feed and toilet train, like his own. He was our provider, barber, first-aid medic, and nurse.

One measure of my trust of him was that I allowed him to pick wax out of my ears with a hairpin. During this operation I held perfectly still while he probed the deepest part of my ear. "Good," he said, in the smooth, gentle voice he used to doctor our cats and dogs, "that's good, almost got it, hold still now . . ." He would give me the lump of wax afterward for a souvenir.

My brother's arm was once burned so badly the doctors wanted to amputate it. My father said, "Like hell!" He worked on that arm night after night, week after week, changing the dressings, making my brother exercise the muscles, bend the joints, lift small weights, then larger ones, until at last the arm healed. It was scarred, but usable, and whole.

He was hungry for knowledge, and carried books with him to work so he could read between jobs. Entirely self-taught, he was deeply suspicious of anybody who had a university degree. Intellectuals made him defensive. Yet he supported my efforts to get an education, caught between his pride in my academic success and his desire to cut me down to size.

Eventually, my mother won me almost entirely to her side. I resented him for his abuse of her. Politics divided us during the Vietnam era—he supported the war, I wanted socialist revolution at home—but gradually I stopped caring enough about his opinions to disagree with them. He told the same stories over and over. I felt that he had betrayed my trust by lying to me during a family crisis, and his stories seemed like a smoke screen to hide his dishonesty. I found his company boring, and hardly talked to him at all.

When he was old, I tried to introduce him to the Buddhist doctrine of emptiness; I thought it would ease any anxiety he might be having about the imminence of death.

"Ultimately," I began, "you never were."

"Maybe not," he said, peering over the rim of his glasses, "but I made a hell of a splash where I should have been."

That was the end of my Buddhist lecture.

I took him to the family grave plots to visit the stones of our dead relatives. This was a ritual my mother used to enjoy. We stood among the monuments for a while. "Well," he said, turning to go, "I don't suppose any of them are gonna get up and thank us for coming."

That was the end of our sentimental visits to the dead.

His major hobby was genealogy. Someone had once insulted his background by implying that he came from an inferior stock of poor white losers. His pride would not let him rest until he had won that argument. He traced our paternal lineage back fairly quickly to our earliest colonial ancestor, Benjamin Butterfield, who entered Puritan Massachusetts in 1636. Then, his hobby escalating into a full-scale obsession, my father spent twenty-five years tracing the lines of Benjamin's offspring into a bewildering maze of branches. A network of contacts across the country funneled data to him from generations of Butterfields, containing thousands of names.

He tried incessantly to recruit me as his research assistant and ghostwriter. I said I was too busy. When he got started on the subject, I would yawn and go to talk to my mother, who thought all Butterfield men, excepting her boys, were ignorant hicks with smelly feet, chips on their shoulders, and no respect for their betters. She was hard at work telling me stories of her Nova Scotia ancestry. "Our people," she said, "had true class."

"Your people," my father would shout at her, "were nothing but a bunch of goddamned Tories, who went up to Halifax because the patriots ran them out of Boston. Read your history, you'll find out who's right." In this bizarre way, my parents were still fighting the American Revolution.

They were fighting while she was in the hospital, a month

before she died. I was past forty by that time. I suggested to him that, after forty years of battle, it was time they made peace. "You mean," he answered, "when I'm surrounded by Indians, I should just hand over my scalp. No thanks."

"You see?" she said. "He'll never change. Always wanting to dominate. I should have left him. But he was your father. I couldn't take him away from you."

I grieved over her death more than a year. I blamed him, and blamed myself for not rescuing her. I could not touch him. I had not been able to communicate with him for a long time, but now his deterioration from Alzheimer's disease made even the attempt altogether hopeless.

When I was a little boy, my father used to wake me up at night for the bathroom. If I couldn't go, he turned on the faucet. The sound of the water started me.

I woke up sick with nightmares and said there were monsters hanging on to my curtain. "They won't let me sleep." He told me to walk right up to them and punch them in the nose, and they would go away. I went back to my room ready to follow his advice, but they were gone.

Now he was a withered, senile old man who got confused and wandered off by himself. I found him standing on a construction site, fumbling with a broken coat hanger.

"Dad, time to go home. Get in the car."

"Wait just a goddamned minute, till I finish the job." He stood there and peed in his pants. The monsters were not gone after all, however much he shook his fist.

I took him to the doctor and had to get a urine sample from him. I led him to the bathroom, unfastened his diapers, and instructed him to urinate into a specimen container. Nothing happened. This was an embarrassing moment. Having broken the biblical taboo against looking on my father's nakedness, I still had no sample. What to do?

I turned on the faucet.

Ironically, the person who brought me back into touch with my father's genealogical work was my oldest son.

Every summer, my son stayed with my parents. While I was preoccupied with my divorces, academic career, union activity, and Buddhist education, my father was taking him upstairs and teaching him how to find and hold jobs, how to cope with an angry step-mother, and what family lore was contained in those notebooks and card files. The old man must have figured that if I did not care enough about the values of my own culture and family tradition to pass them on to my sons, he would make sure the job got done without me.

Eventually I had to put my father into a nursing home. I stored his genealogical records in my attic and forgot about them. One day my son asked me where they were. We dragged them out together.

"Gramp showed me all these books, Dad," he said. "Didn't you ever see these? Look, this is fascinating."

He rehearsed with me the lineage of our direct-line Butterfield forefathers, beginning with Benjamin, who settled in Chelmsford, Massachusetts. They had fought in every New England Indian War since 1675. They included Lieutenant John Butterfield, who enlisted with Rogers's Rangers during the Seven Years' War. In 1759, Lieutenant John fought on the Plains of Abraham at the capture of Quebec.

My sons and I went canoeing on Lake George in New York, to visit the places our ancestor would have seen. My father's work was a thread of continuity holding us together. We talked about him incessantly.

In this way he had converted his isolation, anger, and injured pride into something of priceless value to us. I spent a few days in the Library of Congress, checking the accuracy of his research. He had been meticulous, using vital records to correct the errors of other genealogists as he went along. He preferred truth to legend, always. I found the names of our forefathers on the muster rolls for the French and Indian wars and the Revolution. I read histories of the period so that I could make a chronology of their lives.

The domestic ignorance and aggression that plague the human species were well represented among these forefathers. My great-grandfather was a wife-beater and child-abuser who drove my grandfather, an eleven-year-old boy, out of the house to live on the streets. Great-grandfather was married and divorced twice; grandfather was married three times and divorced twice.

Suddenly I understood why my father should have regarded life as a battle.

While taking volume after volume off the shelves, looking up references, making notes and copies, I felt his presence over my shoulder, smiling and advising, "Check this; I already did that; now you're on the right track." I returned home to Vermont at the end of the week with a briefcase full of new material, having visited Bennington while searching for the site where Revolutionary John had saved a Hessian prisoner. Some kind of expansion was happening to me that I did not fully understand, but I rode this current without resistance, curious where it would lead. I saw the forefathers lined up in a row, their faces creased and squinting from hard work, piling up stone walls, cutting trees, and watching for enemies from the woods. Their features changed slightly from generation to generation, but they all had the characteristic Butterfield glare. I felt lifted out of myself and brought before an archetype in colonial dress, named simply "Father."

The night before my return, I had been reading a biography of Robert Rogers, looking for more clues that would enable me to reconstruct the life of Lieutenant John. In the 1750s Rogers was a dependable and competent leader of Rangers, but he failed in all his business adventures. He died, depraved, drunk, impoverished, and friendless, in a London slum, destroyed by his enemies, his best hopes unrealized. The story overwhelmed me with more than usual sadness at the futility of human ambition. His fate reminded me of my father: strong and competent in practical ways, but always girding his loins for battle, surrounded by enemies real and imaginary, and gradually undone by his own blindness.

I thought, I must see my father right away. I knew there had been some kind of change in his condition. I would tell him, "I see it all now, all your struggle, your longing: I know why this work was so important to you." I felt certain that he would know what I had said, even though his brain could not make a coherent response.

By the time I got home my phone had been ringing for hours. The tape on the message machine was loaded. While I was reading about Rogers's death, my father had died.

Now I understood. My surge of interest in Rogers and Lieutenant John was my father's last attempt to communicate with me in this life. I had imagined sending him a message, but he had been the sender. The story of Rogers was only the medium.

There is no line of demarcation between the normal and the paranormal, or between the mind and the material world. Most communication from the dead probably comes through ordinary events, made significant by their timing and context.

Soon I stood over my father's coffin and touched his lifeless, leathery corpse, faintly odorous with the smell of death. He was haggard and bony, like the rock ribs of the New England countryside where our ancestors have lived, loved, hated, worked, fought, died, and been buried for 350 years. I saw his body lowered into the ground, just as he saw his father's body similarly disposed of, and his father saw his father's before him.

As I sit in my office transferring my father's notebooks onto computer disks and preparing them for publication, I smile to think how he finally hooked me into this job. He did an amazing piece of work, valuable not only to me, but to anyone descended from the same roots. Using the numbering system he invested for keeping track of all these thousands of separate lines, the American genealogy of any Butterfield on the tree can be traced in a matter of minutes.

I smile also to remember how uncomfortable he was with symbolism, even while carrying in his pocket the measuring rule that symbolized his demand for certainty. For him, any job with dimensions could be reduced to a solution. He could not measure the confusion of human life, which is far too messy to have such qualities as dimension and solution: but the product of his attempt—his devotion to his family, and his elegant and precise compilation of our ancestry—illustrates how we transform our confusion into love.

After he turned senile, I did not like taking on the responsibility for his care. I thought about euthanasia. I would not have killed him, but sometimes I wished him a speedy death. Now I can see how his long period of decline gave me a chance to feel close to him again. I needed that chance, in order to dissolve any lingering vestiges of alienation from myself. Sometimes I wanted to deny he was any relation to me, but it was impossible: staff members in the nursing home always knew I was his son. "You look just like him," they said. They reminded me that my father is woven into the very bones of my face and the color of my eyes.

Alzheimer's disease gradually took all the battles out of him. In the end he was gentle as a toothless old cat, smiling and weak, fumbling with his chair. I did not resent him for anything. Whatever had divided us came unwound along with the connections of his brain. If I had been able to dispose of him when he became inconvenient, or was unwilling to be involved in his care, that release may never have occurred.

Despite their battles, both my parents did far more good than harm. In my Buddhist path, I seek a greater vision than the teaching that "life is a constant battle," but no such vision is possible without first accepting the truth of who we are. My father gave me a vital part of that truth. Then he reached past me to make sure it would survive my indifference. He was right to do that. Because of him, both my children and I have a family tradition that we can use to help us transcend our small selves, just as he rejuvenated himself by returning to the woods.

My father was impelled by the same deep desire that impels me, and, I suspect, all others: the longing to continue, from age to age, not merely a blind propagation of genes, but a light of loving awareness, which is never swallowed by death, but only more fully revealed.

CHAPTER FOURTEEN

Ram Dass

Love as a State
of Being

I am in India and I suddenly realize that I have to come back. My mother has died, I have to come back and be with my father in a new way than I was ever with him before. When I came back to Boston from India, I arrived at the airport and I was wearing a beard and I was barefoot, and I had come from India with my tamboura and I was generally a weird-looking being. My father came in his car to pick me up . . . a conservative Boston Republican and a very responsible member of our society. He took one look at me, and his response was, "Get in quick before anybody sees you," which I did, and we started to drive toward the house. Now what he regaled me with all the way home was the fact that he was experiencing a depression, a deep depression, as he approached death. He was seventy-two at the time. He told me about how his life was meaningless and even though he had started Brandeis University, and raised many funds for the Einstein Medical School, and been president of the New Haven Railroad, and done lots of glorious and grand things in his life—he was experiencing the feeling that he was a failure as a human being. That was all there was to it. And he was telling me about his will and the clauses in his will, and all I felt was . . . I was sitting in the car doing my *Om Mani Padme Hum, Om Mani Padme Hum.* And it was like his mind was creating this huge big black cloud of pollution in the car; I mean, this heavy, dark depressed place of "it's all over" and "we'll look through old photographs tonight"—you know that kind of place. And I just did my mantra and off we drove to the house.

We got home and he said, "What would you like to do now?" I said, "I don't care, Dad, anything you'd like to do." He said, "Well, I want to rest. You've had a long trip and . . ." He said, "I'm going to make some raspberry jam," because that's one of his hobbies, is making raspberry jam. So I said, "Well, can I help you?" "No, don't bother." I said, "I'd like to." He said, "All right." So I go in, and we start to make raspberry jam. We're sterilizing the bottles and mashing raspberries, and he's telling me about the horror of his life and how sad it is, and how everybody's forgotten him and, boy, he's got a routine. It's a very heavy story, very heavy story. I feel fantastic compassion for him because I love him very dearly and at the same moment I see the predicament his consciousness is in. I see where he's stuck. So I'm just doing my mantra and mashing raspberries and so on, and I'm saying to him things like, "Should the bubbles all rise to the top? Are the bottles right? Where do we put that?" and so on. And after a while, since I'm giving no reinforcement at all for this fantastic dark cloud that he's creating and holding all by himself, since I'm part of us, but I'm not helping him hold it up particularly, he starts to say, "Well, get all the bubbles up . . ." and pretty soon his conversation is shifting until it's in the here and now. That is, he's talking about how to make raspberry jam, right? And as he starts to talk about how to make raspberry jam—this is a technique you're all familiar with of bringing a person into the here and now—the lines of his face are relaxing and the whole model of himself as somebody who's old and about to die and his life is lived out and all this stuff about his failures and unhappiness and bankruptcy of the railroad and all that stuff, that's all sort of falling into the past and here we are making raspberry jam. We're just two guys making raspberry jam, right? Now we finish making the raspberry jam, and he's happy, see, he's smiling.

So now the question is, "What are we going to do together next?" Right? Because what's happening is he's getting a "contact high" off me, because I'm living in the here and now. All I'm doing is making raspberry jam. And he's coming into that place, and it feels good. Everyone wants to feel good. If we walk away for an hour or two, he'll go right back into the other space again, because that's his karma at that moment to be stuck still in that space. But we start to spend a great deal of time together and as we spend more and more time together, he's living more in the here and now.

To short-cut that whole story, let me explain that eight months later, I gave the bride away at his marriage. Right? He married a woman in her fifties, a beautiful, high, wonderful woman who had actually been one of his secretaries in the Junior Achievement organization, of which he was president. There was another Junior Achievement for him. As he went into the temple, he said to me, "This is all your doing, you know," because what I did was hold his hand all the time because all of his questions would be about the future or the past, like, "Is this wrong in terms of the memory of Mother? Is this going to be a terrible thing later?" All I was saying was, "How does it feel today? Did you have a good time at dinner last night? What are we doing today?" And he said, "Oh, it's wonderful. She's a wonderful person, but I'm just concerned about . . ." As soon as his mind stopped creating all that stuff about then and then, and he lived here and now, it was a gas. He was having a ball. He was writing live songs and they went on a honeymoon in Scotland and Ireland. She is a very high being, in that she lives in the here and now very much of the time. She's a very conscious being. He married a good one. He's in good hands. And when I call, I say, "what are you doing?" "Oh, well, we're . . ." and he sort of laughs, "we're writing some songs at the piano. We're writing some movie routines. We're going to shoot some sound movies and, you know, have some people over." He's having a ball. He's . . . he is no more seventy-four now. Before he was ninety-six and now he's about twenty-three the way I figure it. And he can't walk as well and he's slowing down in all his processes but there they are. The depression has fallen away because he's started to live in the here and now. Now that's how consciousness affected the nature of a love relationship in a sense.

My relationship with my father was a love relationship. He is karmically my father, that is, in this incarnation he is my father. Otherwise, I don't think he and I would have much going with one another. Because he lives in a very different psychological space from the one I do. He has this big estate in New Hampshire and he's a member of this club called the President's Club. It's made up of people like presidents of United States Steel and Bell Telephone and they sit around saying, "You're a president, I'm a president . . ." It's a status reward for having made it in the game, you know. It's an inner club and they play games together. It's beautiful. So they come up to visit him and then he'll always say things like, "I've got this son. He's a little strange, but I'd really like you to hear him." And then he'll say, "Rich," or he calls me "Rum Dum," actually. "Rum Dum, would you come down for a visit?" And I come down and I sit by the fire and I tell ghost stories. I mean I talk about the weird and the beyond the beyond and strange experiences in the Himalayas—the farthest reaches of the Himalayas, you know. And as long as it's not threatening, everybody's having a ball, you know: "Fascinating, absolutely wonderful." And my father, who's listened to the story probably a hundred times now, always sits on the same armchair and says, "Well, damned interesting." He says, "Don't understand a word of it, but if he's doing it, it's OK with me. I guess I'll turn in now." And he always does the same routine. And I know that he's just not ready or interested, or at all involved in hearing the conceptualization or the ability to work with this stuff, but nevertheless the spin-off is very much part of his daily life. I feel that this is a very subtle way in which karma works, and that we have dealt here with a matter of how consciousness changes, because my father and I are closer than we have ever been in our lives together. We genuinely and openly love one another now, in this way. I see the game of father and son as merely another social relationship. We don't have any biological function at the moment, but we do have a karmic connection. And I honor him as my father. The result is, we're very close, and we're not hung up on all the melodramas we always were before.

Yesterday

My friend says I was not a good son
you understand
I say yes I understand

he says I did not go
to see my parents very often you know
and I say yes I know

even when I was living in the same city he says
maybe I would go there once
a month or maybe even less
I say oh yes

he says the last time I went to see my father
I say the last time I saw my father

he says the last time I saw my father
he was asking me about my life
how I was making out and he
went into the next room
to get something to give me

Oh I say
feeling again the cold
of my father's hand the last time

he says and my father turned
in the doorway and saw me
look at my wristwatch and he
said you know I would like you to stay
and talk with me

oh yes I say

but if you are busy he said
I don't want to feel that you
have to
just because I'm here

I say nothing

he says my father
said maybe
you have important work you are doing
or maybe you should be seeing
somebody I don't want to keep you

I look out the window
my friend is older than I am
he says and I told my father it was so
and I got up and left him then
you know

though there was nowhere I had to go
and nothing I had to do

W. S. MERWIN

III

Fathers and Daughters: First Love . . . and Beyond

It must be grand to have a father one can love and esteem, and when the fourth commandment does not confront one with its terrifying spectre "Thou shalt."

KAREN HORNEY (AGE FIFTEEN)

His failure to be reassuring, present even, accessible, approving, companionable, dictated the judgment . . . he became the awesome figure of the no-praise man, creating in me such a need of approval.

ANAIS NIN

. . . I have to break his silence, his taboos; in order to claim him I have in a sense to expose him.

ADRIENNE RICH

. . . knowing now, at forty, what it takes out of body and spirit to go and how much more to stay, and having learned too, by now, some of the pitiful confusions in behavior caused by ignorance and pain, I love you just as much for what you were.

ALICE WALKER

When thou dost ask me blessing, I'll kneel down
And ask of thee forgiveness.

SHAKESPEARE (KING LEAR TO HIS
DAUGHTER CORDELIA)

Introduction

A father is the first and often the longest connection a daughter will have with a man. The father–daughter bond (or lack of bond) shapes her future relationships with male friends and lovers and influences how she moves out in the world.

If he encourages her efforts to achieve, inspires her budding self-confidence, and teaches her competency skills, she will more easily develop an authentic self-esteem. If he discourages her efforts, undermines her self-confidence, shames her body, or discounts her personal opinions, her self-esteem will be marred, and it may take many years for her to learn to believe in herself.

ABSENT FATHERS AND OVERINVOLVED FATHERS

Many fathers are neglectful; they are not actively engaged in their daughters' development. When a father is physically or emotionally unavailable, a daughter may distort in her own mind who and what he represents. An absent father often leads her to idealize him and, later, other men, giving her heroic fantasies more power than a flesh-and-blood experience.

This pattern of pining for the one that got away, or longing for the "man on the white horse" who never arrives, can lead her to have affairs with married men or other unavailable men who live at a geographical distance that prohibits consistent intimacy. The daughter of an absent father typically feels a terror of abandonment, an inability to trust that a man will remain a loving presence in her life.

On the other hand, a father who is overbearing and too intrusive forces a daughter to take a defensive posture to protect herself from him and from other men. Her feelings of vulnerability may cause her to build strong boundaries to distance herself from him and his invasive behavior, whether this is physical or emotional.

The concept of boundaries is critical to understanding how fathers and daughters move toward and away from each other. It's as if a screen stands between their bodies and minds, sometimes thick and impermeable, sometimes thinning and, for moments, even transparent. Traditionally, a father upholds these boundaries and models limit-setting for his children. He does this by how he says no, how he circumscribes behavior such as physical contact and emotional intimacy, and how he respects the privacy needs of his daughters.

If he invades a daughter's body through incest, or cannot tolerate her emotional independence and tries to control her feelings through emotional incest, he violates the boundary. As a result, she cannot feel safe or whole in the presence of her own father. Later in life, the daughter may continue to suffer from porous boundaries, unable to say no to men and their demands. Or she may develop rigid boundaries that communicate, "I won't let you in," leaving her with an inability to share intimacy.

Archetypally, a father's ability to uphold healthy boundaries and become a steadying influence for his daughter is associated with centeredness and order. His task is to walk a path between abandoner and overprotector, critical judge and greatest fan. Fathering a daughter is always a dance of balance, rather than an either-or approach.

A man, if he is lucky, can find a feeling of wholeness when he fathers a daughter. His willingness to honor the feminine both within his daughter and within himself will be tested. Fathering a daughter presents a difficult but wonderful opportunity to cultivate receptive, gentle qualities, which can round out a man's rough edges. The care he takes in handling these tasks sets the tone for his daughter's future relationships.

By the same token, his modeling of some of the more traditional masculine strengths is the best gift a father can give to his daughter. His masculinity assists her development of her own inner masculine qualities, which she needs to be a more whole woman. A father who acts and speaks from his own grounded masculinity, yet also is vulnerable with his partner and with his daughter, helps to provide her with an image of soft strength as she makes her own way in the world.

A Daughter's Developmental Steps

A father can support his daughter best if he is aware of her development process. In his book *Fathers and Daughters,* William Appleton delineates three stages of father-daughter interaction: *oasis* happens when the daughter is in childhood; *conflict* occurs in adolescence; and *separation* takes place as she becomes an adult.

According to Appleton, if a father is too doting or overgiving in the oasis stage, a daughter may always long for a return to that center of attention, that feeling of preciousness. On the other hand, a father's neglect diminishes her confidence in attracting a man and results in feelings of insecurity, detachment, and anger.

During the conflict stage, when the daughter rebels against convention and authority, it's important for the father to acknowledge her anger and disappointment in his imperfection. Appleton believes this will help her to build autonomy and encourage her to have realistic, adult expectations of her male partners.

Finally, in the separation stage, as she gains full autonomy and approaches marriage, a father and daughter may feel the sadness of losing the more intimate aspects of their mutual dependency and emotional attachment. Here, again, the boundaries are shifting. If an overly involved father does not fully release "daddy's little girl," she may be unable to complete the separation stage and break free of the web of her family ties.

There are few universal rules about how to develop healthy family boundaries, but they certainly don't develop automatically. They require a certain amount of mutual effort, open communication, and an exchange of love.

A father's actions speak louder than his words. If a daughter sees her father respect her mother's emotional needs and self-expression, this will leave a lasting impression on her. She will be less likely to accept disrespect from men later in life. If, however, he is sexist or disrespectful to her mother, or if he dishonors the girl's budding feminity, then she is more likely to be accustomed to mistreatment and tolerate it later.

When a father speaks to his daughter, his words should be congruent with his actions. If, for example, an abusive or alcoholic father speaks of trust, responsibility, and reliability, she will feel the depth of the lie. If an absent father speaks of his good intentions, she will feel the hypocrisy.

A father is uniquely positioned to give voice to his vision of life and to pass on meaningful values to a daughter. He is both a limit-setter and the one who gives permission. She is impressionable to him as to no one else.

Different Treatment for Daughters

Fathers tend to treat their daughters differently than they treat their sons. Of course, daughters treat their fathers differently than they treat their mothers too.

Because mother and son are different genders, separation and individuation are early, prominent issues in the formation of a son's identity. His masculine identity is understood through this process of separation from her and identification with his father.

Between mother and daughter, however, there is an acknowledged sameness in their bond: "I and the mother are one." This assumes that the mother-daughter bond is strong and intimate enough to establish a basic sense of trust. Mergence and attachment, rather than separation, are characteristic of the daughter's early identity. Femininity, then, begins to be defined through relatedness, while masculinity is defined through separation.

Because a daughter is more versed in relationship, she may be more available than her brother for an intimate kind of relation with a father. In turn, the father often allows himself an affectionate closeness with a daughter that he may not permit with a son. The reservation he feels with a son may be due to competition or an unconscious fear of homosexual feelings.

The ways in which fathers treat their daughters differently than their sons depend on circumstances as well as on gender. We can make certain generalizations, knowing that exceptions are the rule. For example, fathers tend to be less competitive with their daughters. However, if a father doesn't have a son, he may treat one of his daughters as if she were a son; she then develops into the family tomboy.

Also, the ways in which a mother defines the mother-daughter relationship influence what kind of an alliance is struck between father and daughter. Many fathers feel less isolated from a mother-daughter bond than they do from the mother-son "conspiracy," which Robert Bly has described. The mother–daughter alliance appears to be less threatening to a father. It even may give him permission to spend more time working.

However, the mother–son bond often raises the angst of competition again. A father can feel abandoned when his wife is perceived as choosing another male (his son) over him.

In some families, a father needs an ally in his stand against the mother. If the father chooses a daughter for this inappropriate role, the danger is that, as she becomes elevated by him, she may learn to devalue her mother as he does, and in this way to devalue her own feminine self. In this pattern as daddy's ally, she learns to reject her mother, even hate her, and to side with the world of masculinity.

Fathers typically project distinct expectations onto girls and boys, so that daughters and sons get different lessons in how to achieve love and approval. For example, a father may project his own unfulfilled aspirations onto a son more readily than onto a daughter. In a stereotyped way, she tends to get rewarded for the quality of her being, her attitude and mood, while the son is reinforced for the quantity of his doing, his achievements. So each learns conventional, stereotyped behavior, rather than a wide range of emotional and creative expression.

Fathers see their daughters as more intimately connected to the creation of life. When a father looks at his daughter, he tends more to imagine potential offspring, his grandchildren. He feels this in spite of traditions whereby property is passed down through sons alone.

Fathers tend to be more possessive with their daughters than with their sons. When a father takes an overly protective stance against young boyfriends, he may really be communicating the message, "Nobody is good enough for my daughter because she is mine." Similarly, if a father treats a daughter like a princess, then who qualifies for marriage except a prince among men?

This attitude, of course, leads to the sexual double standard whereby the father encourages a son to explore sexually, while discouraging a daughter from her own search.

In the past two decades there have been tremendous shifts in these more stereotypical attitudes. Some fathers have learned to mentor their daughters through their careers, teaching them to earn a living and to take pride in their workplace skills. And, because of the high divorce rate and the rising number of single women, many fathers have had, to some degree, to come to terms with the nontraditional sexual lives of their daughters. The old "wait until you marry" adage (while her brother is out carousing) is pretty much gone.

Fathers and daughters are left today to carve out their own paths with each other. Fathers who nurture, advise, and mentor their daughters offer them a good start in life. Daughters who love, respect, and communicate honestly with their fathers offer them rich rewards in turn. Fathers and daughters can be each other's dearest allies and greatest friends.

MY DAUGHTER, MYSELF

I feel the need to briefly ground my observations about fathers and daughters in my own experience with my thirteen-year-old daughter. My relationship with her has been a great source of joy. Learning that she is only thirteen, you may chuckle, "just wait." As her hormones and interests change, I anticipate that I will be tested in different, maybe more difficult, ways. I will need to face her falling in love with boys and men. I will need to watch her succeed, then trip and fall. I will need to accept our growing differences, as she distinguishes her own feelings, opinions, and lifestyle choices. I will need to allow her to find her own way.

My daughter's surprise gift has been to help me rediscover my playfulness, spontaneity, and humor, which I had lost during the Vietnam War. My daughter gave me permission to be with her in a way that I wasn't able to give myself directly while carrying the burden and betrayal I felt from participating in that war. Thanks to my daughter, my inner child felt safe enough for me to begin becoming a more self-accepting father. My own experience parallels that of many other fathers, and echoes the wisdom of James Hillman, who wrote, "We all know that fathers create daughters, but daughters create fathers too."

OVERVIEW

Chapters 16, 17, and 20 describe the many dysfunctional behavior patterns between father and daughter. My intent is not to cast the father in a negative stereotype, but rather to illuminate some of the deeper wounds so we can see our way toward collective healing.

We begin Part III with an excerpt from *The Heroine's Journey* by therapist Maureen Murdock, which explores the father's daughter, the high achievement–oriented woman who seeks approval from her father and other prominent men. This adult daughter embarks upon a quest to find male allies. When the father is regarded as a worthy ally, his influence can be inspiring, fostering self-assurance and accomplishment in the world.

The dilemmas that women experience in the workplace are often linked to previous struggles with their fathers about power and authority. An adult daughter may find herself unknowingly adopting compliant or reactive roles rather than actively making authentic life choices for herself. According to family therapist Betty Carter, this passivity may stem from an unconscious collusion between a father and his daughter, which keeps the daughter dependent on male authoritarian expectations both in her personal relationships and in career choices. Carter's article, which appeared in *Networker,* is directed toward family therapists but is written in language accessible to all of us. She urges family therapists to challenge fathers' lack of engagement in the emotional life of the family.

Describing a more subtle betrayal of trust in *The Ravaged Bridegroom,* Jungian analyst Marion Woodman sees addictions as bodily responses to parental domination. According to Woodman, an addiction reenacts a traumatized relationship to the body. She views the anorexic behavior of one of her clients as rejected instincts, separated from feelings, that are trying to make themselves heard.

In an original essay titled "Failing My Father, Finding Myself," editor and author Connie Zweig describes in very personal terms her feelings about not providing her father with a grandchild. She is left with profound questions about motherhood and womanhood with regard to an unlived family life.

With glib humor, author Rosalind Warren portrays a father-daughter relationship revolving around automobiles. "Auto Repair" appeared in *My Father's Daughter: Stories by Women,* edited by Irene Zahava.

In the next article, Jungian analyst Andrew Samuels points to the psychic pain daughters suffer from a lack of physicality with their fathers. This article appeared in *Psychological Perspectives,* published by the C. G. Jung Institute in Los Angeles.

Part III concludes with an original essay by psychologist Tom Pinkson, who shares his own experience of ritually celebrating his daughters' first menstruations. Here is a personal story of a father actively taking a stand in his own family to dispel derogatory cultural attitudes.

In my view, Pinkson's story models a father creating a new current in contemporary male mythology. It is a current in which the father cares enough about his daughter to create a ritual that honors an aspect of her womanhood that our society has denigrated. I believe that a father who aspires to celebrate his daughter's womanhood will never stand taller.

CHAPTER FIFTEEN

Maureen Murdock

Daughters in the Father's World

In spite of the successes achieved by the woman's movement, the prevailing myth in our culture is that certain people, positions, and events have more inherent value than others. These people, positions, and events are usually masculine or male-defined. Male norms have become the social standard for leadership, personal autonomy, and success in this culture, and in comparison women find themselves perceived as lacking in competence, intelligence, and power.

The girl observes this as she grows up and wants to identify with the glamour, prestige, authority, independence, and money controlled by men. Many high-achieving women are considered *daughters of the father* because they seek the approval and power of that first male model. Somehow mother's approval doesn't matter as much; father defines the feminine and this affects her sexuality, her ability to relate to men, and her ability to pursue success in the world. Whether a woman feels that it is all right to be ambitious, to have power, to make money, or to have a successful relationship with a man derives from her relationship with her father.

Lynda Schmidt defines a father's daughter as "the daughter with a powerful, positive relationship with her father, probably to the exclusion of her mother. Such a young woman will orient herself around men as she grows up, and will have a somewhat deprecatory attitude toward women. Father's daughters organize their lives around the masculine principle, either remaining connected to an outer man or being driven from within by a masculine mode. They may find a male mentor or guide, but they may have, at the same time, trouble taking orders from a man or accepting teaching from one."[1]

Psychologists who study motivation have found that many successful women had fathers who nurtured their talent and made them feel attractive and loved at an early age. Marjorie Lozoff, a San Francisco Bay Area social scientist who conducted a four-year study on women's career success, concluded that women were more likely to be self-determining "when the fathers treated the daughters as if they were interesting people, worthy and deserving of respect and encouragement."[2] Women thus treated "did not feel their feminity was endangered by the development of talent."[3] Such fathers took an active interest in their daughter's lives and also encouraged their daughters to take an active interest in their own professional lives or avocations in politics, sports, or the arts.

A young girl's relationship with her father helps her to see the world through his eyes and to see herself reflected by him. As she sees his approval and acceptance, she measures her own competence, intelligence, and self-worth in relation to him and to other men. Approval and encouragement by a girl's father lead to positive ego development.

Women who have felt accepted by their fathers have confidence that they will be accepted by the world. They also develop a positive relationship to their masculine nature. They have an inner masculine figure who likes them just as they are. This positive inner male or animus figure will support their creative efforts in an accepting, nonjudgmental way.

Linda Leonard describes her fantasy of the positive inner masculine figure. She calls him the Man with Heart. He is "caring, warm, and strong," unafraid of anger, intimacy, and love. "He stays by me and is patient. But he initiates, confronts, and moves on as well. He is stable and enduring. Yet his stability comes from flowing with the stream of life, from being in the moment. He plays and works and enjoys both modes of being. He feels at home wherever he is—in the inner spaces or the outer world. He is a man of the earth—instinctual and sexy. He is a man of the spirit—soaring and creative."[4] This inner figure is engendered by a positive relationship with a woman's father or father figure. The inner male will be a supportive guide throughout the heroine's journey.

FATHER AS ALLY

Dr. Alexandra Symonds for the New York University School of Medicine made a study of women who had high commitments to their work and found that they had fathers who stressed the importance of education and taught them how to play the games of the business world. They coached their daughters to keep going in spite of failure and normal feelings of anxiety. They inspired them to be responsible for their own lives. These women were encouraged at an early age to achieve rather than be dependent.

Symonds found that it is fathers who can best cultivate healthy competence in their daughters. Although I don't agree with her findings and feel that mothers have as much to do with the building of their daughters' competence, I do agree with her statement that "if fathers give their daughters the kind of encouragement they give their sons, in sports, in sustained effort, in being self-sufficient, they will have developed qualities which will be important the rest of their lives. Their fathers can help them very much instead of patting them on the head and saying, 'Aren't you cute.' That is not enough."[5]

Women who have received such support have confidence to move *toward* something. They choose a career track that has definable goals and specific steps to follow—law, medicine, business, education, or arts administration, to name a few. Women whose fathers did not support their ideas and dreams for the future or who gave them the impression that they lacked the ability to carry them out meander through life and may *back into* success.

Some women who are successful try not only to emulate their fathers but consciously set out *not* to be like their mothers, whom they perceive as dependent, helpless, or hypercritical. In cases where a mother is chronically depressed, ill, or alcoholic the daughter allies herself with her father, ignoring her mother who becomes the shadow in the upstairs bedroom. The father then carries the power not only in the outside world but in her inner world as well.

THE FATHER QUEST: GATHERING ALLIES

During the second stage of the heroine's journey a woman wishes to identify with the masculine or to be rescued by the masculine. When a woman decides to break with the established images of the feminine she inevitably begins the traditional hero's journey. She puts on her armor, mounts her modern-day steed, leaves loved ones behind, and goes in search of the golden treasure. She fine-tunes the skills of logos. She looks for clearly defined routes to success. She sees the male world as healthy, fun-loving, and action-oriented. Men get things done. This fuels her own ambition.

This is an important period in the development of a woman's ego. Our heroine looks for role models who can show her the steps along the way. These male allies may take the form of a father, boyfriend, teacher, manager, or coach; the institution granting the degree or salary she seeks; or a minister, rabbit, priest, or God. The Ally may also be a male-identified woman, perhaps an older childless woman who has played by team rules and successfully made her way to the top.

"Most women seek power and authority either by becoming like men or by becoming liked by men."[6] This is not such a negative thing at first because seeking male validation is a healthy transition from fusion with the mother to greater independence in a patriarchal society. The young woman who identifies with what could be considered positive father qualities, such as discipline, decision-making, direction, courage, power, and self-valuation, finds herself achieving success in the world. This can be very damaging, however, if a woman believes that she does not exist except in the mirror of male attention or male definition.

LACK OF A POSITIVE MASCULINE ALLY

Approval and encouragement by the father or other father substitutes usually lead to a woman's positive ego development; but lack of genuine involvement or negative involvement on the part of the father, stepfather, uncle, or grandfather deeply wounds a woman's sense of her self. It can lead to overcompensation and perfectionism or virtually paralyze her development. When a father is absent or indifferent to his daughter he indicates his disinterest, disappointment, and disapproval, which can be as damaging to the heroine as explicit negative judgments or overprotectiveness.

In *The Female Hero in American and British Literature,* Carol Pearson and Katherine Pope quote from the diary of Canadian artist Emily Carr, whose father was physically present but emotionally indifferent to her and to her mother. In her late sixties she was still grappling with this indifferent god.

> Sixty-six years ago tonight I was hardly me. . . . I wonder what father felt. I can't imagine him being as interested as Mother. More to Father's taste was a nice juicy steak served piping on the great pewter hotwater dish. That made his eyes twinkle. I wonder if he ever succored Mother up with a tender word or two after she'd been through a birth or whether he was as rigid as ever, waiting for her to buck up and wait on him. He ignored new babies until they were old enough to admire him, old enough to have wills to break.[7]

Inadequate attention from a father on the personal level or from a mentor on the cultural level results in what Linda Leonard calls the "armored Amazon."

> In reacting against the negligent father such women often identify on the ego level with the masculine or fathering functions themselves. Since their father did not give them what they needed, they find they have to do it themselves. . . . The armor protects them positively insofar as it helps them develop professionally and enables them to have a voice in the world of affairs. But insofar as the armor shields them from their own feminine feelings and their soft side, these women tend to become alienated from their own creativity, from healthy relationships with men, and from the spontaneity and vitality of living in the moment.[8]

This type of woman will be seen as professionally successful but difficult to trust in the emotional or relational arena. Her inner masculine figure is not a man with heart but a greedy tyrant that never lets up. Nothing she does is ever enough; he drives her forward "more, better, faster" with no recognition of her longing to be loved, to feel satisfied, or even to rest.

ADDICTION TO PERFECTION

A young woman may appear to succeed while bleeding herself dry internally. Because of an innate fear of female inferiority, many young women become addicted to perfection, overcompensating, and overworking because they are different than men.

We live in a culture that does not trust process and is intolerant of diversity. Therefore we are all expected to be perfect, and beyond that, to be perfect in similar—if not the same—ways to one another. We are supposed to "live up" to standards of virtue, achievement, intelligence, and physical attractiveness. If we do not, then we are expected to repent, work harder, study, diet, exercise, and wear better clothes until we fit the prevailing image of an ideal person. Thus our unique qualities [in this case being female] are likely to be defined as "the problem" that we need to solve to be OK.[9]

Some women take great pride in learning how to think like men, how to compete with them, and how to beat them at their own game. Such women become heroic, but many are left with a gnawing sensation that they will never be *enough*. They continue to do more, out of the need to be the same as men. Having grown up in a Catholic household I often wonder if a woman's sense of lack stems from the fact that she was not made in the image of God. The experience many girls have with their fathers is the same they have with the father God: loved but held apart, even feared, because they have different genitalia.

Nancy is a woman in her early forties who has returned to law school after twenty years as a performer and political activist. When she does her assignments for school she realizes that she wastes an enormous amount of time and energy trying to do each assignment perfectly. She puts much more effort into each problem than is required. Because of this she never has enough time to finish all of her work, and her grades reflect assignments finished late. Nancy doesn't lack intelligence or the ability to do the work; she overdoes it.

When I ask her who she writes the perfect answers for, she responds, "Dad." She tells me about the memory of a recurring dialogue she had with her late father when she was a little girl. He was a truck driver with a great sense of humor who treated her, the first daughter, like a son. "Well, I wish you were a boy," he'd say, "but since you're not, what's nine times nine?"

"I always had the right answer to any question he asked," recalls Nancy. "I memorized sports statistics, the longest words in the dictionary, and the capital of every state so I would never be off-guard. It was great for my memory, but I had no concept of what it meant to be a girl. All I knew was that something was wrong with me because I wasn't a boy, and I had to figure how to make up for that."

Nancy was defined by her father's ideal of what it meant to be a female. Since she already lacked the physical equipment to be male, the next best thing was to be smart and do things perfectly. My own father puts it this way: "If you can't do it right, don't do it at all"— which I internalized as a dictum not to try anything unless I could ace it.

Learning the Rules of the Game with Dad

Little girls learn early on which games to play for their father's approval and attention. They may have to act smart, cute, coy, or be seductive. Power and authority are daddy issues inside the bedroom as well as out. The first man a girl flirts with is her daddy. How he responds to her is critical to a girl's sexual development. A father's warmth, playfulness, and love are very important to a girl's healthy sexuality; otherwise, her primary love object will remain her first attachment, her mother. On the other hand, a father's dominance, possessiveness, and criticism can undermine or destroy a girl's heterosexual development.

More abusive is the father who ignores his natural role as protector of his young daughter's sexuality and, because of a need for male dominance, violates her normal sexual development through incest. She will spend the rest of her life reclaiming her sexuality and the fact that as a woman she *does have rights.*

Other girl children learn that it is best not to act too smart around dad. They might become a target for ridicule, criticism, disapproval, or physical abuse. They learn not to be "smarty pants" around men who can't fill the pants in the family. They quickly learn to let dad win in cards, checkers, or free throws in basketball and tennis. They forget their own ambitions and become women who make their bosses look good. They end up feeling bitter, passive, and cynical about what has happened to their lives.

Girls who suffered from the denial of positive attention from their fathers in childhood look for him in each relationship they have. Loretta, a woman in her late thirties, idolized her handsome sportscaster father but was unable to get his attention. She grew up with three athletic brothers who monopolized his interest. As a girl she was quiet and dreamy and loved to spend time in the woods, but she had no athletic ability and little interest in sports. Loretta's father made fun of the stories she wrote and ridiculed the games she played with her animals. Her mother was quiet and depressed. Loretta didn't know how to enter the all-male world around her so she married into it.

"My first husband was a baseball player in the minors, so I went to the games and invited my dad to sit in the box with me. Dad followed my husband's career closely but had no interest in mine, and the more time I spent with Jon off-season, the more I realized that we had nothing in common. So I married Mike. He was older and looked just like my dad. He was also an athlete but not a professional one, so I thought things would be different. He was a writer like me, but he always told me I had no talent. After three years of listening to that, I realized I was beginning to disappear just like my mother.

"I left Mike, and it took me awhile to heal, but after we had been apart for a year I woke up to the fact that I was marrying guys in an effort to fill a giant hole left by my dad's reflection of me. I stopped seeing men altogether and focused on my writing. Now I'm seeing a high-school teacher who looks nothing like my dad, doesn't follow sports, and is interested in what I have to say. We really enjoy each other; it's the first time I've felt good about being a woman. I don't know if I'll remarry, but I do know that I no longer need to look for dad."

Part of the heroine's quest is to find her work in the world, which enables her to find her identity. It is important for a woman to know that she can survive without dependence on parents or others so that she can express her heart, mind, and soul. Skills learned during this first part of the heroic quest establish a woman's competence in the world.

CHAPTER SIXTEEN

Betty Carter

Fathers and Daughters

In today's society, the relationships between fathers and their daughters are often full of mixed messages and contradictions. A father may spend a fortune on his daughter's education, yet not expect her to achieve much. She may admire his achievements, and then push her husband or son, instead of herself, to match them. Priding himself on strength and independence, father rewards helplessness and compliance in his daughter. She values direct emotional expression, but uses flattery and deceit with him.

These contradictions have increased as women's roles have changed. The supportive father is confused about what expectations and hopes to hold for his daughters. The authoritarian father holds desperately to the past to escape redefining his own new role. His daughter, for her part, wants her father's approval, even for behavior she knows he cannot accept. She may become distant with him, unable to discuss her life choices for fear of his angry disapproval. Or, she may seek autonomy through reactive defiance and rebellion.

Among the wealthy, father's iron rule may be disguised by the apparent benevolence of his material gifts. His authoritarianism may be excused by society on the grounds of his "importance" and "busy" schedule. Daughters of any social class whose fathers are physically or emotionally absent often adopt negative and condescending attitudes toward the men in their lives. Or, in the place of a flesh and blood mate, they may develop a fantasized "ideal man" who remains forever desired, forever sought in vain.

Traditional psychological theories obscure rather than clarify the tangled nature of the bonds between fathers and daughters. Many therapies echo the popular wisdom that *father* is the key to the daughter's success in love and work. Women with inadequate or missing fathers are expected to have difficulty sustaining intimacy, marrying wisely and well, or achieving sexual happiness. At the same time, these truisms about fathers' profound influence in their daughters' lives raise a curious question—why do so many women blame their mothers for their problems? In our patriarchal culture, it sometimes seems father gets credit for daughter's success, and mother gets credit for the blame and failure.

Many of the conflicts between fathers and daughters arise in therapy in disguised form. For example, therapists often fail to recognize that the dilemmas women experience involving work and career are often linked to old struggles with their fathers about power and authority. Around the issues of work and career revolve all the questions of power, authority, entitlement, and expectations that embroil fathers and daughters. A father may expect his daughter to work, but not want her in a demanding career, or he may deem some careers more suitable for her than others. Whatever her work, he may, like her husband, expect her to quit when she has a baby or finesse career demands so that these will not "interfere" with family life. For daughters, the question centers around entitlement: is she entitled to pursue her own ambitions if they conflict with her father's expectations? Does she need his permission? His help and approval? Can she get along without them?

Throughout history, men have held almost all the world's power and prestige, women almost none. Within the social microcosm of the family, fathers have commanded, daughters obeyed. Traditionally, the good father has been required only to protect his daughter from other men; if he abused his own power at her expense, there was no one to hold him accountable, no one to protect her from him. For many centuries, daughters could consider themselves fortunate if their fathers protected and provided for them until they were old enough to be handed over to a husband who continued the job. First father, then husband, then adult son, made all the decisions about the daughter's life, from childhood through old age. What is startling is how little, not how much, these patterns have changed, until this generation.

The following is an outline of four major dysfunctional father-daughter patterns: cut-off, distant, enmeshed, and perverted. Each major pattern has both conflictual and non-conflictual variations and should be conceptualized as a part of a triangle rather than as a purely dyadic interaction and as a multigenerational, not merely a nuclear family pattern. It should be kept in mind, of course, that even this conceptual unit (the transgenerational triangle) is a minimal view of the relationship problem, which is actually embedded in a much more complex family system, with all its members, themes and rules. And, of course, beyond the family level, the relationship is influenced by the complexities and mandates of the social, cultural, and political system that shapes the family. The formulations given here are meant to suggest a conceptual approach or handle on the problem, not to provide a total analysis of it. The theoretical framework is derived from Bowen Family Systems Theory with revisions or adaptations that explicitly include the factor of gender and its connections to the social values in which the family system is embedded.

The Cut-Off Father-Daughter Relationship

Bowen Systems Theory and feminist theory are in agreement about the importance of emotional connectedness and the dysfunction that results when significant relationships are disrupted or cut off.

Cut-Off by Death

If a father dies when his daughter is very young, the chances are that he will continue to exert a strong influence on her life through fantasy. It is very common in this situation for father to be idealized by his daughter, who then conducts an impossibly perfect relationship with him in her mind. The more the father is idealized, the more negativity may be directed toward the mother, who is, after all, "merely human." And of course, if mother remarries, there is an extremely high likelihood of intense conflict between daughter and the man who tries to take her father's place.

In these interlocking triangles, father is flash-frozen in perfection, daughter's attitude toward the stepfather is "you are not my father," and mother is caught in the middle. The most insidious characteristic of this situation is that since the father is probably not often spoken of, the adults may not be aware of the daughter's fantasy relationship with him. Almost any move, positive or negative,

that the stepfather makes toward the daughter will be fiercely re-
sisted by her out of loyalty to her "real" father.

Resolution of this situation can be brought about by encouraging the family to talk to daughter about what sort of person
her father was or, if daughter is an adult, coaching her to find out
about him.

Cut-off by Divorce

Divorces may also result in a father-daughter cut-off. In this situation, the daughter often assumes that the father doesn't care about
her. In their mutual anger at father, there is a collusive element in
mother and daughter's relationship, and, if they are isolated from
extended family and social networks, daughter is a prime candidate
for the emotional caretaker role.

THE DISTANT FATHER-DAUGHTER RELATIONSHIP

In this pattern, daughter may experience her distant father either
positively or negatively.

Distant and Positive Father-Daughter Relationship

Predictably, the daughter of an emotionally distant father often feels
more warmth towards him than towards her mother, to whom she
is actually closer. This is one of the most common family triangles,
largely because so many fathers give most of their attention and energy to their work, leaving their wives to struggle with child rearing almost alone. Feelings of guilt or lack of familiarity with the
complexes of parenting often lead father into adopting the "Mr.
Nice Guy" role leaving mother to play the bad guy. The so-called
"distant but nice" father may be suffering the emotional consequences
of having established a polite but distant relationship with his own
mother.

The less clear the communication in the family, the more covert
the father-daughter alliance and the more unclear its base. There are
several possible varieties of father-daughter alliance. Daughter may

sense, without being told, that she is the father's favorite child, or that he prefers her to mother, or she may be similar to father in ways that annoy mother. The secret alliance is revealed when daughter stands up to her mother in ways that father never does. Daughter understands that her conflict with her mother doesn't really upset him; quite the contrary, the more conflictual the daughter's relationship with her mother, the deeper the warmth and sympathy for dad for "having to put up with her." If you ask her which parent she is closer to, she will answer "father," mistaking the feeling of alliance for closeness. Actually, you will usually find that she knows next to nothing about father or his family. In this triangle, daughter has little understanding of the parents' *mutual* dependency and mother's dilemma is invisible because of this triangulation. It is common for this daughter to choose a husband who reminds her of "dear old Dad" but then to fall into conflictual marital patterns that are a repeat of her relationship with her closer parent—her mother.

The Distant and Negative Father-Daughter Relationship

In this variation, daughter has an alliance with mother and feels very negative toward her distant father. Typically, father functions over-responsibly somewhere on the spectrum from boss to tyrant. He may have had a doting mother from whom he learned early compliance or special attention from the women close to him. His wife accepts his dominance, placating him when he's upset and acting out the put-upon role.

Daughter feels sorry for mother and allies with her; father receives her anger and contempt. She blames him for not giving more to mother and herself. However, father is not very involved in her life, and since they are so distant, the tension between father and daughter may well remain covert during daughter's adolescence. She thinks the negative thoughts about dad that her mother wouldn't dream of. She will be cold and distant, refusing to placate him and refusing his attempts, often blunt and tactless, to advise or take care of her. If they arrive in the office of a family therapist, very often father's concerns will be seen as reasonable and mother and daughter's warm relationship will be scrutinized for overinvolvement and made the focus of the therapy. When daughter leaves home, she'll stay as distant as duty will allow. If the stress gets high enough, however, their emotionally loaded relationship may explode into open conflict or total cut-off.

The movie *On Golden Pond* provides an excellent illustration of this pattern and how it can be resolved. Mother (Katharine Hepburn) encourages daughter (Jane Fonda) to come to terms with her father (Henry Fonda) from whom she has been angrily distant and is on the verge of cutting off. Father has never been able to relate to his daughter in a way that got through to her. Daughter's interpretation of her difficulties with her father is that he wanted a son and doesn't love her. Mother reminds her that her father is old and will not live long and daughter decides to try again to relate to him.

First she approaches him and takes the risk of being vulnerable. She tells him important personal news—the fact that she has gotten married. Much to her surprise (in a distant relationship people don't know each other well enough to accurately predict behavior), his response is positive. Now daughter does something else that is different in their relationship. Instead of insisting that her father change *his* way of relating to her, perhaps through talk or through entering into her world, daughter accepts her father for who he is and moves toward him in *his* way. She reminds him that he used to try to teach her to do a back-flip dive, but that she couldn't ever do it right. Now she will show him that she can.

Daughter's willingness to drop the power struggle over who needs to change, and to approach her father in a way that he understands and values, is her step into maturity. Such a step couldn't be taken as long as it is seen as capitulation, which is how it might appear to a rebellious adolescent or a young adult. Nor could such a step be taken by a daughter overwhelmed by feelings of hurt, rejection, or anger, which is how his daughter previously reacted to her father. Now, giving up the need to "win" her battle with him, she is willing to accept his nonverbal, sports-oriented ways of relating as being his best or only way of moving towards her.

It is thus with a lot of unspoken but understood emotion that he gives her his old college diving medal. As she leaves, she calls him Dad instead of Norman. Daughter has changed her approach to her father instead of continuing to insist that he change. She seeks his support and a connection with him through the metaphor of the dive he had wanted to teach her, and he responds positively, using the same metaphor, by giving her the diving medal. Their closer relationship is sealed with a hug, and by calling him Dad, she signifies that she has come to terms with who he is, and accepts him.

The above is a good example of the resolution on a personal and family level of a problem that relates to issues on the social level. Thus, sexist social values that might lead a man to be disappointed that his only child is a daughter, or that permit him to remain so distant and inflexible that he can't figure out appropriate ways to relate to a daughter, have to be understood and resolved on the personal level without putting down either father or daughter. If we take our movie example, for instance, as a real family, one would hope that now that daughter has healed the breach with her father by demonstrating her willingness to enter and accept his world, he can be helped to find ways to enter her world and to connect to her in ways that *she* values.

ENMESHED FATHER-DAUGHTER RELATIONSHIPS

Daddy's Little Girl

In enmeshed father-daughter relationships, father has made an ally of his daughter and is, therefore, most influential in her life. Like some other dysfunctional patterns, one of its most pernicious characteristics is that it is generally experienced as benign by daughter and is so intended by father. Its problematic aspects may thus be invisible to mother (and to therapists) because it comes closest of all father-daughter patterns to the culture's ideal. The bargain is this: Daddy will give his daughter everything in his power to give, and, in exchange, she will never reject or challenge his authority. In other words, she may grow old, but she will never grow up.

In the parental triangle, father and mother fight over their daughter's upbringing, with mother feeling left out and angry, or mother may acquiesce in daddy's wishes, becoming more like a sibling than a mother to her daughter, with both of them equally oriented toward daddy's wishes, his rewards, and punishments. In either triangle, daughter has been promised a rose garden. She has been programmed to expect a good life without any effort on her part except compliance. Many divorces are precipitated by women who don't know any intermediate way to assert themselves with their husbands, as they never were permitted to argue with daddy. Therapy for daddy's girl must begin with an extended course of "assertiveness training," and reconciliation of mother and daughter.

The Conflictual Father-Daughter Relationship

In this extremely common pattern, father is once again the boss and mother typically assumes a placating or peacemaker position regarding her own and her daughter's relationship with him. However, daughter is a lot like her mother in some way that annoys father and a lot more outspoken in her defiance of him. She may also refuse to cater to him in the way he was trained to expect.

While his daughter is young, father is quite involved in directing her life, either on his own or through mother. During adolescence, when her growing independence threatens his role, father increases his efforts to control her and she rebels all the more. Although mother's alliance with daughter is covert, daughter knows on some level that she is fighting the mother's battles with father as well as her own and this adds fuel to the fire. What entirely escapes her, however, is her own collusion with father, whereby their battles protect him from having to deal with his wife.

The greatest pitfall for daughter is that she will devote her life to being or doing the opposite of what her father wants for her without really finding out what she wants for herself. The biggest pitfall for father, on the other hand, is that he will let his marriage stagnate or die as he focuses on the battle with daughter, and his wife either distances or cuts herself off totally from him.

This pattern of conflict is very hard to overcome. In the first place, by directly expressing a lot of anger to a man, [the daughter] has broken a cardinal taboo for women and she will feel like a bitch for doing it, no matter how justified she thinks her anger is. Secondly, during the heat of the battle, conflictual fathers and daughters will have said and done so many hurtful things that their list of grievances seems endless. Worst of all, the conflict is a power struggle and giving it up feels like "losing." An adult daughter's motivation to extricate herself from this pattern without cutting off may depend on the ability of the therapist to reframe her change moves as "winning" in some way (e.g., "Won't he be totally bewildered if you show up looking happy and successful instead of depressed and down-and-out?").

The Perverse Father-Daughter Relationship

In this father-daughter pattern, generational or personal boundaries are blurred or eradicated to the extent that even the most basic responsibilities of parenthood are neglected or transgressed. Incest is one of the most damaging transgressions. Until very recently, incest was a social as well as a family secret with most cases going unreported and even mental health professionals denying its widespread occurrence across economic and class lines.

Mental health professionals have most commonly blamed mother for incest, though some experts also blame daughter's "seductiveness," regardless of her age. Mother is cited as having certain negative personality traits, and for failing to protect her daughter or report the abuse. However, none of these factors is sufficient to explain incest, for which the most significant triangle is three-generational: father, daughter, and one or both of the father's parents.

This triangle, connecting father to the parent who abused him in childhood, should not be relegated to "past history," but seen as an intense, smoldering, arrested, perverse relationship to which the father is still reacting in the present. Therapeutic treatment should focus on this relationship, but should in no way seem to excuse father's behavior or eliminate the need for him to take personal responsibility for his actions, quite the contrary. However, mental health officials typically concentrate on the nuclear family, scapegoating the mother and child-victim, while ignoring the chaos in the extended family and its intense current influence.

Socially, incest and other childhood abuses are rooted in our patriarchal attitudes, particularly the centuries-old belief that children are the legal property of their fathers. In our more enlightened times, this subjugation to the father still receives subtle approval in society's designation as "ideal" a family structure comprising a dominant father, the "head of the household," and his deferential wife and children. This pattern is still idealized, even though the basic economic structure that long sustained it—father as sole breadwinner—no longer holds.

The stage is set for incest when two emotionally deprived dependent parents play roles that the patriarchal society has assigned them. He demands, she defers; he blusters, she placates; he threatens or beats her, she backs down or withdraws. Then this domestic tyranny isolates all the members of the family from each other, he molests his daughter, and calls it "love." Over time, his behavior becomes compulsive, and is triggered by any tensions in his life, inside or outside the family.

Father tries to convince himself that his behavior does no harm. Mother, when she finally admits to herself what is happening, finds herself in a double-bind similar to that of an alcoholic's wife: she can openly confront the incest and plunge herself and her children into shame and perhaps destitution, or she can try to convince herself it won't happen again. Like an alcoholic and his wife, the parents may spend years exchanging idle threats to leave and empty promises to reform, both too dependent on each other actually to end the marriage. The daughter, feeling that only her silence holds the family together, may thus keep her "secret" for years, even forever.

If the incest is current, the family's denial of wrongdoing must be challenged if therapy is to succeed, even if that means jailing the father and/or assigning him to a sex offender's program until he admits he has a problem. No change is possible in a family until the father accepts personal responsibility for his behavior, just as if he were an alcoholic or drug abuser. Individual or family therapy aimed at the "psychological" or "systemic" factors only, expecting the abuse to cease automatically as a result of the sessions, just reinforces the abusive behavior.

The restoration of a positive mother–daughter relationship is crucial to the treatment in incest cases and often the best place to begin therapy. Next, the marital relationship must be rebalanced, with the wife acquiring more power. Finally repair of the father–daughter relationship should be addressed, to the extent possible. Thus, again, compassion, understanding, reconciliation, and forgiveness may be personal and family options, though at the social level, they are not enough.

Abusive Relationships

In a typical triangle, father's abuse of daughter may be aimed as much at his wife as at the daughter. In this pattern, father has been abused by his father in childhood and has a "macho" or petty tyrant approach to male roles. There is often open and ongoing conflict between husband and wife, in which daughter gets caught. Whatever the circumstances in which the father first shoves, harangues, threatens, or strikes his daughter, a negative reaction by his wife may challenge him and fuel a further escalation on his part, with more intensity from her, and on to explosion. Whoever initiates it, the sequence ends with daughter being beaten or tongue-lashed and mother thus defeated by father. As in alcohol abuse, incest, and wife-beating, this cycle is followed later by the parents' exchange of idle threats and empty promises.

Whether the abuser agrees to a program aimed at behavior change or not, it is essential in cases of physical abuse that the child protective service be notified, as required by law, to root the therapy firmly in open acknowledgment that a crime has been committed and that the therapy will not serve to by-pass the social constraints created to deal with the problem. After the abuse has stopped, if this pattern is not fueled by drugs or alcohol, and if the adult participants want to change it, it can be altered by helping each adult find a specific way to change behavior before the conflict becomes a runaway. Children cannot change such a pattern on their own by any method. Behavioral contracts and other methods of helping couples to avoid situations that lead to violence will seldom hold for long if there is an intergenerational pattern of abuse, and this triangle—abuser and his parents—should be the focus of therapy.

Women who report that their husband's abusive behavior is associated with alcohol or drug use should be told frankly that there will be no control of the physical abuse until the alcohol or drug abuse stops. Therapeutic work should focus on helping these women and their children leave the man until he gets substance abuse treatment.

Daughters with abusive or aggressively intrusive fathers may marry someone who is so unlike their father that they subsequently complain of their husband's lack of initiative; or conversely, they may duplicate the intensity of the father-daughter relationship in endless marital conflict with another tyrant. The relationship with father may remain the most intense one of her life, with daughter alternately placating him and fighting with him as they remain locked in intense mutual emotional dependency. Severe stress easily leads to complete cut-off, which may last for years or a lifetime.

The Therapist's Role

It is time for family therapists to take fathers more seriously and to recognize their emotional importance to everyone in the family. Over and over, I see fathers written off by therapist in collusion with others in the family, because of men's supposed "incapacity" to relate more fully. I see fathers excused from therapy sessions because they are busy, and I see them courted, flattered, and deferred to so that they will remain in treatment. I see peripheral fathers dismissed, post-divorce fathers forgotten, and "distant" fathers ignored (supposedly in hopes that they will join voluntarily; actually, I think, in hopes that they won't disrupt the therapy).

The failure to challenge fathers to engage in the emotional life of the family and in the process of change is a major stumbling block to successful therapy. Worst of all, such negative expectations in therapy are isomorphic to the father's greatest danger on family life—that he will settle for status in place of emotional participation.

CHAPTER SEVENTEEN

Marion Woodman

Betrayal of Trust and Addiction

Parents may triumph over a child, but ultimately there is no such thing as triumph by force, even if that force is elegantly disguised. Domination is domination and the body that has been tyrannized has learned its lessons well. It becomes a potentate, abandoned, outside the civilizing influence of love. In its desolation, it compensates by becoming possessive, clinging to objects or people, investing them with magical powers. Dependent on these talismans for any sense of vitality, the body becomes ferocious in its demands to possess and control them, trying to perpetuate a phantasm in which it no longer believes.

I do not mean to make parents guilty. We are all products of our cultural situation, which encourages competition and dominance. We scarcely understand what love in the body is. We confuse it with sexuality and need. Genuine love, however, permeates every cell of the body. It is immediately recognized by animals, children and even some adults who were either born with it or have found it through suffering and surrender. Gilt-edged guilt merely compounds the abandonment. Our task is to work to change the dynamics.

The overwhelming sense of abandonment which terrorizes so many people is rooted not in the parents' abandonment of the child, but in the abandonment of the child's soul. By projecting their own image of their child, they obliterate the actual child who then goes underground, abandoned not only by the parents, but by the child itself. Out of this habitual abuse arises the sense of shame connected with some unknown crime for which the child feels guilty. Dreams of a murder being committed, or a corpse lying hidden, reveal the betrayal that is perpetuated into adulthood. When a relationship is endangered, for example, the adult again abandons the underground child, who is impossibly honest; then the persona takes over, trying to please, hoping to save the relationship at any cost. The guilt is two-fold: "I am guilty for being who I am," and, at a deeper level, "I have abandoned myself."

The abandoned one becomes the victim of the magician who exploits the loneliness, connects with the rejected essence, produces magic in a realm where soul seems to be lived, then shatters the illusion. The dark side of the magician takes the addict deeper and deeper into his or her secret death-dealing world; the light side, as wise old man, can take the released soul into its own creativity. The razor's edge between those two worlds is genuine feeling. "I am wrong, I am guilty, I am a victim, I deserve to be punished," leads to magic and addiction. "I will not abandon myself, I am not guilty, I will be who I am," leads to mystery and creativity.

Julia is an addict whose childhood faith in her father was repeatedly betrayed by, of all things, his laughter. He was the magician who every night at storytime wove spells that made her forget her sadness, but at the same time led her deeper into it.

Lest it be assumed that every father who reads to his young daughter at bedtime is unconsciously drawing her into his own unacknowledged erotic fantasy, something needs to be said about this particular relationship as it gradually came into focus in the analytic process.

The father was a charming *puer* whose imagination created palaces where others saw poverty. Alienated from his wife, who found his idealism a threat to the material welfare of herself and her family, he turned to his daughter as his chief psychic support. In her infancy he had sought to protect her from the sudden, irrational outbursts of her mother's physical violence. As a result, Julia accompanied him wherever he went and spent the happiest days of her childhood working beside him at her small desk in his study or rocking on his lap to the rhythms of poetry or song. The two of them seemed bonded against a world largely indifferent, if not hostile, to the spiritual splendor which they together brought to it; her imagination fed his aspirations.

The world the father and daughter shared, while reading together, was a secret, treasured world, associated with a forbidden "high." The father magician was psychically seducing his daughter.

The child felt shame, but the shame was compelling because to be in that intimacy with her father was numinous. Together they were caught in a strange, mysterious rite. Repeatedly, the child tested the magic to see if she could restrain her tears until she was alone. Controlling her body in this way gradually cut her off from body awareness. While Julia has no memory of physical abuse, the psychic betrayal split body from soul as surely as actual incest.

Perhaps alarmed by the intensity of their relationship, the father continually punctured it in a manner that radically betrayed his daughter's boundless trust. Her favorite story reveals, as all favorite stories tend to do, her psychic situation. She loved to hear "The Little Match Girl," which tells the tale of an abandoned child who on New Year's Eve uses her last match to keep warm and to light her fantasies. When it goes out, she freezes to death. This story, which summed up the daughter's relationship with her mother, against whom her father was her sole protection, served a healing function. She believed that in reading this story to her, her father was not only acknowledging her plight but assuring her of his understanding and support. When, therefore, he responded to her tears with explosive laughter, her trust was brutally betrayed. She was the little match girl whose last match went out with her father's laughter. The terror was compounded by the intervention of her mother who slapped her, declaring "I'm not raising a crybaby."

These episodes constituted a childhood trauma that repeated itself in her intimate relationships. As she surrendered to the magical world of unboundaried intimacy, at the same time she anticipated the killing blow that would sever her from the magician and from her own body, frozen in unexpressed emotions. Already fading into unconsciousness, she disappeared when her mother struck. This trauma later manifested itself in her unconscious setting up situations in which she manipulated men into what she experienced as acts of betrayal. Food and sex became for her a box of matches which, if emptied, would lead to starvation. She ate and made love in an attempt to fill a hole—her traumatized body—that, because of its alienation, was always empty.

After Julia had stabilized at a healthy weight, she attended body/soul sessions in which she encountered overwhelming vulnerability without her body fat and a resultant terror of being abandoned by the man she loved. Repeatedly she had been dreaming of a handsome man dressed in a broad-brimmed black hat and flowing black cape, a magician who had the power to give life and to take it away.

In the following dream, it is the father whom she adored and strove to please who finds her guilty for being who she is. The childhood relationship that kept her alive now shows its other face. The projection she had put on men comes home to roost.

> I am on trial. The courtroom is my church. My father is the judge in the pulpit. I am resigned. The verdict is inevitable. I know I will be found guilty for being who I am. I stand dignified before my father-judge, but I am terrified because I can hear the barking of starving dogs in the graveyard and I know the punishment for my crime is to be thrown to the dogs.

We can see in the dream how the father, albeit quite unconsciously, betrayed his child's essence. Trusting him to understand her empathy with the abandoned child in the story, she was totally cut off when he laughed at her tears. Her feelings were repressed in her body, which became the tyrant dogs that threatened to eat her as ravenously as she ate food to try to avoid their rage.

Significantly, the father appears in the dream as a patriarchal principle—judge, bishop, father-god—without personal love for Julia. The outer man has become the inner magician. In reality, the power she once projected onto her father she now projects onto her lover; the lack of grounding in life (abandonment by the mother) now makes her cling to her lover as mother; her terror of loss activates her eating compulsion (sweetness, nourishment from mother). The dogs in the graveyard were hungry for all she had denied herself—feelings, tears, sexuality. But were they to come out, what then? To have angered her father would have dismembered her world. Therefore, she took the blame for the bewildering outcome of their magical times together and split off her feeling heart. To anger her lover was once again to watch the dying of the light in what she experienced as her last match. Thus she suppressed her real feelings but anticipated the death sentence.

The punishment the father complex metes out in the dream comes from the place of his, now her, own rejected feelings rampant in the ravenous instincts locked in the church graveyard. At this point, Julia had neither the masculine strength to control the dogs nor the feminine ego in a grounded body to contain them. Having dealt with her perfectionist ideals on one rung of the spiral with food, she was once again flying with perfectionist fantasies in her relationship. She was resisting matter, resisting life. Thus her body, instead of being a loving container, counteracted her rejection of herself as an imperfect, passionate woman by becoming rigid, impervious to light.

In her desire to be "beautiful enough" for her lover, Julia was moving into anorexia. *No* to food became an eroticized *no,* charged with the euphoric high of starvation. *No* to her feelings, *no* to her instincts, all produced dreams of passionate lovemaking with the magician or her lover. As long as she was starving, she experienced herself as lovely, healthy, pure, worthy of her beloved. At the height of her fasting, she once heard the demonic laughter of her magician father who was claiming her for his own, taking her into the perfection of death. Just as she once looked to her father to bring the light, she now looked to her lover. In projecting the action of a god onto a human being, she was creating a magician who flung her from inflation into despair. Again she was catapulted into binging, unconsciously communing with the mother she yearned for, and raping her instead. The rape was the compulsion to possess the loving mother even through death, her own death. Thus the demonic is appeased while the soul, under the anesthetic of carbohydrate, passes out into the very darkness that through some magic may yet become light.

Any addict knows these extremes. The body-in-control is an unloved tyrant, resistant to light because it exits without love. The starving dogs in the graveyard of her body are rejected instincts trying hard to make themselves heard. Julia needs to connect to them with consistent, loving discipline. Being victimized by rampant instincts can result in promiscuity, which, like insane eating, is a manifestation of instinct cut off from feeling.

CHAPTER EIGHTEEN

Connie Zweig

Failing My Father, Finding Myself

My father dreamed of walking me down the aisle, slowly, grandly, to the hum of Mozart or Bach, in a black tux, satin-trimmed, with his upright athletic walk, his graying hair, his authoritative eye, and me in pearl-trimmed, cream-colored lace, radiant with hope, my arm resting on his, lightly.

My father dreamed of walking me down the aisle, slowly, grandly, until we reached an altar of flowers, high and full of the colors of spring. My father dreamed of the moment when he would lift my arm and place it on another, lightly, stepping back then to leave me, his daughter, standing in the next moment as a wife.

My father occasionally stopped at hotels in his travels looking for the ideal wedding site, imagining the aisle walk in every grand hotel lobby, hearing the sounds of music fill the air like flocks of white birds.

He imagined evening dinners with long tables full of food, hot and fresh, the colors of autumn. His children and his children's children laughing and teasing one another, while food disappeared amid the raucous sounds of play, the intimate noise of family life.

Family life—an elusive dream, always just out of reach. Family life—to my father, an unrequited love, whom he has wooed and cherished, battered and bloodied in an effort to shape it to his own idiosyncratic needs, formed in his soul during a childhood of drought, absence and longing, shame and thirst.

Family life—to me, the unlived life. As wife, mother, grandmother, it's been taken from me, a stolen plum.

And so it's been taken from him. My boisterous, charming, warmhearted, lovable father looks at me now and sees an unmarried, childless woman. He sees the end of his line . . . and wonders what he did wrong.

My first memory of my father is taking a shower with him in a blue-tiled stall. I must have been six or seven years old. I remember the feeling of his tall, strong body next to me, standing by this great presence under the water, feeling no fear.

I remember a special birthday when he alone took me out to dinner. I was in a pink organza dress and we went to a restaurant for prime rib and candlelight. I felt like I was his girl, his special date. It seemed to me then that he knew so much about everything. I could ask him any question and, inevitably, he had lots of answers.

At college in Berkeley I explored my own sexuality, altered my awareness, and engaged in radical politics. On the day I called to tell him to stop sending me tuition money, my mutiny was complete.

My father had become the enemy. I rejected his values wholesale—his reverence for family, his striving for financial security, his faith in the democratic process. I joined ranks with the shadow-heroes of the day, the Black Panthers.

Later, I turned another corner, giving up on the dream of political solutions, and turned toward an inner life and a spiritual solution.

When I went to live in a spiritual community, my father commented, "I don't know why you need that guru. You already have a father." It took me fifteen years to see the wisdom in his insight.

My guru was a shadow-father, representing for me the opposite values of my dad: the material world is fleeting and holds no permanent value; attachment to it is fatal; desire and sexuality impede the growth of consciousness, which is the only worthy goal.

Without realizing the full implications of my choices, I had become a nun, a lover of God, unable to love individual human beings. My fear of intimacy was reinforced by a credo that trivialized human love. While other women my age were finding mates, I was burning with holy longing.

When, after several years, I left this community and reentered the social world, my father welcomed me. For as long as I can remember, he lights up when I walk into the room and opens his arms for a hug.

Today, my dad and I understand that we have been caught in a web of love, that the fibers which connect us have been too tightly wrapped. We have come to see that, even while living many miles apart, even while making very different choices, our love has shaped and molded our souls.

And so we have tried to let each other go, giving up our illusions of each other, and letting other loves come first. We find it difficult to care deeply for each other in a way that does not bind. And so our relationship becomes like a spiritual practice: loving and letting go.

As he has released me, I have been left to feel both a child's abandonment and an adult's relief. Now I turn toward male lovers with more freedom and more hope, no longer seeking my father's twin or my father's opposite, but simply a man who can give and receive love.

As I write this piece I am in midlife, sitting by the warm fireplace in my mountain home. I add a log to the fire and step back into the soundless container, pen in hand, facing the empty page, feelings of grief and loss welling up into squiggly lines meant to transmit this moment of my very private life to another, an unknown other. I write this to a woman like myself who also has no demands of feeding schedules or dirty diapers, no breasts that fill at the cry of a small one, no baby-sitters to find or preschool to choose. Someone perhaps who is grateful for the absence of these messy interruptions but who wonders, too, in her quiet moments, about small smiles missed, small hands and feet unseen, silky skin untouched, and the first step not taken. Does she feel as I do that she has taken from her father his most precious dream?

To my father, childlessness is a stain on my womanhood, a blemish on my worth, a failure of maturity. Adulthood for a woman means in some profound way to birth and care for young ones, helpless and dependent ones, so that to remain childless means to remain a child.

To remain childless means to avoid fulfilling a female mandate, to betray a biological gift. I refer here to an inner wound, as if we were meant to grow two arms but only grow one, an amputation to our potential as women.

The feminist in me rages—I was not born to breed! I am enough as I am.

But as a single woman coming to terms with not having a child, some time soon to be incapable of having a child, I carry a secret terror of meeting new men, assuming they all seek to impregnate the one they love, they all seek to re-create themselves, they all dream the dream of family life.

And I carry a secret shame that no matter what I produce or create, I have utterly failed my father because he has no young ones playing at his feet as he grows old.

This is my fate; and so it is his.

And I ask myself in this moment: How do I stop seeing the world through the eyes of a daughter without becoming a mother? How do I become a woman who did not give birth to children—but did give birth to herself?

CHAPTER NINETEEN

Rosalind Warren

Auto Repair

There's no place to go in Detroit that's half as fun as getting there. Expecially in my daddy's Olds. The closest thing to heaven on earth is being on the freeway when Aretha comes on. Her soaring voice is telling me to floor it. I turn the volume up until the music is coming from inside me and go as fast as I can.

I don't want you to think that I don't drive responsibly. I am a responsible driver. Responsible, but accelerated. I go to the community college, though I'm just seventeen, because I'm accelerated. I still live at home, though. So I can drive my daddy's Olds.

My father taught me to drive when I was fourteen. He took me to the parking lot at the Tel-Twelve Mall, told me to get behind the wheel, sat back in the passenger seat, and lit a cigar. "Do your worst, babe," he said.

He put on the country-western station and Earl Scruggs and Ricky Scaggs sang love songs as we lurched around the lot. Dad slouched back in the reclining seat and gave me advice. "Don't squash that poodle, honey." "Watch out for the Winnebago." One morning he gave me a key ring with the keys to seventeen cars. "They're all yours, mercy," he said. I gave him a bear hug and smiled. "Sure wish your mom could see you now," he said.

Mom died when I was only two. She died in her car, a red Trans Am. Coming home from the supermarket one night, she was broadsided by a drunk car-door salesman in a Lincoln Continental. The car was totaled. She was killed instantly. The groceries in the trunk survived.

Dad didn't junk the car. He had it towed home. He rebuilt it. He wanted to salvage something, he says. Repairing the car made him feel better. He started collecting them. He buys wrecks and puts them back together again. It's like a hobby. He tells me it's therapy. "Auto repair—the poor man's analysis," he says. He must have over twenty cars now, plus junkers he keeps for parts.

Some of Dad's cars are stashed in friends' garages; some are out in our driveway or sitting in the backyard. We've got a peach-colored Studebaker down in the basement, because he took it apart in the driveway one summer and reassembled it down there, just to see if he could. Everything in Detroit comes down to cars. If you don't work on the line like my dad, you work for a company that makes car-door handles or cruise controls. Or plastic saints for the dashboard. Or you're that company lawyer, or the shrink the auto execs go to, or the funeral director that puts them all in the ground. Remember that guy who was buried sitting behind the wheel of the Caddy? He wasn't a Detroit man, but he had the right idea. Detroit is all auto showrooms, muffler shops, and intersections with a gas station on each corner. Motown babies are born groping for the steering wheel, and by the time a local kid is five she can call out the model and year of every car that drives by.

My dad never remarried. He's got girlfriends. He's got me. He's got reconstituted Chevys, Fords, Pontiacs, a Studebaker in the basement, and job security. He's got pals on the line to go drinking with.

When he gets too drunk to drive, he phones me from a bar and I drive out to get him. His friends help him into the backseat. He sits with his feet up and lights a cigar.

"Where to?" I ask.

"East of the sun, west of the moon," he'll say if he's really sloshed.

"Dad?"

"Anywhere you want, babe," he says. "It's all the same to me."

The streets around Detroit—long, wide roads under a big midwestern sky—are made for cruising. I'll drive down Woodward Avenue. We'll put the radio on or just sit quiet and watch the world go by. Woodward is the main drag—miles of glittering neon signs and fast-food stands. Everybody in this city learned to drive on this street. Sometimes we'll cruise all the way out to Dearborn to see Ford Motor Company World Headquarters, a complex of gleaming skyscrapers sitting all by itself in the middle of nowhere. Or downtown to the Detroit River to see the Renaissance Center, which was supposed to revitalize the inner city but didn't. Or to Canada, crossing through the tunnel under the river, driving through sleepy down-town Windsor, and returning across the Ambassador Bridge. I drive by my mom's cemetery. Over the entrance is a sign in lovely pink neon script—Roseview Cemetery—that I remember from way be-fore I had any idea what it meant.

Eventually Dad falls asleep and I drive home.

I fell in love with Todd in his daddy's Eldorado.

My daddy didn't take to Todd at first. "He's too short for you," he said. "He looks like a hoodlum." Dad was wrong about that. Todd was a rich kid from Bloomfield Hills. He wore faded jeans and a beat-up leather jacket because it looked cool, not because he couldn't afford better. He had long dark hair, beautiful gray eyes, and loads of nervous energy, and he played lead guitar in the Clone Brothers, a local band. He was at our place watching television with a crowd of my friends. A girl I didn't like brought him, so I started flirting with him.

I could sense Dad lurking by the front door later on as I walked Todd to his car. The girl he'd been with was long gone. Todd got into his Eldorado, and I leaned in the window of that gorgeous black car and kissed him. That's when I fell in love. Todd didn't seem too surprised—as if strange girls leaned in his car and kissed him all the time.

"Call me," I said, dizzy.

We gazed into each other's eyes. Then he turned the key in the ignition and the engine blew up.

The next thing I know I'm sitting on our front lawn, with Todd and my father running around the car yelling instructions to each other, trying to get our old fire extinguisher to work and swatting at the burning Eldorado with blankets. A crowd of neighbors came out to cheer them on, but the Eldorado burned to a crisp.

Dad decided to like Todd then, either because he felt sorry for him or because he wanted the car for parts.

But Todd didn't phone. Maybe because our kiss had set his car on fire. I didn't see him till months later. His band was playing at a bar out in Ypsilanti, and Dad went to see them without telling me. I guess he was getting sick of my moping around the house telling him how the love of my life had passed me by. Dad ended up having a pretty good time. After the last set, Todd drove my father home.

Todd rang the doorbell. It was late, and I came to the door in my pajamas. He was the last person I expected to see.

"Guess what?" Todd said.

I didn't have to guess—I could hear my Dad snoring away in the backseat of Todd's new Chevy.

"Let him rest," said Todd. He got out his guitar and I put on a bathrobe, and we sat on the warm hood of Todd's car, where he re-cycled all the love songs he'd written for his last girlfriend. Between the songs we kissed.

Hours later the car door opened and Dad stepped out. "What a night!" he said.

He squinted at us sitting there on the hood, stooping to admire the whitewalls, tracing the chrome with a fingertip. Finishing, he bowed to us and shuffled toward the house, still wrapped in the blanket I'd thrown over him. He looked like a drawing in my grade school civics textbook of Pontiac, the Indian chief for whom the city of Pontiac and later the car were named.

He paused on the front steps. "Call me if you need help putting any fires out," he said.

Todd phoned the next night.

"Want to come over?" he asked. He gave me directions to his house. It wasn't till I got there that I recognized the neighborhood, a posh subdivision that had gone up a few years back. When it was new, my friends and I used to cruise through and laugh at how silly the houses were. They were all monsters, each flashier than the last. And Todd lived in the grandest one. It was a little castle, complete with three turrets, a (waterless) moat, and a fake drawbridge.

Todd met me at the door with a skinny girl with wild red curls and thick glasses. She looked about twelve.

"I'm baby-sitting," he said. "My parents are out of town. This is my sister Gladys. She's a computer nerd."

"Computer hacker," Gladys corrected. "Want me to access your school records and change all your grades to A's?"

"They already are."

"Cool." She grinned. "If you're so smart what are you doing with my brother?"

Todd gave her a friendly shove. "Come on," he said to me. He led me through the place, which looked like something out of a magazine, to his room, which was ten times the size of my room at home. Guitars and stereo equipment lined one wall, and his record collection took up half of another. I'd never seen anything like it. We sat down on his bed.

"Where are your parents?" I asked.

"Geneva." He sounded almost apologetic.

Silence.

"I missed you," he said finally. Then we started kissing, and I felt at home again, even in that outlandish place.

We got to the point where if we'd been in a car, we'd have dusted ourselves off and gone to get coffee someplace on Woodward and talk. I'd never known anyone whose parents vanished to Geneva and left them a castle to hang out in. I wasn't entirely comfortable about it. I began wondering how I was going to get out of this. Did I really want to?

Then Todd stopped kissing me and looked into my eyes. I waited.

"Want to climb a tree?" he said.

Climb? a tree?

"We have to take Gladys, though. I'm responsible for her."

"A tree?" I asked.

"You'll see," he said. "It'll be fun."

It was. The three of us drove to Ferndale, a small residential neighborhood. "We used to live here," said Todd as we cruised through the quiet streets. "Then Grandpa died and Mom inherited." We got out of the car at a sleepy little park. There was an old beech with thick, sprawling branches—perfect for climbing.

"This is my favorite place," Todd said when the three of us had climbed up to the top. We sat in the branches, looking out over the park and talking. When we ran out of things to say, Todd and Gladys sang me Elvis songs. I'd never been happier.

"And what have you been up to?" asked Dad when I got home.

Todd and I started going out. We usually took his car. I'd sit beside him, my head against his shoulder and the radio playing. He'd chain-smoke and we'd cruise and talk for hours. Or I'd just sit, quiet, feeling so happy I wanted to freeze the whole thing and stash it in a time capsule somewhere.

All this bliss made Dad a little nervous. "Don't get in over your head," he warned me one night while he and I watched the Tigers pulverize the Red Sox on television.

"Too late," I said.

"He's a real nice kid," said Dad. "But he's got a few problems." I got a kick out of that. Dad spoke as if Todd were a faulty engine that needed a few days in the shop.

"What kind of problems?"

"You think that boy spends a tenth of the time thinking about you that you spend thinking about him?"

"This is a relationship, Dad, not a see-saw."

"Do you two ever talk about anything besides his music and his band and his plans? Ever talk about *your* plans?"

"I don't need to talk about my plans."

"That's the point," he said, "and you know it."

Of course I knew it, though I wasn't going to tell him so. I wasn't stupid. I knew deep down that I was in love with Todd and that Todd was in love with me being in love with Todd. As neat and talented as he was, he was too insecure and unsure of himself to be able to focus on me. But that would change. I'd make it change.

It was as if Dad could read my mind.

"That boy's a do-it-yourself model," he said. "You deserve a finished product."

I blew up at him. "I'm not one of your cars!" I said. "Don't try to take me apart and put me back the way you want."

He smiled. "Okay, honey," he said. "I'll back off. But maybe you'll listen to an expert." He took a folded-up piece of yellowed newspaper from his wallet and pushed it across the table to me. It was an old Ann Landers column about how to tell love from infatuation. I asked how long he'd been carrying it around.

"Five, six years," he said. "You never know when something like this could come in handy."

"I was only eleven when you clipped it?"

"Just thinking ahead," he said, rummaging around in his wallet. "The concerned single parent."

"The overprotective single parent," I said. "The nosy, interfering single parent." I told him I didn't give a hoot about what some old lady had to say five years ago about love. I was happier than I'd been ever with Todd. Dad would just have to trust me.

He kept poking around in his wallet. Finally he took out my mom's high school graduation photo and sighed. "You're the spitting image," he said. "On the outside. But on the inside you're just as pigheaded as your old man."

"I could do a lot worse," I said.

A few weeks later Todd and I were sitting in his car parked in our driveway, and Todd told me he wanted to break it off. "It's getting too serious," he said.

I had the feeling that wasn't it at all. He'd found someone new to listen to his love songs. He just didn't have the nerve to tell me. I tried to joke.

"You want it to be more shallow?" I asked.

He stared at me, looking as if he were about to cry. I could tell he wasn't enjoying this, and my heart went out to him. Then I realized that if I didn't stop myself, I'd end up comforting *him* for leaving me.

"Ann tried to warn me about you," I said. I got out of the car, slammed the door, and went to my daddy's Olds, parked right behind Todd's Chevy. I started her up and began searching for a good radio station.

Todd came over and leaned in my window.

"Where're you going?" he asked. "You live here."

"East of the sun, west of the moon," I said.

"Can we be friends?" he asked.

I was so angry I wanted to back up my daddy's Olds, floor her, smash right into Todd's beautiful car. You break my heart, I'll wreck your Chevy. But I'm my father's daughter—I couldn't do that to an innocent auto. Instead I found Stevie Wonder on the dial and took off with a squeal of tires. Todd ran after me, but I floored it until he was just a tiny dot in the rearview mirror.

The music was good. It carried me through our subdivision and the quiet side streets over to Telegraph Avenue. I decided to drive down Telegraph, past all the Mile Roads. Ten Mile Road, by the all-night kosher Dunkin Donuts. Eleven Mile Road, by my old high school. Twelve Mile Road. All the lights were with me and I was cruising. I love this car, I was thinking. Nothing can get me in here. It's when you get out of your car that the trouble starts.

There was a groan from the backseat, and my daddy's face appeared in the rearview. "Apparently a man can't take a little nap in his own Oldsmobile without getting hijacked?" he said.

"What on earth are you doing back there?" I asked.

"I was sleeping," he said. "It's usually real peaceful back here."

I glared at him. I didn't need this. Not now.

We rode a few minutes, silent. I could see it was funny. And I knew he loved me. Still I had planned to drive for hours—a heartbroken blond racing down the freeway at night with tears in her eyes. A real American cliche.

Having Dad pop up in the backseat like that kind of ruined the picture.

"Are we headed anywhere in particular?" he asked a few miles later.

"Nope."

"Care to talk about it?"

I didn't really. I wanted to drive. Alone. I wanted to drive for miles and miles and dwell on my sorrow. But it was too late for that.

"There's a twenty-four-hour car wash out on Lone Pine Road," Dad said. "Your mom and I used to go there to talk. If we couldn't get things straightened out, we figured at least the car would get clean." He smiled. "We don't have to talk if you don't want to. But the car could use washing."

Of course, on the other hand, the car did need washing. It couldn't hurt to wash the car. At the next intersection I turned toward Lone Pine Road, switched over to the country station, and gave the full weight of my foot to the accelerator. Dad leaned forward to squeeze my shoulder, then settled back in his seat, smiling. "No rush," he said. "We've got all night."

It wasn't that I stopped feeling sad. There was a heaviness in my chest that I knew would stay with me awhile. But as we cruised along, the idea of driving in the middle of the night to take a beat-up Oldsmobile through a car wash for a heart-to-heart talk with my old dad didn't seem too bad.

CHAPTER TWENTY

Andrew Samuels

On Fathering Daughters

At the height of the Cleveland affair (a child molestation scandal in England) my next-door neighbor confessed to me that he was frightened to cuddle his two-year-old daughter in public. The moral panic over child sexual abuse was reinforcing difficulties which many fathers have about physical aspects of their relationship with daughters.

Years later, when some daughters enter analysis, past inhibitions about bodily contact and the apparent failure to establish a warm, shared, physical contact with the father turn out to have been very wounding. In a sense, these wounds are the opposite extreme from incest and generate their own brand of profound psychic pain. The stress on avoidance and detection of incest masks this other, more subtle problem.

Boys have an easier time of it than girls. This is because their mothers are so used to being physical in relation to children of either sex that they are not as alarmed by the bodily dimension and by their feelings about their sons as fathers generally are by their feelings about their daughters. I am thinking of the physical experiences of pregnancy, childbirth, feeding, and so forth.

Analysts and therapists have had relatively little to say about the father. The positive aspects of fathering have been neglected and, for the past thirty-five years, interest has been in the mother–infant relationship.

There is little to be found in analytic writing about the direct relationship of father and infant, not even a description of what ordinary, devoted, "good enough" fathering might look like. Hence the difficulty of communicating the evidence from the consulting room that many daughters are suffering from a denial and not an exaggeration of the bodily dimension of the relationship with their fathers.

What kind of damage results from the exclusion of physicality from the father–daughter relationship? There are three issues to consider here. First, when the girl is a baby or small child, her father's inhibition, expressed in his handling of her, cannot help in the formation of a positive attitude towards her body, a sense of its "rightness," beauty and integrity. The image many women have of themselves as weaker than they are may stem from this particular lack.

Second, when the girl reaches adolescence, the physically inhibited father can have a destructive impact on her emerging sexuality. This can be seen happening in many ways: excessive prohibitions about her activities with boys, mocking her sexuality, and general up-tightness. Of course, a degree of "jealousy" may be no bad thing in that it confirms to the daughter that her father does care about her. For there is no doubt that one sort of attack that a father can make on his daughter's emerging sexuality is to ignore it altogether, leaving that sort of thing to the mother.

The third kind of damage that results from physical inhibition between father and daughter is more difficult to portray. It has to do with what Jungian analysts regard as the positive side of romantic, even sexual fantasy, such as is typically found in most families— wishing to marry the parent of the opposite sex or to have babies with them. This normal fantasizing is not to be confused with actual incest, though—and this is the problem with writing about these matters—actual incest may result from incest fantasies which have gotten out of control.

Jungians do not accept that such fantasies can be adequately understood as the child wanting intercourse with the parent. We need to understand these fantasies on the part of the child symbolically and metaphorically. Jung's idea was that the child's fantasies and wishes concerning the parents express a longing to grow by means of being regenerated, reborn even. The purpose of such fantasy is to make contact with the grounds of one's being, a kind of refueling that makes subsequent maturation easier. The parents represent the fueling station.

Getting really close to someone who is psychologically more

developed than you are leads to enrichment of the personality. We grow inside to a very large extent by relating to someone outside. In childhood, that "someone" is usually mother or father, though in single-parent families, for example, the child often involves other adults to aid the growth processes. But what is it that enables us to get that close in the first place? The answer is the physical, bodily element in our relationship, family life, is the factor that helps growth to occur. We could refer to this factor as "sexual" or "erotic" but, by so doing, we probably only confuse things. Nevertheless, because the bodily factor is also present when the disaster of actual incest happens, it would be excessively cautious to leave the sexual aspect out altogether.

The physically inhibited father is going to be useless as an assistant in his daughter's inner growth. He cannot actually stop her from fantasizing, but he can send a message, on a bodily level, that such fantasies are not welcome.

There is a social, cultural, and political importance to all this. Acknowledgment and acceptance of the daughter's bodily integrity and sexuality helps her to differentiate herself from the mother. In other words, the father acts as a liberatory influence on the daughter so that she can begin to explore her full potential, not restricted to the role of "mother." For instance, the spiritual path, the vocational path, the path of solidarity with the travails of other women, the path of an integration and acceptance of her assertive side, the path of sexual expression all become open to her.

A good father-daughter relationship supports the overthrow of restrictions placed on women. Once a girl, or woman, learns in the relationship with her father that she is something other than a mother, she can begin to explore just who it is that she can be.

Women have suffered enormously from narrow definitions of what it means to be female, from the requirement that they be unaggressive and selfless creatures who relate, who are responsive to the needs of others, who react but do not act. True, as mothers maybe (just maybe) something like this has to be done. But as persons, women can sniff out other vistas and ways of being. It is the young woman's apperception of herself as a physical creature, facilitated by her bodily connection to her father, that enables her to spin through a variety of psychological pathways, enjoying the widest spectrum of meanings inherent in the ideogram "woman." The father's first fertilization helped to make the female baby. His second helps to bring forth the female adult, who is then free to drop her father when and if she needs to.

There would be little point in replacing a feminity which pleases Mummy with a feminity which pleases Daddy. Moving beyond mother and father, though obviously in relation to them, today's female adult can develop, more than before, into a multifaceted, plural woman-person, able to grow in all manner of unpredictable and exciting ways.

CHAPTER TWENTY-ONE

Tom Pinkson

Honoring a Daughter's Emergence into Womanhood

My eighteen-year-old daughter left home today. She walked out the door and broke my heart. Somehow it seems so unfair that after all this time and effort of raising, nurturing, and caring for her, she just up and leaves. She has been a vital and intimate part of my life every day since she was born—loving, enjoying, being driven crazy by, playing, worrying, watching her grow, being grown by her. Now she is gone, moved away to pursue her dreams. I feel grief and sadness, my heart torn open. I miss her laughing smile, her usually joyous presence, and even her incessant jabberings about things I wasn't usually interested in.

I think back to what my parents must have gone through when I left home at seventeen. Then, I didn't have any awareness about what feelings were stirred in them by my leaving. I was totally caught up in my adolescent self-absorption and the adventure that lay before me. Now I feel what I imagine was their pain along with my own. I feel very joined with them.

I give thanks for the bountiful blessings of my two wonderful daughters, while surrendering into the ache I feel with their departure from home. I give myself permission to face and honor my feelings, and the process reminds me of the healing power of letting go. Looking out my office window, I see the beautiful springtime plumage of blossoming flowers and fruit trees, new life emerging from fertile Mother Earth. The new growth seems to convey the message: Holding on to what has been destroys the new growth of life. The old has to die, it has to be released in order for the new to come through. It's an operational law of the universe we live in. "You can't have one without the other." I take a deep sigh and release my contracted breath.

I think of my younger daughter and remember the growth forces pulsing in me as a teenager that took me out on the road to pursue my vision. If I had been stopped, or if I had stopped myself, something very deep and vital inside of me would have begun to wither and die. And so it is with my daughter. She leaves the safe harbor of her home and loved ones, her security, to pursue her vision of who she is and what she can do and accomplish with her life. I'm proud that she has the courage to step out of her comfort zone and push her dream to a reality test. She has crossed a major threshold and begun her hero's journey—stepping out into the unknown to be with her own fears and doubts and find out what she is made of by facing the tests and struggles that await her. I respect her for it— my little baby, my youngest child, growing up.

It was precisely the quality of listening to and honoring the inner call with respect, responsibility, and inner strength that my wife, Andrea, and I wanted to empower in her and her sister as they were growing up. As their adolescence approached I was eager to create some kind of rite of passage for them that would take them into the challenges of the teenage years with a positive thrust. In my youth I unconsciously hungered for some kind of rite of passage that had meaning to me. In its absence, my teenage peers and I created our own form of initiation through drinking and various delinquent acting-out behaviors. I certainly didn't want this for my daughters. Instead, I wanted to give them affirming messages about their new state of being—womanhood, with their first menses.

I was distressed by the disrespectful messages and treatment that girls and women receive in our society. I wanted my daughters to be honored, to be blessed for who and what they were, young women just coming into their power and responsibility for creating their lives. I thought back to stories I had heard from some of my Native American women friends describing their rites of passage into womanhood, and I wanted to offer my daughters something that would touch them as these women had been touched in their youth by the rites they had undergone. As a practicing psychologist interested in the development and potentials of a healthy psyche,

I had been studying with Native American spiritual leaders and Elders for many years.

I listened raptly as my friends and teachers related dramatic accounts of rituals, ceremonies, ordeals, and celebrations accompanying the rites of passage into womanhood. Through my association with these Native Americans, I learned many perspectives and attitudes different from what I had learned in my culture. Attitudes about a woman's menstrual period are a perfect example. The socialized messages I had received were all negative—the woman was "on the rag," menstruation was dirty, something to be embarrassed about, kept secret. Furthermore, a woman's period was a burden, a mess, the curse, a limitation, certainly not something to be proud of. Yet pride was exactly the attitude I found among the Native Americans with whom I spent time in various settings around the country.

I remember a time I spent with the Shoshoni people out in the Nevada desert. As was the custom of the Shoshoni, a woman went off to the woman's lodge and stayed there until completion of her menstruation. The woman's lodge, or moon lodge, was a teepee away from the main part of the camp and could only be approached by other women. While in the lodge, the woman was totally free to pursue her own creative process however she saw fit—no chores, no jobs, no tasks to perform—only to honor her "moon time" without having to bother with anything else, a time to relax, listen to her dreams, and be with her creative "flow." Meals were prepared for her and she was served by the other women. Husbands or other relatives watched the kids, cleaned house, and took care of chores usually handled by the woman.

This treatment was accorded the woman not because she was dirty and had to be separated from others; just the opposite. The woman was considered to be in her most powerful state, open to the universe and the Great Spirit. She needed to be allowed this important time both for her own rejuvenation as well as for the good of the tribe. The dreams the woman had during her time of the moon were considered most sacred, and the entire tribe depended upon them for guidance. As her body purified and prepared itself for the next cycle of new life, her power was so great that it could draw power away from the medicine man or the hunter. In respect for this power, the menstruating woman went off to be in the company only of other women in the moon lodge. In practical terms she got a monthly vacation from her husband, kids, and housework!

These thoughts were uppermost in my mind as I thought of my daughters and the approaching time of their first period. I very much wanted to share the positive outlook on this significant development in their maturation that I had learned from the Shoshoni and other Native peoples, who all seemed to share a reverence for the woman in her moon. I also wanted to affirm their sexuality and their creative power to bring new life into the world and to honor these gifts as sacred, to be held in a respectful and responsible manner at all times. I knew that as attractive young women already drawing the interest of the opposite sex, they would run into plenty of men who would not hold them and their gifts in a sacred way. It was vitally important that my daughers respect and care for themselves so as to not tolerate disrespect from others. I especially wanted them to get this message of self-respect from a man, their father, who in fact was the first man in their lives. I hoped it would afford them a model that would be helpful in the choices they made about men in their future.

I pondored and thought, asked for guidance from dreams, talked with wife and women friends, most of whom were excited about the idea of a rite of passage and said they wished someone had given them such support when they had their first period. The vast majority of women I spoke to had minimal if any real communication about menstruation prior to its onset, let alone any positive messages. Some were even taken by surprise and were frightened and embarrassed. None had received any sense of empowerment and encouragement from those around them. I wanted a different experience for my daughters.

I decided to speak to them beforehand and told them that I wanted to spend some special time alone with them when their first period took place. Ever since they were little I would sometimes take each of them separately on weekend adventures shared just by the two of us. We took plenty of other family camping trips and other outings all together, but I felt it was important to have some time alone at least once a year. So they were used to being outdoors and they were used to special time alone with me. They also knew about my interest in Native American spirituality, since I had been sharing many aspects of what I was learning about as they were growing up. They had also met some of the people who were teachers for me, and so none of what I proposed was completely foreign to them.

My proposal was this: the first available night after their period began, we would camp out together. All I told them was that we would perform a ceremony to honor their "coming into their womanhood." They weren't quite sure what to expect, but they were emphatic that they wanted the "news" kept quiet and that the ceremony was to be just between them and me. I agreed, though I would have loved to have had some of our family friends over to help celebrate their passage too.

In the meantime I was busy trying to come up with a special gift I could give them. I wanted it to be symbolically significant and something they would value as well. For my first daughter I chose a beautiful hand-decorated gourd that I had brought back from a Peruvian trip years before. It was in the shape of a womb, and the incised decorations were happy and joyous ones. I intended to use the gift as a visual aid to help her be conscious regarding her own womb that was just coming into its time of fertility.

For my second daughter, I chose a fire opal that I had brought back from a pilgrimage with the Huichol Indians in Mexico. The outside of the stone looked like an ordinary rock, gray-brown and dirty with no distinguishing marks. But turn it around and inside was a rainbow-colored opal that danced and sparkled in the light. My thought was that this gift served as a reminder not to judge the depth of things by their outside appearance. Even though her newly arrived period might bring a certain amount of physical discomfort, she could try to stay open to the deeper aspects of it that were beneath the surface—the gifts of dream power and of knowing through intuition rather than just with the intellect. Having gathered my gifts, I now sat back and awaited the "good news."

Several months went by, until I returned from work one day and Andrea said, "Get ready, Kimberly started her period today but she wants to tell you." Then my daughter came out of her room where she had been sharing the news with her best friend and said, "Hey, Dad, I started my period this afternoon!" "That's great," I replied and gave her a big hug. "Now let's set up the night for our ceremony!" We scheduled it for that coming Friday night. I still wasn't exactly sure what I was going to do, but I trusted in my intention to honor her.

When Friday night arrived we waited for sunset, then went to a campsite with a fire pit. I started up the fire and we laid down our sleeping bags and got comfortable. The night air was chilling, so we huddled together close to the fire and enjoyed the flickering play of light and shadow as darkness descended and took us into its embrace. I listened inside for guidance about how to start and what to say. For a long time we sat together in silence with only the sounds of the crackling fire to keep us company while far overhead the stars shone in brilliance and slowly the moon crept up over the eastern horizon. That was my signal, so obvious now but I hadn't even thought of it before—the cycles of the moon. Yes, how obvious.

I used the moon's appearance and movement across the night sky to start talking about the new cycle in her life. I asked her how she felt about it, how her friends felt about their period (she was the youngest of her peers) and if they talked about it among themselves. Yes, they did talk about it but none of them expressed any notion of empowerment, pride, or saw it as a sacred gift. At that point I began to share what I had learned about the power of women among the Native American people I had known. I told her that I wanted her to have another perspective than what she received from her friends, from the dominant culture, and from the media via advertisements for this or that menstruation product. So I explained what I knew and then sang her an "honoring song" that I had learned to use when honoring another person one cares deeply about. I gave her my gift of the gourd and told her how it represented the sacred container within her. I then went on to share my hope that she would welcome and respect the sacredness of her body, her feelings, her sexuality, her creative power and beauty, and the wisdom within her that was her heritage as a woman. It was now her responsibility to hold these gifts with the greatest respect and to care for them always.

We stayed up late into the night talking and enjoying being together. I spoke about the importance of inner listening to her truth, of caring for life and nurturing it, of dating and mate selection, of childbearing and marriage, of family, of being active in the world to improve it, and of taking responsibility for developing her talents and abilities and bringing them to fruition. I explained the important connection of her bodily rhythms and those of the earth beneath her and the moon above her, always emphasizing listening with respect. I encouraged her to explore as she saw fit, to grow into all that she could be and to always be thankful to the Great Spirit for the gift of life. Then I said a prayer for her future dreams, and I gave thanks for her being in my life.

At this point I broke down and cried. With tears running down my cheeks I told her how much I loved and cared for her. She cried too. We held each other, and I felt such joy for the wonder and blessing of having such a daughter to enrich my life. We finally fell asleep in the wee hours of the morning after more discussion, questions, and sharing of our hopes and dreams, our fears and worries, our joys and excitement. The next morning we greeted the new day with thankfulness prayers and hiked back home for a hearty breakfast with the rest of the family.

It was a rich night for me, one that was repeated several years later when my younger daughter had her first period. We basically went through the same ceremony of being out around the fire, the giving of the gift, the honoring song and prayers, and the wonderful sharing of hopes, dreams, fears, and aspirations. Both nights were warm and wonderful, deepening our relationship and laying down a pattern for open and honest communication throughout the teenage years.

Recently I asked my daughters how they remembered their rite-of-passage night and what it meant to them. Their responses were similar. They didn't remember much of what we talked about, but they appreciated that I had taken special time to be with them and that none of their friends' fathers had done so with their daughters. They also expressed thanks that I had helped give them a different perspective on their menses, as well as appreciation for the interest in their growth that the ceremony demonstrated. Their rite-of-passage gifts are still meaningful to them and hey, guess what? They are out there pursuing their dreams!

My attention drifts outside once again to the blossoming flowers and a new life of spring. My daughters too are blossoming flowers of great fragrance and beauty. I hope that I have given them roots strong enough for them to achieve their full potential. The rites of passage continue onward as they reach out to create their own ceremonies of growth and expansion. A warm glow slowly spreads through me as I fondly recall those special nights around the fire and the birthing work we performed for each other.

IV

New Images of
Fatherhood:
The Challenges
and Opportunities

There is no good father, that's the rule. Don't lay the blame on men but on the bond of paternity which is rotten.

JEAN-PAUL SARTRE

The words a father speaks to his children in the privacy of the home are not overheard at the time, but, as in whispering galleries, they will be clearly heard at the end by posterity.

RICHTER

You must teach your children that the ground beneath their feet is the ashes of their grandfathers.

CHIEF SEATTLE

We never know the love of our parents until we have become parents.

HENRY BEECHER

The child is the father of the man.

WILLIAM WORDSWORTH

Introduction

Recently I was in a playground with my son. I saw a couple of other dads there and remembered my feeling of isolation years before when I was often the token father represented at playgrounds. Today many fathers, rather than feeling like aliens in the playground, initiate conversation with each other. So I moved in on a swing next to a fellow dad, or possibly a granddad, who was with two children about the same age. I asked, "Both yours?"

He replied, "More or less. The younger one is mine and the older is my daughter's child."

I commented, "That must present some interesting situations."

He was silent for a minute, then replied, "Although my daughter and I have different child-rearing styles, our intent is pretty much the same. And we've both learned to suspend judgment of each other—but we still say what is in our hearts."

I asked, "Does she still see you primarily as her father or in your new role?" "Both," he said. "They seem to enrich each other. She accepts that I'm both the same and different from the man who fathered her. Hey, she trusts me enough to leave her kid with me while she's working, and I know she can afford whatever child care she wants."

I pondered how challenging and rewarding it must be for this father and daughter to pursue their relationship. It brought to mind the amount of flexibility that is called for by new variations on traditional fatherhood.

Fathers come in varied guises. We live in a time of many options as to the form fathering can take—divorced single fathers, stepfathers, gay fathers. Most of the stigma around divorce, and some of the stigma around homosexuality, has vanished.

But this freedom for fathers has made it easier to change our relationships than to change ourselves. The work required to overcome our resistances and sustain active, nourishing bonds with our children has not gotten any easier.

When I reviewed the literature on stepfathers and noncustodial fathers, for instance, I was struck by how much pain men feel in these roles. We cannot underestimate the grief and guilt of the divorced father who has lost everyday contact with his children. And the hurt is not short-lived. When divorced fathers have not grieved and accepted the losses of previous relationships, they carry their pain into new ones, and this carry-over can reduce their emotional availability.

Most fathers desperately want to be important in the lives of their children, but adopting the role of an outsider seems to be an easy and familiar trap to many men. This pattern, of course, is particularly true when their own fathers were not available for intimacy. And the tendency can be reinforced from outside by cultural biases, such as judicial decisions, so that in the end, personal and social patterns of resistance support each other.

Those fathers who seek to be positively involved in the lives of their children need to get past these resistances. I suggest they make an internal declaration as to their commitment, then express it to their spouses, ex-spouses, and children. For many fathers this affirmation of commitment to partners and children needs to be invoked on a daily basis. An individual or family ritual, such as holding hands before dinner, helps to focus this intention to participate fully in each other's lives.

When a man marries a woman with children and becomes an instant father, he faces other issues. Stepfathering has its own rites of passage, such as protecting the marital bond with the mother, befriending yet sitting limits for the children, adjusting to different styles of parenting, making agreements about discipline, chores, and other tasks.

Everyone is challenged to adapt in a blended family. And it takes time for children to adjust to a stepparent especially if a biological parent had been in the household. A caring stepfather typically will need to have patience until stepchildren can accept his authority and his love.

In my father's group, one man recently related how he had asked permission from his stepchildren to take their mother away alone for the weekend. He met with anticipated initial resistance. Then he asked them if they had noticed how irritable and impatient he had become. They nodded. He continued by explaining that when he and their mother returned after the weekend together, he would be in a much better mood and more able to give them what they wanted. They accepted the proposal, and he was there to deliver when they returned.

In my work with fathers, I hear that "alone time" for stepfathers and their wives is often sacrificed, becoming a source of suffering for both partners. Whether this sacrifice is due to guilt, avoidance of adult intimacy, or perceived lack of time, in the end it is not beneficial for the parents or the children.

When I was single after my divorce, I enjoyed the flexibility that joint custody provided me. I was able alternately to work and parent in depth. My week developed a rhythm in which my work and personal life could be pursued without restraint. Then when my daughter joined me she became my major commitment. I felt like a family man and yet was free to explore relationships with other women.

When my daughter was with me, I liked being the total parent. While I did not replace her mother, I could perform mothering activities as a father. Part-time single parenting softened me and gave me permission to be more nurturing. Instead of dividing responsibilities with my wife as we did while married, following more traditional roles, I felt the freedom and need to be more comprehensive in my approach to parenting.

Now in my second marriage, when my daughter is with us, our new family unit feels more complete and whole. The four sides of the dining table are occupied. The television is turned off. Dinner becomes a more meaningful ritual, and the words *brother* and "sister" return to our language. Our toddler son is so enamored with his older half-sister that he wants her here all the time.

Regardless of the form and circumstance of fatherhood, being a father brings profound changes. The voices in this section speak with pride, concern, loss, exhaustion, commitment. I believe compassion for our co-parent, our children, and ourselves fuels our willingness to sacrifice our self-absorption and care for another.

OVERVIEW

Part IV covers these new images of fatherhood: the stepfather, the single father with full custody, the single father with or without joint custody, the gay father, and the grandfather. In the following selections certain themes emerge: acceptance and rejection, fear and hope, gratitude and surrender. These personal accounts highlight the poignancy of the sociocultural issues. Fatherhood offers men the chance to experience the full range of emotions, the chance to become fully human.

I have not included in this section the "second father" or the mentor. Finding a mentor is the responsibility of a son or daughter, although in some traditions a godfather is chosen by the parents. Mentors step in where the father has little or no knowledge. They act as a guide to the son or daughter in their particular area of interest. And, conveniently, it's not necessary for our mentors (writers, for example) to be alive for us to be inspired by them.

While there are new cultural standards that have the expectant father playing a more active role in pregnancy, birth, and child care, at the same time psychology professor Jerrold Lee Shapiro believes that men are given the message that they are outsiders. Feelings such as anxiety, anger, sadness, and fear are often unwelcome. This leaves the father-to-be in a kind of double bind that says, "Be involved, but keep your feelings to yourself, particularly if they are not upbeat." If the expectant father is to fully participate in the pregnancy and birth, Shapiro contends in this article, which originally appeared in *Psychology Today*, then his feelings need to be recognized by all, including himself.

Chapter 23 is excerpted from Kyle Pruett's book *The Nurturing Father.* This noted child psychiatrist focuses on what he calls a dangerous opportunity (a term from the I Ching) for noncustody and joint-custody fathers after divorce. He views custody as an internal, emotional commitment as well as a judicial arrangement. According to Pruett, the father's feelings of loss, anger, sadness, and guilt after divorce are real and enduring. He offers some important guiding principles regarding the many decisions that might affect the child, including such issues as visitation rights.

"Just Visiting," by teacher Kip Eastman, recounts a single father's transition from a painful sense of loss of daily contact with his daughter to his fighting for and winning joint custody. Eventually, he felt empowered and transformed by the love generated in his newly formed relationship with his daughter. Now he prefers his present life to his previous married life.

Becoming a stepfather is a long and trying process. Drawing on his personal life, author Warren Farrell portrays the "two-year syndrome," the rejection of the stepfather by his new children for about two years. During this time, the stepfather wonders whether he can be a true male role model for the children and whether he can be loved for himself, rather than for the home that he might provide. In his own case, Farrell describes how his wife was supportive when he experienced his fears and she understood and accepted the reasons for them. This excerpt is from *Why Men Are the Way They Are.*

A gay married man, P. Gregory Springer found that fatherhood broadened and challenged his concept of gay identity. In this article, which appeared in *The Fathers' Book: Shared Experiences,* the author is saddened that most gay men are deprived of the joy of raising children and receiving children's affection by "too closely associating their lives with their sexuality."

In an article that first appeared in *Mothering* magazine, William F. Van Wert, a teacher, tells about the trials of being a single father of three young boys without family or role models to lean on for support. His development as a father contradicts arguments that men are not capable of sustaining nurturing care. With a generous spirit, Van Wert describes the gift of parenting.

While the subject of grandfathers deserves separate and thorough exploration, I chose to include them in this section as a variation of fatherhood. The grandfather is uniquely positioned to be less competitive and less emotionally entangled with his grandchildren than the father is. He is also apt to be less busy career building, allowing him more availability to pursue leisurely activities like going fishing, taking walks, and telling stories. A grandfather's considerable experience can serve to guide and enrich the lives of his grandchildren. Becoming a grandfather gives fathers another chance in the life cycle to present the mysteries of masculinity. Also, seeing and hearing about a father through the eyes of *his* father helps children to develop a little more objectivity and understanding of their parents.

Journalist Perry Garfinkel finds that the grandfather–grandson relationship is often close, conflict free, and a source for understanding hierarchical power and learning to surrender control. Fathers get a second chance in grandfathering, without the power struggles. Based on his research in *In a Man's World,* Garfinkel portrays the grandfather as potentially available for intimacy and wise about the ways of the world.

I believe that obstacles in relationships invite us to move beyond blame and guilt and to enter a new field of heartfelt connection. Even with such external obstacles as an unfavorable outcome of judicial renderings regarding custody, what is essential is the emotional commitment fathers bring to their children's lives. If fathers allow personal and cultural patterns of the status quo to lull them to sleep, then they may lose their children in the process. If fathers truly want deep connection with their children and are willing to do the work, I believe it will come to them, although its form may surprise them.

Whatever course our lives take with respect to fatherhood, there remains some opportunity to deeply touch another soul. Although we may feel loss or even relief from being removed from the everyday tasks of fathering a child, the question still remains, how are we to play the cards we hold?

Good fathering transcends our belief systems regarding fate. This fatherly presence is revealed at least as much in the feelings exchanged between fathers and their children as in the form or role that fatherhood takes.

CHAPTER TWENTY-TWO

Jerrold Lee Shapiro

The Expectant Father

The sentiment on the front of the pastel greeting card was innocent enough: "Congratulations on the birth of your daughter." The zinger was handwritten inside: "To the proud parents, especially the mother, who did all the work."

The card was sent by three members of my family who, since they lived thousands of miles away, had never met my wife. Their card expresses an entire cultural phenomenon in a few words. We truly value motherhood and child rearing. We pamper pregnant women. Strangers give them seats on the train, stop on the street to chat about their own pregnancies and exchange theories as to the sex of the unborn child. Our culture loses its paranoia and its boundaries in the presence of pregnancy.

This is as it should be. A woman feels more vulnerable as well as more special when she is pregnant. There is a new life inside her. Her hormones are acting in novel ways. She clearly needs and deserves substantial support. But what of her spouse? He shows no physical signs of pregnancy, but in some ways, emotionally and psychologically, he is as pregnant as she is. This is particularly true in America today, where society expects fathers to play an increasingly large role during pregnancy and birth.

My experiences as a new father several years ago introduced me to these feelings firsthand and made me wonder. If a clinical psychologist who specialized in marital and family therapy found it difficult to deal with expectant fatherhood, think how hard it could be for someone who did not make a career of dealing with relationships and stress. In the years since then, I have observed, in my practice, the father's part in the process of changing from a couple to a family relationship.

In addition, from 1981 through 1985 I completed a series of interviews and tests with 227 expectant and recent fathers from all walks of life. They ranged in age from 18 to 60 and in family income from recipients of public aid to some earning more than $100,000 a year. Overall, the group mirrored the general American population except that they had a higher median income ($26,500) and there was a slightly higher proportion of men with Asian and Pacific island backgrounds.

Not too long ago, pregnancy was strictly "woman's work." An expectant father didn't have much to do until the day of the birth. Then his job was to get his wife to the hospital on time, smoke cigarettes and pace a well-worn circle in the hospital waiting room, anxiously awaiting the nurse's report on the sex of the child and on the health of the wife and baby. It was rare for a father to be present at the birth. Apocryphal stories of fathers who handcuffed themselves to their wives as they were being wheeled into the delivery room are still part of the folklore passed on with a chuckle in childbirth-education classes.

Times have changed. Today it is the rare husband or hospital that expects the father to be absent. Fathers also expect to play a much greater role in child care than their fathers did. "Help around the house" is no longer limited to keeping the family car in running order and the lawn well-trimmed.

Such major changes in cultural expectations have naturally brought with them new problems for the fathers-to-be. From the moment he knows of the pregnancy, a man is thrust into an alien world. He is encouraged, instructed and cajoled to be part of the pregnancy and birth process, something he knows little about. He is expected to become the coach or supporter for his wife, who has the leading role in the drama. He has no role model, since his own father almost certainly didn't do what he is expected to do.

These difficulties, while troublesome, can usually be overcome with care, education and preparation. Another problem is far more serious and confusing. I call it the cultural bind. Men are encouraged to participate fully in the pregnancy and birth of their children but are simultaneously given to understand, in a multitude of ways, that they are outsiders. Most of all, it is made clear that while their presence is requested, their feelings are not, if those feelings might upset their wives. Anxiety, anger, sadness and fear are unwelcome.

I first became fully aware of this double bind during a child-education class I attended with my wife. As the class toured the labor and delivery rooms, the instructor gave a thorough description of the facilities. She discussed the use of surgical implements and tables, stressing how well the hospital was equipped to deal with emergencies. When we returned to the classroom, she asked, "Now, doesn't everyone feel more comfortable?"

It was clear to me that several of the men were anything but comfortable, so I said to the instructor, "Actually, I feel much more nervous now." To my surprise, my comment was ignored, and within thirty seconds the topic of discussion was female reproductive anatomy. When I later asked the instructor about this privately, she looked at me with dismay. "What did you expect me to do, get all those pregnant women upset?" The message was clear. Fathers shalt not express nervousness about childbirth.

The double bind results from inconsistency between what fathers are told—"please be involved"—and the unspoken afterthought—"except for your negative feelings." But when he does, not all of them are positive. At times, he will be frightened, concerned, sad and angry at his wife. He needs to share these feelings and fears.

A young woman, about to have her first child, is expected to be frightened and ambivalent. Furthermore, her changes and feelings are supported and explained by the biological alterations in her body. The father-to-be has neither the support systems nor the cultural sanctions for what he experiences. He can't even be "out-of-sorts" for fear his negative feelings will affect the mother-to-be. Some men unconsciously compensate for this by developing physiological aspects of pregnancy, but such symptoms are generally treated humorously by family and friends.

This indifference to fathers' feelings extends to the media. Publishers produce a host of books and articles each year to help new parents adjust to their new roles and to gain better understanding of their children and themselves. But while there is excellent material on motherhood and child care, information for and about expectant fathers is limited. On television, the father's role in pregnancy and birth is still usually played for laughs, much as it was in the I Love Lucy days thirty years ago.

This TV stereotype has its ironic side. Men's increased participation in pregnancy, birth and child rearing grew out of the push for equality fostered by the feminist movement. Yet during this crucial transition in a couple's life, women are reinforced for being "the little woman," understandably a bit helpless, and men are rewarded for keeping quiet about their feelings. Both reactions encourage sex-role stereotypes.

When I analyzed the tests and interviews done in my study, I uncovered seven major fears and concerns that men usually keep to themselves. All were described by at least 40 percent of the men.

Queasiness. The most universal fear was the birth process itself. Desire to be part of the event did not reduce discomfort with the daunting prospect of blood and other bodily fluids. The men wondered about their ability to "keep it together" and truly help their wives through the process. Quite a few were afraid of fainting or getting sick. The same points came up when recent fathers talked about the birth of their children. Immediately after describing it as "wonderful," many mentioned their surprise and pride at coming through the procedure without becoming nauseated or fainting.

The fact that very few men actually have such trouble does not diminish their concern, which at times is increased by the insensitivity of the medical people. Some doctors and nurses show clear distaste for fathers' presence during deliveries, warning them that they may faint and get in the way.

Increased responsibility. "One day I was going along happy-go-lucky. The next day I was the sole support of three people." More than 80 percent of the fathers agreed with the feelings expressed by this 22-year-old father of three days.

Usually both husband and wife work before the first pregnancy. The birth of a child means financial as well as physical and emotional adjustments in the relationship, along with changes in the role expectations and feelings of responsibility. In my own case, when my wife was pregnant I found myself unconsciously allowing my carefully limited private practice to expand steadily. I was working longer hours to build a "nest egg"—a peculiarly appropriate term in this case. Other men told me of switching to more reliable jobs or working a second job to bring in more money.

Obstetrical-gynecological matters. Medicine that deals with "female" issues remains mysterious, discomforting and alien to many men. For years, women have told about the dehumanizing quality of much gynecological care. They cite the stirrups, examination positions and the embarrassing and insensitive attitude of many physicians. Expectant fathers often experience these feelings for the first time during contact with these medical people.

Several men who accompanied their wives to prenatal pelvic exams told that they felt coldness and nonacceptance from the same members of the obstetrical staff who earlier had praised them for being so involved. The men were made to feel out of place in the examining room and offices. Their questions about what to do were frequently silenced with looks that implied, "Only a fool wouldn't know that."

Uncertain paternity. "I was joking when I told my wife that if the kid has blond hair and blue eyes, I'm gone."

The surprising fact behind this "joke" is that more than half of the men surveyed acknowledged some nagging doubt that they were really the child's father. For most of them, such fears were based less on any real concern that the wife had been unfaithful than on a general insecurity brought on by being part of something as monumental as the creation of life. The questioning of paternity sometimes also reflected a general feeling of being left out. When a man is pressured by the cultural double bind, his unconscious mind may compensate by giving him a way—not being the real father—to be present physically at the birth and at the same time be absent psychologically.

The feeling of inadequacy to create life sometimes manifests itself in both men and women in psychological denial of the pregnancy—a phenomenon that may last for men until after the birth—and in strong concern that the hospital staff has mixed up the babies in the nursery.

Loss of spouse and/or child. "All of a sudden, I was filled with fears of JoAnn and the baby not making it through the pregnancy. I think it was the conversation with my mother, and her reminder that my grandmother had died in childbirth. Now that I think of it, so did her sister. I just can't get these thoughts out of my head. I'm afraid to tell JoAnn. I don't want to upset her. She's young, healthy, the hospital is good. Why am I so worried? I don't know how I'd go on without her."

Such fears begin for most men during the second trimester. They may seem groundless on the surface, but they are part of our cultural heritage. Only two generations ago, childbirth and its complications were a major cause of death for women of childbearing age. And since a man's wife is normally turning toward the infant and away from him at a time when he is feeling particularly insecure, it is easy for his unconscious to transform her temporary turning away into a sense of permanent loss.

Almost every expectant father I interviewed also talked about a related fear—that the child would be brain-damaged or defective in some way. It is a rare parent who neglects to count a newborn's fingers and toes.

Being replaced. "The one thing that really scares me is that the best of our lives together will be gone as soon as the baby is born . . . in some ways, I'm already feeling displaced by the turtle [the couple's pet name for the fetus] . . . it's already harder to get physically close. I am less vigorous in lovemaking, and when she becomes quiet and I know she's communicating with the turtle, I really feel left out. It's almost as if the primary relationship is with him, and I'm the fifth wheel."

It is important for pregnant women to turn inward and begin bonding with the life growing inside. So it is not surprising that so many men in our study felt left out, particularly since most of them used their own parents' relationships as a model. Usually, their fathers earned the living and their mothers took care of the house and children. The primary relationship was indeed between mother and child, with the father pushed into the background.

Today's expectant fathers are more likely than those of previous generations to know divorce, their parents' or their own, at first hand. That experience can have a powerful impact on expectations of how likely a marriage is to survive the additional stress of a child.

This fear of losing the relationship may play an important role in a much-publicized phenomenon, the late pregnancy affair. While they don't happen often, these affairs can be devastating to a marriage. In my work as a clinical psychologist and researcher I have interviewed twenty-seven men who admitted having such affairs.

Most of these relationships had certain common aspects. There was usually no history of previous affairs. The men felt abandoned during the pregnancy. They had a strong need to talk to someone about their feelings and chose a woman because men often find women more understanding than other men. The woman was usually someone the wife knew well—often a friend, but in one case a sister, in another a mother—who was also feeling estranged by the wife's pregnancy.

There is no way to excuse or minimize the impact of such affairs, despite the great remorse and guilt the husbands reported. In every case the affair severely damaged both the marital relationship and the wife's ability to trust her husband and her friends. One unexpected aspect was that feeling of rejection seemed to be a stronger motive for the affair than a lack of interest in the wife's pregnant shape. Nearly all the men insisted that their sexual attraction to their wives did not diminish during pregnancy.

Life and death. "I became aware when Mary was pregnant, that I no longer had any right to die. . . . I stopped taking huge risks. I found myself driving slower, avoiding rougher areas of town, actually listening to a life insurance salesman. . . . All for the reason that I was now important to this little thing, and I couldn't die because he needed me."

Of all the changes, fears and novel experiences a wife's pregnancy brings to a man, none is so subtle and yet so dramatic as consciousness of the biological life cycle. Several men said they felt closer to their own death after being so intimately involved with the beginnings of life. They also described an increased connection to their own fathers. Most of the men with living fathers made efforts to become closer to them during the pregnancy.

Since death is usually ignored in our youth-and-action culture, most men I talked to were surprised by their sudden feelings about human fragility and their own mortality. Until a man is a father, he remains identified as a member of the younger generation, a man with time to spare. His living parents or grandparents act as psychological buffers against death, since he expects to outlive them all. When he becomes a father, there is now a new, younger generation, one he cannot expect to outlive.

Most of the fathers dealt with this and their other concerns largely by themselves. Normally, they would have turned to their wives for support. But, believing that their worries were unique and afraid of making the pregnancy more burdensome for their wives, they usually kept the fears to themselves. Unfortunately, this further isolated them and made close emotional connections more difficult for both spouses.

I found that the number and severity of the fears increased under several conditions: if the man's wife was increasingly unavailable emotionally, physically and sexually; if he felt a need to reflect on the changes in his life and had no close friends or family with whom he could share his concerns; if he believed that he should be strong enough to handle matters without help; if he wasn't aware that the pregnancy, rather than financial or job concerns, was the main source of his worries.

If fathers are to get a solid psychological start on parenthood, they must learn to accept their natural fears during pregnancy. If men are to be involved in prenatal matters, their own negative feelings must be accepted by others. A cultural double bind that only partially and grudgingly accepts men's participation in pregnancy and birth restricts intimacy between the partners at a time when both of them need more communication rather than less.

One fact that emerged clearly in my study was that when men did share their concerns with their partners, the relationship deepened and closeness increased. As men become more involved in the process of fatherhood, we must expand our understandings of their needs and fears. The father-to-be cannot be fully a part of the pregnancy and birth unless these fears are fully recognized by himself, by his spouse, by his family and by a society in general.

CHAPTER TWENTY-THREE

Kyle Pruett

Divorce and the Nurturing Father: The Dangerous Opportunity

Nearly half of all United States families are wracked by serparation and divorce at some point. A few work things out, but most are torn apart. Divorce occurs so frequently, we prefer to numb ourselves to its lacerations of the spirit. When it does come, the family changes its complexion and integrity, never to be the same again.

One particular statistic bears stark witness to this change. The number of single fathers in America mushroomed by over 125 percent from 1970 to 1984 in homes that care for 1.5 million children. The reordering of this new life and its relationships constitutes a major crisis of our time. The word *crisis* evokes our attention and concern, but it need not imply hopeless destruction. Crisis, as defined by the I Ching, is a "dangerous opportunity." I think many fathers and others would agree.

Most fathers who divorce lose custody of their children, but some share it. Depending upon the divorce decree or agreement, they may have ongoing contact with their children through "visitation" (a most unsatisfactory word). The time a father spends with his children in such arrangements may not be much less than he had before. It may even be experienced by both father and child, after the initial shock of the "moveout" has eased, as "better" time, since it is usually less constricted by the depleting, conflicted misery of a painful marriage. Thus freed, father and children may embark on new explorations of the territory of their lives and relationship. This is the opportunity part.

The dangerous part comes later, especially for the father who loses custody. Most major studies of divorced families conducted over time show that after five years, fewer than half of noncustodial fathers still maintain "actively nurturing roles" in the lives of their children.[1] The rest either have been actively excluded from their children's lives by courts or mothers or have slowly suffered a kind of paternal erosion or drift, slipping inexorably out of the main current of their children's lives.

This loss of contact with one's children is a huge loss, whether sudden or by slow degree, that wreaks much profound devastation upon both fatherhood and childhood. Since the majority of custody arrangements favor mothers, this situation clearly qualifies as a major problem for fathers. One father likened the loss of his children from his daily life to being "slowly disemboweled." Not surprisingly, many men are radicalized by such experiences.

I have encountered many men who are plagued by guilt years after potential court battles because they "didn't try harder for my kids." Yet those who do try often watch in pain as their finances, property, and emotional lives are devastated by interminable legal maneuverings, when the odds are they will lose anyway.

Given the large number of affected fathers, it is absolutely amazing that we know so little about how divorced men actually feel about losing their children from their daily lives and the havoc that it wreaks on their sense of fatherliness.

We do know that divorced fathering starts very painfully much of the time.[2] It begins with a period of numbing, often bitter, shock and sadness for both father and child that can "feel like death," as one 25-year-old accountant described it. The sadness may vary in intensity for the father whether he feels he "won or lost." It is more uniformly painful and sad for the children, as they feel they've usually lost either part or all of a father. It is painful for the father because he's just experienced a lengthy, depleting emotional battle that often leaves his self-esteem in shreds.

Such hurt is rarely short-lived. It often forces competent, well-functioning, caring parents into atypical, obstructive roles vis-à-vis their children and each other. Intimacy, affection, self-esteem, and communication are frequent casualties during this early period. Fathers take flight into the Santa Claus stance, becoming givers of *presents* in lieu of their frightened, uncertain *selves.*

As men become increasingly aware of the enormous damage that divorce (whether they sought it or not) can inflict on their fatherhood and their children, a growing number are seeking sole custody. However, the single father, not unlike the single mother, once embarked can expect heavy weather. Exhaustion, boredom, worry, confusion, and disappointment are all fellow travelers. So are exhilaration, emotional rewards, and pleasures unique to this experience never before felt or thought possible.

Career advancement is often put in cold storage while adjusting to the enormity of the new responsibilities and drudgeries. Women, because of sexist role expectations, are *expected* to put children first; but when a man does, balancing career and parenthood can feel very precarious indeed. Although the single father, because he's still a rare (supposedly even heroic) species, is more likely to receive offers of community or family help than the single mother, his independent—even antidependent—nature will usually cause him to shun help more often than he probably should, making things harder for him and his children.

Some important questions are beginning to be answered as we begin to study and understand single fathers and their life situations. In 1983, more than 1,000 single men with custody of their children responded to an interesting Parents Without Partners survey about single parenting.[3] Their biggest worries were not about their competence in child care or homemaking responsibilities. Their largest concerns were about the juggling of careers and parenthood. When asked what they felt would help them resolve their real-life difficulties, they gave the following solutions: (1) more time flexibility in the workplace, (2) more legal and mental health support for themselves and their children, and (3) wider, less stigmatizing acceptance of men as sole parents.

But for each father who "won" custody, there are ten who lose the irreplaceable dailiness of life with their children. Some are granted joint custody, which permits them some say in important life decisions such as schooling and medical care (access to which often comes with a huge price tag in terms of child support payments).

But many fathers have only "visitation." Not unlike the concept of "baby-sitter," "visitation" is a bizarre term that consigns the parent to the designation of remote relative or circuit rider who comes into the child's life not to "father" (or to "mother") but merely to "visit."

Making "visitation" work as an ongoing arrangement for a life with one's child is very difficult indeed. One young journalist father described it this way. "At first the relationship is so vastly affected, it's like nothing mattered from before. It's a grotesque artifact of what used to be. It's like death, and this is some sort of afterlife or painful 'out-of-body' experience."

Such men find themselves scrambling, reaching, maneuvering, and manipulating to find what the young journalist called a "strong second place" in the life of their children.

Competition with the ex-wife over importance as an abiding, effective presence in the child's life is nearly universal and almost as universally damaging to the relationship with the child. The children, depending upon their age and level of sophistication, may be initially titillated by the competition, which involves the giving and denying of affection as well as material goods and services. But eventually the children are less and less impressed. One eleven-year-old boy "divorced" for three years said, "It's not that I don't want an all-terrain cycle—I do! Who wouldn't? But what I need is for my dad and mom to stop the silly Santa Claus stuff. It's like a dumb TV game show. It just doesn't mean anything after you watch it for a while."

Eventually, many a man comes to realize that part of the competition does not come from his ex but comes instead from another part of himself—that part that clings tenaciously to the image of the full and perfect father, the giver of life, goodies, wisdom, protection, and happiness.

But the fight for *importance,* no matter what its individual source, is ongoing, and many men feel it is never confidently "won." The young journalist: "It's really like a guerilla action aimed not at a complete overthrow of the regime but just to win a presence in the governance of the life of my child. I am secondary and I'll never be primary—I know that. But goddamn it, I still want to be *important!* And I'm not just fighting my ex in the jungle, I'm fighting the inevitable drift out of my growing child's life. Her independence from me, no matter how much I want to make it happen well for her, seems like an enemy, too."

The guerilla action is a heavy drain on resources, mental and economic. Of course, some men, those who leave or quit their children's lives, never start, or eventually stop trying. They just stop fighting. No one knows how much that costs them, but it usually costs the children plenty.

But what happens to "visitors" who do visit?

One of the longest-running myths about divorced fathers is this: A father may be a good protector or breadwinner, but his innate (stereotyped) inability to respond to his child emotionally leaves him to feel little, if anything, of depth about the impact of divorce on his fathering. His role as husband and provider certainly is affected but *not* his fathering.

How wrong, how wrong. This witless view has made it much easier over the years for attorneys and judges to dispense wisdom and justice in contested divorces.

Staying involved as the "visitor" is a job that usually changes with time, although more radically for the noncustodial than the custodial father. E. Mavis Hetherington of the University of Virginia found that noncustodial fathers were in progressively less and less contact with their children as time passed.[4] Of the 48 fathers in her study, she found that after two years, 19 men saw their children once a week, 21 saw them every two or three weeks, and 8 saw them once a month or less. Remarriage, resistance on the part of the custodial parent, and child drift were all variably responsible.

For the joint-custody father, things are quite different. Los Angeles psychologist Ann D'Andrea found that joint-custody fathers stayed actively involved well beyond this two-year dropoff point.[5] Fathers on such regular visitation schedules not only kept more current with child support payments, but they expressed greater satisfaction and self-esteem as fathers than did those who did not keep to a schedule. This of course could be a cart-before-the-horse finding, but the fact remains that the men who stay involved *are* more involved.

Such involvement may not be without its price. David Chambers of the University of Michigan Law School has found that men who wished to "visit regularly" with their children paid court-ordered child support payments that were significantly higher than the average: the "put up or shut up" visitation/child support syndrome.[6] The lowest payments were made by those men who had no contact. He concluded that money and involvement seem to come from the same source—"affection and devotion" to one's children.

But the investment is hardly risk free. One 42-year-old father, a successful commercial real estate broker who had joint custody of his two twelve-year-old sons, had "suffered a lot since the divorce of six years ago. Every time I come to pick the boys up, it's like running the gauntlet with my ex. She just never lets go of the opportunity to be mad at me. I think of visitation rights sort of like beach rights. When you get down to the water it's great. But if the neighbors don't like you, and they make it plain they don't like you over and over again, pretty soon you start thinking about not going. That's why I hate calling it visitation *rights.* It's God given that I ought to be in their lives. Hell, I helped to make 'em! Why do I have to pay over and over again for it? Once she offered me back half of my child support check if I'd cut down on 'visitation.' That would have made my cash flow problems disappear, but it would've wrecked me in my kids' eyes, in my own eyes, and in the long run, made things even worse for my kids."

One of the most respected ongoing studies of the children of divorce, by Judith Wallerstein and J. B. Kelly, shows us repeatedly that the absence of the father is a serious, sometimes dangerous condition.[7] They found that most of the children in the study missed their fathers painfully. "Two-thirds yearned for the absent parent, one-half of those with an intensity we found profoundly moving." Depending on the sex and developmental stage of the child at the time of the breakup, children who never saw their fathers again, *regardless* of the reason, frequently developed emotional and behavioral difficulties. Such difficulties were very often quite serious and emerged immediately, but some appeared and reappeared later on as well.

One of the few things on which students of divorce and child development agree, even across disciplinary lines, is that father absence makes for a lot of potential trouble in the evolution of the child's personality and sense of self.[8] Poor control of aggressive behavior in boys and girls, difficulties in establishing unconflicted gender identities and roles, impaired intellectual and school functioning, depression, and troubles in the regulation of self-esteem are all more common in children from divorced families than from intact families, even unhappy ones. Although most responsible researchers stop short of attributing such problems to linear cause and effect, their prevalence among the children of divorce is very sobering indeed. If the child, however, is guaranteed an open, continuous relationship that stays essentially protected and unchanged over time, the *probability* of such unhappy results is greatly reduced.

Now that we have begun to pay attention, we have found that

fathers who want to be involved after the divorce have their own list of vulnerabilities. These may be especially obvious during the early months of the breakup (and may be shared with the children). Such things as depression, troubles in the maintenance of self-esteem, impaired work function (impaired school performance for kids), occasionally even poor control of behavior show up early. Fathers often have feelings that are much more than they bargained for.

Some of what fathers feel so intensely is certainly linked to the end of the marriage. These strong emotions are also often related to the threatened termination of the effect their children have on their lives, and vice versa. Much of this feeling is based on the fear, hardly irrational, that the power of the father to affect his child's life and to "feel affected" by the child's life is slipping out of his grasp.

This capacity to be affected by the life of the child is what divorced men discover painfully is so seriously threatened by the event of the divorce.

How is the divorced father to make his presence best felt, and usefully so, in the life of his child?

First, custody, however it's carved up judicially, is largely an internal, emotional commitment. Children *feel* that sense of "belonging" to a father and mother, not as property but as beloved kin. They watch carefully, no matter what the State says, to see if their fathers *act* as though they feel that sense of belonging, too. So here's some advice I shall address to divorced men to preserve that sense of mutual belonging.

The first and foremost guiding principle regarding any decisions about visitation or changes in your life that might affect your child should be made with what is best for your child, not just you, in mind.

Second, be guided by your child's developmental needs, and especially his or her different sense of time. Frequent brief visits are a lot better for toddlers with short memories than are long visits at greater intervals. Older children with successful social and school lives (about which you would feel understandably proud) need more flexibility about visits with you.

Third, live close to your children if you can, especially when they are younger, for obvious reasons.

Fourth, honor your "visitation" rights. "Bite the bullet," run the gauntlet, but don't give up and stop seeing your children, no matter who tests you, your ex or the kids. Your life together is preserved in and by the mundane tasks, such as changing diapers, blowing noses, helping with homework. Be with them whenever you can. The door may close if you don't keep going through it.

Fifth, pay your child support. If you don't, you are the real loser. Skipping may deprive your kids of something, but it deprives you of much more—your self-respect as a father.

Sixth, do not overindulge your children. No matter how many "I wants" you hear, children of *all* ages inherently *want* you to define, guard, and keep the limits for them. That's how they learn what to expect from life, and they see you as one of the experts, whether or not you think you are.

Seventh, don't press for talk about the divorce. Your job is to figure out how you and your kids can fit into one another's lives, not cross and recross-examination. All your kids want to know is that you are not going to quit on them. The details are usually not as interesting to them as they may think they are, anyway.

Finally, crisis need *not* spawn failure. Though divorce can be dangerous to the leaving father, and to his staying child, some opportunity lies in the shadows of all that sadness. A man may define his fatherhood to himself for the first time in honest and intimate terms. He and his children may also struggle to shape together in some way a vision and understanding of what they have taken for granted in one another's lives and then to decide whether or not to protect it. When accomplished by both father and child, the rewards can sometimes reach beyond words. When our whole society learns to understand and value these relationships, that part of the father problem which plagues divorced men and their children can fade quietly, namelessly away.

CHAPTER TWENTY-FOUR

Kip Eastman

Just Visiting

It is the little things
that hurt the most:
The vacant place across the table,
the dolls aligned along a shelf,
one sock left there on the floor.
Melancholy thorns adorn the rose
that blooms on visitation days.

Visitation weekend number 104 is over. My daughter, Chelsea, is again "home" with her mother. I sit alone in the garden we have planted, weeded, watered—a ritual we perform when we are together. I watch the young plants struggle to reach the sun.

Eventually, one or another tendril will make the essential contact with the trellis, and the plant will thrive. But some shoots will remain in limbo, not quite useless, not quite needed. It is this feeling that washes over me after nearly every visitation. (I hate the word— like being in prison or a psychiatric institution.)

Am I still Chelsea's father when she is not here? In my heart and my gut the answer seems to be no. My mind knows better. We share the pattern of freckles across the nose, although in most other ways she resembles her mother. She calls me when she is hurt, cuddles with me in the quiet times, judges my women and my cooking. We finish sentences for each other, laugh and cry in synchrony. When we are together, none can mistake the relationship.

But we are together so little. Every two weeks we make the transition from estranged correspondents to father and daughter.

There is a brittleness about the first few hours; there is a melancholy about the last few. It leaves a painfully sweet day or two in between, a time that makes the repeated assault on both our sensibilities worthwhile.

Longer visits are even more difficult for us. The parting leaves us feeling betrayed, yet each of us misses the patterns of our separate lives. I miss the woman-comfort, creative grumbling, and independent time of my single adult world. Chelsea misses friends and mother and baby brother. Besides, the pain is more than parting— we are made aware that our lives cannot run in the same channel even while the times we share show us how good it could have been.

Seven years ago I cursed the fact of my daughter's coming, in fear of losing my mate to a difficult pregnancy. I can remember standing at the window of the intensive nursery, and feeling bubbled to the surface. At that moment I vowed that all my life, all my health, all my power, was that child's, if she would be OK.

Chelsea lived, her mother lived. I had made the transition from nonparent to parent, with a vengeance.

I blundered into and through the father/spouse/provider/ protector role. I read the books, had the best of intentions, and failed. That failure cost me the dream of domestic bliss I had nurtured from age thirteen. I was thrust into a schismatic existence, the life of a divorced father without custody.

I was not so deeply hurt by my wife's leaving me as by her taking my daughter. I knew that for years to come I would be making the transition over and over from the single existence (which I had every intention of taking full advantage of) to that of either a committed single parent or a Disneyland Dad.

It was not in me to absolve myself of all but financial responsibility for my daughter's growth. I fought for, and won, joint legal custody. I refused to be a vendor of weekend holidays. The financial and emotional costs of that battle were significant, but the rewards were worth it.

Chelsea and I wash dishes, cook (after a fashion), and commit ourselves to taking care of whatever business needs attention, in spite of our limited time. There are occasions, however, when I cannot interrupt my concentration on a project to join in an activity with her. Since age four, she has been able to work contentedly on her own for longer periods than I usually can.

In the four years since our schism, I've read over six hundred children's books, many of them repeatedly, reintroducing myself to that amazing fantasy world. I've arranged to volunteer at Chelsea's school, to increase the time spent with her, but I get so much more than just "time." I've come to accept shared love—I bear the title "Daddy" jointly with the man who married Chelsea's mother. While I once thought of him as "that S.O.B.," now, through Chelsea's love, he has become co-father.

I have grown to care about women in ways my own relationship with my mother, my adolescent exploitation, had never allowed. Participating in Chelsea's effort to grow up female has contributed immeasurably to my effort to grow up male.

But, of course the waves of change have not come without great cost. A few episodes are typical of the catalytic forces of my intermittent parenting.

My wife and I had been separated but a few days. I'd honored her request for total isolation while she settled into her new apartment. One afternoon she came to the house unexpectedly, carrying Chelsea who was not yet three. I greeted them as calmly as I could and bent down to kiss Chelsea. She turned her face away and began to cry. Nothing, nothing before, not even the demise of my first love, nothing since, hurt me more, cut me deeper. That was the bulldozer that took my relationship with my daughter back to bedrock.

On a week-long trip, after a tiring day, hassling over sleeping arrangements for four adults and four children, Chelsea began to wail, "I want my Mommy." I overreacted, yelling at her, threatening never again to take her anywhere, never to see her again if that's how she felt. The impact was staggering—for both of us. Awash with guilt, I tried to hold her close, but, hurt and angry, she would have no part of it. Only after much talking and crying was an accommodation reached. I still blush over my frailty.

Finally, another time of tears, but for a much different reason. Chelsea and I sat in a nearly empty theater moments after the show was over, holding each other close and trying to staunch the flow of tears. We had sniffled our way through the last part of the movie, but when the alien assured the little boy that he would always be there for him, inside his head, we both lost control. Like fools we sat there crying. Then we looked each other in the eye and burst into laughter. We knew. We knew!

Crying seems to come easily to us. It is often the finale of our weekends together, although we both try to keep it in check. Most of our time together is just too damn good to have it end. Assurances that our love remains inside do not make it easier. I rarely leave Chelsea without the sense that something important has gone unsaid, and I always depart awkwardly.

The chronic state of transition brings some concrete hardships as well. I drive a fair distance to pick up and return Chelsea. There are all the usual difficulties with school, parties, lessons. I sometimes find it hard to adapt to the demands of being a father-in-fact after two weeks of furlough, particularly when I'm in the midst of a complex project. Then there are the schedules, revised schedules, and revised, revised schedules. They provide security, probably for all of us, and sometimes inconvenience that requires delicate negotiation.

From this alternating current I derive tremendous power. I live in the present; I've become unashamedly physical and affectionate; I fight and apologize unabashedly; I savor the moment. I treasure the past and try to communicate it more intimately. I have a concern for the future that goes far beyond the ecological abstractions of my education. There is a subtle force generated by Chelsea's unconditional love and trust that lingers when she is gone. It has transformed my life for the better.

CHAPTER TWENTY-FIVE

Warren Farrell

The New Fear: Stepfathering

Fourteen million children in the United States now live with only one parent. *Because over 90 percent of these children live with their mothers, men are approximately nine times more likely to become step-fathers than women are to become stepmothers.*[1]

Stepparents of either sex (instead of saying *step,* I will use *new*— as in "new father," "new mother," and "new parent") face realities that previous generations rarely faced when married: they must deal with their new partner's children, visiting privileges, several sets of grandparents, and the relationships among new siblings. Into his complexity are blended the adults' conflicting theories of child rearing and the balances between discipline, love, everyday schedules, fairness of treatment, and egos. This all requires such a change from the single life that it might give pause to a single person of either sex.

On one hand, it is amazing that these "blended family" relationships last an average of almost five years.[2] On the other hand, a relationship likely to last only five years can help us to understand the special fears faced by men—the sex most likely to make a five-year investment in children who are not his to begin with and whom he may never see again should the commitment end.

NEW DAD AS REJECTED DAD: THE TWO-YEAR SYNDROME

The nine-times greater likelihood of women to have custody of children after divorce means that a man is much more likely to experience the "two-year syndrome": the almost constant rejection of him by his new children for approximately two years (experts say this is the average length of time it takes for a new parent to be accepted by the partner's children). For the hundreds of thousands of men who have never before been fathers, the "two-year syndrome" means that their introduction to fathering is two years of rejection. And no one can reject more subtly and powerfully than a child.

I have gained a special feeling for the hurt experienced by a new father during my three years of living with Anne and her daughter Megan. When I met Anne five years ago, Megan, before meeting me, thought of me as "the man Mommy stayed out with longer than she said she would—the man who made Mommy keep the baby-sitter waiting." Megan picked up on her mom's special interest immediately.

The result? When I first met Megan, her three main responses to me were "I don't know," "I don't care," and "It doesn't make any difference." She and Mom had been alone together six years. The first time her dad had remarried, his new wife showed very little affection to Megan. And Anne had fallen in love only once before during those six years (to a man who lived five hundred miles away); Megan saw that as "Mom was gone a lot more often. . . . If Mom falls in love again, I'm going to be deprived of her love again."

So I was to be rejected before Megan got rejected.

To casually say that it took four or five months to move out of this stage is to minimize the extraordinary pain I felt with every overture that was unresponded to: the unspoken "get out of here— you're just trying to be nice to me because you want to take my mother away from me"; the distrust in the eyes of an eight-year-old who seems to be saying, "I know what you're really up to"; the kiss goodnight with the cheek turning the other way and the hands preparing to wipe away the residue of any possible contact; the present received without a thank you; the response to the offer to take time away from writing to pick her up from a friend's when her mom was too busy—"I want Mommy to pick me up [not you, Warren]."

Each rejection made each day of deeper commitment a day in which I wondered whether I was setting myself up for years of rejection. Each day eroded my image of myself as a loving, giving man with enough patience and creativity to develop a balanced and loving interaction with a child. Was I inadequate, was I a masochist, or was this a stage? It was easy to know intellectually that it was a stage, but calling it a stage feels like telling an army private who has just engineered his way through a minefield—every second know-ing that one careless step could destroy everything he's worked for—that what he just moved through was "just a stage."

I know that while I was in the midst of this minefield it would not have helped if Anne saw my caution and told me I was afraid of commitment in an accusatory tone. Yet it would have been equally off-putting for Anne to have said, "I'm glad *you're* not afraid of commitment like most *other* men are." That would have been an "ego bribe" to deny my feelings. What I wanted was that my feel-ings of fear be acknowledged and the *reasons* for them understood. I felt caution was a sign of maturity—and of respect for myself, Anne, and Megan. When I felt understood on that level, I came to trust that I had met a woman who understood my feelings even when they were feelings she would ideally prefer I not have. *That* told me a lot.

In turn, it would have been unreasonable for Anne to do this if I were not understanding her minefield in the process: attending to the fragility of her new relationship and the fragility of her child; the bind that if she understood me, Megan might interpret it as proof that my inclusion meant her exclusion (which would only force Megan to reject me longer); and the haunting fear that if she didn't take my side, she would lose a man she loved and resent Megan for it. I guess the more she understood me, the more I under-stood her, the more she understood me—but most of all, I felt good about commitment growing out of the cycle of understanding rather than pressure.

CHAPTER TWENTY–SIX

P. Gregory Springer

Is Daddy Different?

Ten years ago, I was a confirmed gay man writing with pride and self-assurance for gay liberation newspapers, and marriage was simply not on my agenda. Children were an even more remote possibility.

Today I still write for those newspapers, sometimes with my son Henry—soon to be three years old—sitting on my lap in front of the computer screen. When Lee and I decided to marry, we both knew the situation could not be easily labeled. Neither of us believed I would ever change or that I would need to.

For the first years of marriage, Lee insisted upon only one rule. If I were sexually active outside the marriage, I must agree to take the battery of cultures necessary to test for sexually transmitted diseases before we could resume relations. This was sometimes bothersome, but it was an arrangement she insisted we work out between us.

There were slip-ups, arguments, flare-ups, doubts. But unlike many gay men, I never actively sought a gay lover. I could be drawn physically to a man, but family had supplied me with most of my important emotional needs. Even before the unwelcome arrival of AIDS into the gay community, I had virtually ceased sexual activity outside our marriage. But it was not always easy.

There are hundreds of gay fathers in this country. Many of them keep their sexual feelings secret, whereas others are—to my way of thinking—more fortunate in being able to share the truth with friends and family. One particular difficulty in living a "disclosed" life is in finding a way to explain yourself to your children when they inevitably ask: Is daddy different?

In the early seventies, my female friend Lee and I lived together, sharing rent and space and occasionally the bed. When I confronted my true sexual feelings—with some difficulty—I left Lee for Richard, someone I needed for a while, in order to discover and open up the feelings I had repressed for years. Lee, also with some difficulty, accepted this, and we lived apart.

I began to get writing assignments from gay periodicals. Several years later, on a tour of Iowa for *Blueboy*, I invited Lee along for the ride. Between interviews in Des Moines gay bars and a tour of hot spots at the Iowa State Fair, we discussed the possibility of merging our friendship into a permanent relationship.

Soon after marrying Lee, I wrote an article for the *Advocate* about such mixed-oriented marriages. We discovered there are hundreds of couples in this same situation, unhappily typed by media-drenched labels, floundering in a state of being both happily married and sexually specialized. For a brief moment, it appeared that such marriages would constitute "a trend," the topic appearing on book shelves and the "Phil Donahue Show." In retrospect, the serious studies conducted by Dr. David Matteson and Michael W. Ross (*The Married Homosexual Man,* Routledge & Kegan Paul) have revealed that the problems faced by gay married men are not very different from the ordinary difficulties in any marriage.

The gay organizations and magazines I was affiliated with did not always respond favorably to my marriage. On some staffs, I'm the token straight. Others simply rejected me. A prominent gay bookstore in New York still refuses to stock publications related to gay married men.

Parenthood follows patterns. Gay men learn to change diapers with the same trepidation and fumbling as nongay fathers.

When Henry was born, new worlds of identification opened before me. Suddenly, those movies about children and fathers brought tears welling inside me. (They still do, even something so remote as a well-edited telephone commercial can reach out and touch me into blubbering.) My feelings for and understanding of my own father shifted from one of tenured indifference to genuine appreciation. Watching him play grandfather also unleashed a new feeling of sameness. I see myself in him, and him in Henry. At first, I experienced these psychological connections to some age-old, mainstream masculine habits and attitudes. Nervousness, pride, cuddling, roughhousing, and protectiveness were there for me to accept. Mostly, fatherhood turned my world on its head with joy.

As with all new fathers, pains of responsibility must follow in the wake of delight. Discipline and nurturing aren't the exclusive right of heterosexuality. By the ordinary means of procreation, one is granted the status of father. But true fathering entails many more years of follow-up.

Even now, as I attempt to explain the importance of naptime to a three-year-old, hints of a future communication gap surface. How could I ever be able to explain my voyeuristic visits to a gay bathhouse to someone who can't comprehend the simple sharing of a toy truck?

I'm not particularly worried about it. I have no grand plan or expectations as to how to handle the question that inevitably will arise. Henry plays with "guns" now, shooting people and beasts and bad guys in imitation of television. Some of this playacting is unavoidable, and without owning any guns myself, I avoid flustering and overemphasizing his behavior. Someday, he will be able to reason for himself. I must wait, with as much patience as possible. He may follow the lead of my behavior, or he may not. We can teach only so much.

Henry's first word was *ball*. Before he was two, he could recognize and name every sport played in North America. He insisted on owning a football, baseball, soccer ball, tennis ball, and various others. Suddenly, I found myself thrust into a world of competitive sports, which I had managed to elude all my life.

It's confusing, how different we can be already, yet how closely bound we are. Observing the differences doesn't clarify a thing. It only raises more questions about environment, heredity, learning, models, and influence.

Children are, as Freud claimed, highly sexualized beings. Changing diapers, sharing bathtime, slobbery kisses goodnight, and the minimum requirement of daily hugs enrich any parent's life. How tragic when those moments are curtailed or completely denied because of a parent's sexual insecurity. In only one occasion have I felt some strange vibrations from friends, concerned about my gayness and my willingness to hug their children. Although the overwhelming majority of sexual abuse of children is committed by heterosexuals, the explicit sexual component of homosexual rhetoric may cause the question to surface more quickly.

I would sooner deny a child water than a daily dose of affection. We starve and wither without touch. I suffer, too, knowing that so many gay men are denied or deny themselves a child's kisses by too closely associating their lives with their sexuality.

Loving children can fill many gaps in life in profoundly satisfying ways. Many gay fathers have married in order to experience fatherhood. In a few of these successful marriages—Freud notwithstanding—it would seem the drive to raise children outweighed the sexual drive itself.

How will Henry and my new baby, Ernie, respond when they learn daddy is gay? It is something we must wait to face. Homosexuality in our house is discussed with the same lack of passion given to the mention of potato salad. It is not an issue—not yet. Any concern that possibly the children would reject me for having a minority sexual identity seems—impossible. And if one of my sons should be gay, I probably will have to relive much of the difficult self-examination that I went through for myself. But in that case, the boy will have a supportive, loving father who can at least offer some advice on the subject. He need never fear my rejection of his feelings.

For myself, most of all, being a gay father has altered my conception of what it means for me to be gay. I speak for myself when I say it has been neither an immutable curse nor admission into a social club of outsiders.

In many ways, I expect that the extended self-acceptance period on my life will help me watchfully groom my children to adulthood. Tolerance, pain, reflection, individuality, confusion—these are some of the less subtle traumas of growing up, traumas that gay people sometimes are forced to face again and again in their lives.

Since becoming a father, I have come to know two things more deeply than ever before: my homosexual feelings are an undeniable presence, but the ways in which human feelings can be explored are manifold. The fact of being gay doesn't have to mean giving in to a stifled or stereotyped life. The fact of being a father is a creative challenge that draws from the very depths of being.

My gayness, like my fatherhood, has an undeniable biological component. But there is so much more. The other aspects are the important ones: growing, learning, seeing, sharing, knowing, loving. Until we deny these, there are no constrictions on the conditions of life.

CHAPTER TWENTY–SEVEN

William F. Van Wert

The Transformation of a Single Parent

Becoming a single father felt anything but natural. It was as though I had been tossed around in a whirlpool and thrown into the role by default. The birth of my third son preceded my mother's death by two weeks. From the start, the new baby was up every night, crying from the pain of ear infections. After nine months of amoxicillin, our doctor determined that the best solution was to have tubes put in both ears. At that point, my wife went into an emotional and physical tailspin and was advised by her therapist to leave her family. To me the therapist said bluntly, "As for the children, it's you or foster homes."

So there I was, still grieving over a dead mother and now grieving over a departed wife. In addition, I was suddenly the single father of three boys under five—two of them still in diapers. I had no immediate family in the area, no support group, no baby-sitters, and no role models.

I did have a few things going for me. First, I was a tenured full professor, well established in my career. My two-day teaching schedule allowed me to minimize on baby-sitters and time away from the boys. Second, because the children had been born at home, I was incredibly bonded with them. And third, the grief over my mother's death brought some clarity of vision. In retrospect, I am grateful for these things, but at the time I had no idea how much they counted.

SINGLE FATHERHOOD

I did not take on single fatherhood gracefully. My image of parenting had convinced me that children needed their mothers, not their fathers. I had little self-esteem, felt rejected, and was so out of touch with my feelings. I sighed a lot, made lists and lost them, talked to myself, cried some. Moreover, I was a horror in the kitchen. My oldest son Ian, who was four at the time, knew the difference between food that was burned and food that was not. While he did not condemn my cooking, he wouldn't lie about it either. "You tried," he would say, urging his younger brothers to give my spaghetti a second chance.

My father came for a visit. His plan was to stay a week; instead he stayed two days. With tears in his eyes, he muttered, "This is not man's work." I resented that. About the same time, my therapist told me the boys would probably be "damaged children." I resented that too. I resented the ineptitude of men in general—not to mention their aloofness, their foolish pride, and of course, my own.

Women, on the other hand, found me "noble." I was not feeling noble at all. Some women I knew glorified the notion of holding a job while raising children; others resented their husbands' preoccupations with jobs and careers. One mother even told me: "Women are always single-parenting, even in their marriages, but a man . . ." These women judged my ex-wife more harshly than I did.

Some things actually became easier. Gone were the arguments about whose turn it was to cook, do the laundry, go grocery shop, or walk the baby. It was always my turn. Gone too was the awkwardness about whether to spend the late evenings relating to another adult or preparing for class. The time after my children went to sleep was suddenly all mine. "All my time," however, took on a strange new quality. After orchestrating harmony for my sons all day, I would sit alone at my typewriter—and with no inspiration left for writing, simply let feelings of chaos wash over me. I worried about money. I worried that I might never feel sexual again. I worried that my boys would grow up to be gay from too much father-exposure. Often I would break down and cry, then try to harden myself. When I gave in to sadness, it weakened me physically. When I did not give in, I felt numb emotionally.

Most terrible were the bouts with a kind of loneliness that I had never before encountered. I realized that I had been in some sort of relationship with a girlfriend, lover, or wife from eighth grade to the age of thirty-five, and I had no idea what it meant to be fully alone. I scared myself. I bored myself. Stubbornly, I sat with myself night after night, until my time alone did not bother me anymore. My reasoning was, if I couldn't learn to enjoy being with myself how could I expect anyone else to enjoy being with me?

After about two years of single fatherhood, I stopped feeling like a victim of circumstance and realized that I liked being a full-time dad. I looked forward to the middle-of-the-night ritual of walking the baby, singing him songs, and feeling him fall asleep at my neck—only to wake up needing a change, a bottle, more walking, more singing. It was not unusual to open my eyes in the morning and find all three of my sons asleep in my bed. I took strength from our closeness and from the little things they said. One day, for instance, Ian told me: "Daddy, everything you say and do is right and true." Its rhyme alone gave it the ring of prophecy.

We read books, and when I got bored with them, I would invent new dialogue. Eventually I got caught in the act. "Daddy," one of my sons blurted out, "Babar doesn't talk like that." We made up little ditties—the grosser the better—for long car rides. Our most famous verse went like this:

> *Who put those poops*
> *in my ice-cream scoops?*
> *Chocolate-y-gloops.*
> *I ate those two brown poops.*
> *Whoops.*
> *BLEAH!*

We all screamed the BLEAH! as loud as we could and broke up laughing. Within minutes, one of the boys would invariably suggest singing it again.

Each time we traveled out of town, I packed twenty to thirty bottles of milk and/or juice, which were usually finished off in the first two hours. I changed diapers on the turnpike turn-outs or on top of picnic tables at rest areas. Our favorite motel stops were around the Midwest. Here, Ian saw his first hygienic display of paper across a toilet seat, and declared that it was a slingshot for doodies, "so that lazy maids wouldn't have to clean the toilets." Sometimes we used the motel beds as trampolines and had pillow fights and stayed up late running racehorse through all the cable channels—all things we did not do at home.

As fathering encompassed more and more fun times, I decided that we were all healthy enough for me to leave for a lecture, a movie, or even a date. The only thing holding me back was that I had not yet, after almost three years of single-parenting, tapped into that rich resource of information and support: the neighborhood mothers' network. Here was a 24-hour hotline of crackerjack parents who knew the existing pool of baby-sitters backward and forwards; who knew about toys, secondhand clothing stores, museums without entry fees, and all the inexpensive entertainment available on weekends. Although I knew who these women were, I had not had the courage to approach them. So I finally set aside my pride and embarrassment and called them and began teaming up with them for visits to the zoo, the arboretum, and the mall. Shared outings evolved into shared confidences—horror stories of divorce, financial woes, discussions of parenting styles, even gossip.

My contact with these mothers was refreshingly nonjudgmental and sexually uncharged. At first, I worried about the lack of sexuality in my new relationships. Was I so beaten-down that I had become desexed without even knowing it? Or was I simply relating to women in a new way—casually, free of posturing or innuendo or other assertions of sexual difference? The truth was I was making friends with women, lots of women all at once. And suddenly I was no longer the loner, no longer the exceptional single father. Happily aware of the great number of single-parent families in my midst, I exchanged single fatherhood for single parenthood and drew sustenance from this new source of support.

Still, dating was difficult, awkward, sometimes even silly. One woman proposed to me on our first date because she liked the look of my sons. Another asked me to make a baby with her. Others, who had me tabbed as a caretaker, were frustrated at my unwillingness to caretake them. They did not understand that my three children satisfied all of my caretaking needs, many of my touching needs, and some of my conversational needs.

Several women were put off when I canceled dates when one of my boys got sick. I thought that surely anyone who was single-parenting would understand that children come first, but not everyone did. One mom even offered her own willingness to go out—

despite having a sick child at home—as a role model for me to emulate; if I didn't, it meant that I didn't care for her, not that I was being
a good parent.

Most times, I would silently question why I was going out at
all. The energy it took to arrange for the sitter, see to the boys'
needs, and get dressed up and psyched up was often too much, especially when I spent the entire evening yawning, missing the boys,
or worrying about the money I was spending. The underlying
problem was that I was oversensitive about being a single parent.
While married, I had maintained a deliberate distance between public life and private life, but as a single parent, much of my private life
had gone public.

Although I did not post homilies on the refrigerator, I did keep
some in mind—especially those that gave me incentive to endure
the hard times. When reason failed to explain my broken marriage,
for example, I recalled a Willie Nelson line from the film *Barbarosa:*
"What cannot be changed must be endured." A Japanese haiku—
"Even with devils, we prefer the ones we're used to"—also proved
apt. As did a cliche reeled off by my grandmother: "Play the cards
you're dealt." When I felt victimized and angered by my ex-wife's
freedom and lack of responsibility, I remembered a line from Maya
Deren's book on Haitian voodoo, *Divine Horseman:* "Great gods
won't mount little horses." Or the ditty my boys used to say when
they decapitated dandelions: "Mommy had a baby and her head
popped off." Or the old saying: "What goes around comes around."

When I felt drained to a stupor, the image of my mother would
emerge as a role model. She had raised seven children, so who was I
to squawk at raising three? Setting aside my male pride, I welcomed
this nurturing role model. In the process I forgave my father for his
absenteeism, emotional distance, and inability to help me. And having done that, I forgave myself for similar forms of male patterning.

Fathers have acquired a long history of learned helplessness.
They are still at the mercy of cultural indoctrination, religious
dogma, and outmoded educational beliefs. Why can't high schools
encourage boys to take home economics instead of shop or mechan-
ical drawing? Even Hollywood perpetuates false images. The movie
Kramer vs. Kramer was a fairy tale for fools, full of lies and over-
simplifications. And after seeing *Three Men and a Baby,* my boys
wondered if the movie industry would be ready for *One Man and
Three Babies.*

Numerous men have confided in me, "I would leave my marriage," they said, "but I wouldn't know how to cook or do things for myself." Or "I would leave my marriage, but she would move and then I'd lose sight of the kids." Or, "I would leave my marriage, but I wouldn't know how to handle the kids on my own." These confessions exude tragedy. Most men are willing to accept their ineptitude, willing to believe in the primacy of the mother, and willing to keep her as a buffer between themselves and their children. While it is true that men can't biologically birth children, they can psychologically own these births.

Put simply, I discovered that children need parents, not genders. To construe the single father as a symbolic or mythical figure of any sort is to severely distort the reality of the work involved. I also discovered that the "single" part does not exist. As a parent of growing children, whether you are separated or divorced or widowed, you and your children come as a package. Over the course of ten years, I finally learned to dissolve "single father" into "single parent" and "single parent" into "parent."

PARENTHOOD

Ian is now thirteen, David is eleven, and Daniel is nine and I am two months shy of having three children in double digits. The boys know how to cook, do laundry, and shop for groceries. Ian now wants more privacy than before and less affection. David is in a collector phase, with a strong passion for baseball cards. Daniel likes to charm and manipulate me into letting him stay overnight with friends, or into buying him treats, or upping his allowance.

Although the mechanics of parenting have become easier, the psychological aspects have become more challenging. For one thing, I can no longer keep ahead of my sons. I realize, fait accompli, that they are watching too much TV, not eating enough vegetables, and stalling on their homework to delay bedtime. While we have had two "birds and bees" talks, I know that I am also their foil—the authority figure against which they must rebel. I reproach myself for not taking enough pictures, for hurrying bedtimes, and for not being able to afford better vacations. I do not take my son to the library enough, I have not insisted on long-term violin lessons and I forget sign-ups for Little League. I yell too much and forget to light candles for the supper table. Sometimes I can feel our apartment shrinking as they grow and take up more space. My life, like that of any parent of preteens and teens, revolves around trying to keep up with it all.

Fortunately, I feel no constraints about touching my children or being there emotionally for them. I lay-on hands whenever I can—hugging them when they let me, roughhousing with them when they do not, and giving them foot massages at bedtime when their guard is down. I listen to them and encourage everything from talking about their day to singing, acting out, playing cards, and working at my typewriter or computer. I shift tactics and change rules when old strategies wear thin. I apologize and ask their forgiveness when I screw up. What I do not do is send them to their rooms, insist that they finish dinner, get involved in their bickering about who started a given fight, or let them pit me against their mother.

I parent simply to parent. I encourage their independence, insist on respect in their relationships, and try to minimize their stress and maximize their sense of humor. Imposing punitive or guilt-provoking measures to prevent undesirable behaviors is not my style. Instead, I make workable contracts with my boys: in exchange for their promise to avoid drugs, for example, they can wear their hair however they please and put up whatever rock posters they wish on their walls. Nor do I censor what I do not like. Instead I might ask Ian to translate Easy E's rap music into language I can understand, or I might ask Daniel to sing a heavy metal song for me.

Now that my children are becoming teenagers, I am beginning to realize that parenting is a privilege—a very temporary one, at that. My sons owe me nothing. The gratification I get from parenting comes with no deferred debts. A librarian friend once put it this way: "Children are like books on loan. We can lose them, we can be distracted from reading them during the time allotted, we can retain them beyond their due-dates and pay the penalty, or we can read and enjoy them while they are with us. What we cannot do is keep them." The consolation is that we can always keep the joy, if not the books themselves.

CHAPTER TWENTY-EIGHT

Perry Garfinkel

Grandfathers: Bridge to the Outside World

Fathers—absent or present—are not enough. Nor should they be. Throughout their lives men pick up valuable pointers from other men about the basics of the masculine connection, and how men act with each other. A boy needs and gets messages from elsewhere about the mysteries of masculinity; and while each new man in his life may add new depth and breadth to his understanding of himself in relation to other men, he also begins to recognize familiar lessons learned at his father's feet. These are lessons about power and control, and male hierarchy, and closeness and distance between men.

As a boy begins to look around in his life for other male role models, he finds two men—his grandfather and his mentor—who contribute in significant ways to his development. In his grandfather, and later his mentor, he finds two men whose partial appeal is that they are devoid of the emotional entanglement and competitiveness that arises with his father—at least at first.

If we have learned anything, it is that the source of male power and empowerment comes down to us from the father. The man above him—the father's father—must, we can only assume, have manifold power. We are pulled to grandfathers as a connection to our male lineage, and as a key to understanding our fathers and ourselves. They are drawn to grandsons as perhaps their final opportunity to assure the continuation of their names or at least their wisdom. In grandfathers we see our past. In grandsons we see our future. The link between the two was explained in a gripping fashion in a dream told to me by a thirty-two-year-old Boston attorney:

> In the dream my grandfather had just died. We were at the funeral, except my grandfather was still alive: I guess it was that state before the soul is supposed to leave the body. Anyway, he was dressed in a white tuxedo sitting in a white wheelchair, surrounded by white walls and clouds. My father was pushing the wheelchair and I was walking next to it at my grandfather's arm; we were dressed in white tuxedoes too. My grandfather directed my father to a door and into a room that looked like the basement of my grandfather's house. My father used to haul winter storm windows up from there for my grandfather when Grandpa got too old to do it himself. He told my father to start bringing the windows upstairs. Then my grandfather turned to me—and I'm not sure here whether he actually said it or told me with his eyes—but the message was clearly, "You're the one." It was a strong image and a strong message. I was the inheritor of the family chalice, the family name; he was passing the family reputation down to me. I felt my father was bypassed.

Memories of grandfathers frequently came up in interviews as the soft spot in their man-to-man relationships. This, I realized, was quite possibly one of the very few men in a man's world with whom you were practically guaranteed to be free of power struggles, competitiveness, and ego-clash. Why? The difference in generations accounts for a relative lack of assumptions and expectations of what constitutes success in the world—two factors that engender conflict between father and son. Lower expectations produce higher satisfaction; they allow for emotional interchange but with a lot less static.

Also contributing to the relative emotional neutrality of the grandson-grandfather bond is the old man's power position in the world at large at a time when the boy is growing up and watching him intently. While the boy's father struggles to define and maintain his power/position at work, the grandfather may well be into the power years of his life—those fifties and sixties in which he is part of the command generation—in which he has clearly established his domain. But apart from his position in the outside world, his unquestioned role as the elder male in the family hierarchy may be enough to assure his superior position, both to himself and his grandson, rendering competition out of the question.

On the other hand, when the grandfather is "past his prime," retired, physically weak, and viewed by the rest of the family as a dependent figure, the boy may feel no threat of being overpowered and may be, therefore, much freer to open his heart, fears, and hopes to his grandfather.

So though the boy may be drawn to the grandfather's power, it is exactly the lack of competition for power that makes this such a rewarding conflict-free relationship. For both people it is distance that affords closeness.

This distance/closeness theme was reinforced in the two most commonly recalled images that surfaced when I asked men to tell me about their grandfathers. In both, the grandfather appears as a less-than-real, remote figure.

One view came in romantic sepia tones and diffused lighting, in an oval cameo, blurry at the edges. Here is the man with the largest, most inviting lap in the world, with all the time in the world. A warm man full of deep laughs, deep personal contentment, and always those deep sparkling eyes gazing adoringly at us. Clearly out of focus, it was the vision of a man so loved, so idolized, that I suspect these young boys never really got to know the man in a clear objective light. He remained a distant and distorted image—his own kind of stranger.

The other picture of the grandfather was quite different but no less distant. In cold, dark lighting we now see a dour grumpy man with a long gray beard, speaking perhaps in a foreign language—a man who smelled funny, and never seemed to be paying full attention to us. He was the tyrannical patriarch whom everyone feared. When this man turned his attention to us—for however briefly—a shiver went up our spines. He too was a stranger.

Here again—as we learned from our fathers—we find built-in distance and separateness in one of our closest male-male relationships. With all its richness and warmth, the grandfather-grandson relationship brands us with that message. Nonetheless, a deep longing for closeness that all humans share draws men to each other, urges them to break down those barriers.

Closeness to one's grandfather also holds out the hope of closeness to one's father—though, ironically, sometimes the man who may attempt to block that hoped-for connection is the father himself. A father's attempt to thwart his son's knowledge of the grandfather may reflect the father's own unresolved anger, pain and frustration with his father. Boys watching their fathers for clues as to

FATHERS, SONS, AND DAUGHTERS

how to relate both to father and all men pay careful attention to the interaction of grandfather and father. What they may find is a mirror of what they're encountering themselves.

Feeling ostracized from the interaction of father and grandfather only adds more confusion and a sense of inferiority—a feeling of being the outsider—in the shadow of "grown-up men." But, a boy craves to understand himself through understanding his own history—and in most cases that understanding comes through the lineage of men in his family—so he pushes through father to reach grandfather. Even when the grandfather has been long gone when the boy arrives, his craving is so strong he will find out about the man—if not from his own father, then from other relatives (usually the women).

There are some men whose grandfathers made more than brief appearances, or came in dreams or retold stories. In the last century and early in this one, men left their families for months or years for jobs that would make them enough money to send for the rest of the family or to retire early back to their homeland. The education of the man's young son, left at home with his mother, fell to the grandfather. I was told of such a relationship by a sixty-three-year-old Greek restaurateur living in New York City. I asked him, "What was the most important thing your father gave you?" "My grandfather," he answered. He explained:

> I didn't spend much time with my father because people at that time, in that area of the world [Greece], migrated or went to sea, or wherever there was work. Sometimes I wouldn't see him for a few years. It was kind of strange. Since my mother was rather young and busy raising the family, it was my grandfather who really brought me up. He had the time, he had the interest and he knew so much. I was in awe of him, held him in the highest regard. I remember how people from different villages would come to talk to him, seeking advice. My grandfather would take me for walks and inject me with his philosophy of life. He talked about religion and war and Greek history. I admired him so much.

When I asked this man what he learned from his grandfather, he emphasized three points. The first was discipline. The second was what he called "worldly wisdom—he gave me a sense of the scope of the world, and what I had to know to be in it." And the third was the importance of lineage: "Our family structure is based on patriarchy. Everything is spelled out quite precisely. I understood that anything my grandfather told me came from the same source as my father."

Another kind of relationship between grandfather and grandson emerged through the interviews—a type of bridging relationship that helps the son who is revolting against his father nonetheless maintain contact with the men in his family. The young man, usually in his early or mid-twenties, is looking for a friend and approaches his grandfather for solace, camaraderie, conversation, and intimacy, and as a means of staying in touch with his own lineage. The grandfather, somewhat more dependent, himself lonely with his children preoccupied making a living and his own peers slowly dying off, appreciates an "ear." A thirty-six-year-old Los Angeles school administrator, Craig, described such a relationship:

> My grandfather's eighty-seven years old. I wasn't that close to him when I was a kid. He was your basic immigrant who killed himself working. He started with nothing and built up a pretty successful business. I really have a great deal of respect for him for that. Our closeness started about six or seven years ago, just after my grandmother died. I used to walk him to the dentist and he and I would walk and talk. It was beautiful. He talked about his childhood. He was so generous with his feelings, in a way that I couldn't be. And I was so responsive to that. I started to feel so open to him. We became very close, a deep friendship—without any regard for the older-younger thing or the fact that he was supposed to be my superior. He never moralized like my father. I couldn't share with him many of my contemporary experiences but we maintained a good level on lots of things and personal issues. I just spoke with him the other day on the phone for forty-five minutes. It was heaven. I feel very lucky to have contacted him again.

"He never moralized like my father." Here is a key to the grandfather's role in a young boy's life—he can reminisce with, love, and enjoy the boy without feeling, as the father does, the need to create a fledgling man who reflects well on himself as masculine standard bearer. Through the old man the boy tastes the freedom to relate to a grown man on his own terms while still remaining anchored safely to the family.

Fifty Males
Sitting Together

After a long walk in the woods clear cut for lumber,
lit up by a few young pines,
I turn home,
drawn to water. A coffinlike band
softens half the lake, draws the shadow
down from westward hills.
It is a massive
masculine shadow,
fifty males sitting together
in hall or crowded room,
lifting something indistinct
up into the resonating night.

Sunlight kindles the water still free of shadow,
kindles it till it glows with the high
pink of wounds.
Reeds stand about in groups
unevenly as if they might
finally ascend
to the sky all together.
Reeds protect
the band near shore.
Each reed has its own thin
thread of darkness inside;
it is relaxed and rooted in the black
mud and snail shells under the sand.

The woman stays in the kitchen, and does not want
to waste fuel by lighting a lamp,
as she waits
for the drunk husband to come home.
Then she serves him
food in silence.
What does the son do?
He turns away,
loses courage,

goes outdoors to feed with wild
things, lives among dens
and huts, eats distance and silence;
he grows long wings, enters the spiral, ascends.

How far he is from working men when he is forty!
From all men! The males singing
chant far out
in the water grounded in downward shadow.
He cannot go there because
he has not grieved
as humans grieve. If someone's
head was cut
off, whose was it?
The father's? or the mother's? Or his?
The dark comes down slowly, the way
snow falls, or herds pass a cave mouth.
I look up at the other shore; it is night.

ROBERT BLY

V

Renewing
the Bond:
Healing
Within and
Without

When one has not had a good father,
one must create one.

FRIEDRICH NIETZSCHE

Very little is needed to make a happy life.
It is all within yourself, in your way of
thinking.

MARCUS AURELIUS

Forgiveness is . . . the remembrance of
wrong transformed with a wider context.

JAMES HILLMAN

And when you make the inner
as the outer, the outer as the inner,
and the upper as the lower,
and when you make male and female
into one, so the male shall not be
male and the female shall not
be female, then shall you enter
paradise.

THE GOSPEL OF THOMAS

Introduction

Fathers seem to evoke a certain ambivalence. We love them, we hate them, we want them, we reject them. We desperately yearn to find some common ground of connection with them. The father-child relationship can be difficult because fathers were a part of our lives when we were the most vulnerable. And, inevitably, they made mistakes. They were invariably too hard or too soft, too distant or too overpowering.

We may have grown from wanting to be like them, from wanting nothing to do with them, to accepting them as both like us and different from us. That's considerable mileage for a relationship to cover without a breakdown. And indeed, for some of us, a breaking down may be what is required to renew the bond based on accepting our differences and honoring our shared history.

As a leader of support groups, I meet people for whom father issues have become critical to their well-being. They suffer from feelings of rage, loss, and betrayal about their own fathers and may feel a lowered sense of self-esteem and emotional availability as a result. Their unexpressed grief and anger form a wall of blame between them and their fathers, through which love cannot pass.

In addition, many feel a sense of shame and self-criticism about how they themselves parent the next generation of children. Unable to understand and accept the limitations of their fathers, they cannot accept their own.

With insight into a father's wounds and empathy for his life's journey, we begin to forgive him his shortcomings—and to see ourselves in a different light. Once the hurdle of blame has been crossed, we may feel, especially at midlife, an increasing interest in reconnecting with our fathers. A passionate desire to reach out toward our fathers seems to be a prerequisite for healing the father wound. With reconciliation, we feel a new sense of aliveness and his presence permeates our lives.

In this way we discover the inner father who has been living in our souls all along. The inner father, whom we internalize as young children, can represent mastery and balance, or tyranny and chaos. He can be described as one voice among a cast of inner characters, or subpersonalities, which make up our inner world. He may be a kind, encouraging voice, or a harsh, domineering one. The critic, the judge, the "top dog," for instance, are often associated with the difficult inner father.

Healing the father wound at some time involves identifying and building a relationship with this inner figure. As Linda Schierse Leonard writes in *The Wounded Woman,* "Ultimately, redeeming the father entails reshaping the masculine within, fathering that side of oneself." A healthy inner father is like a reservoir that makes us feel full, generous, and calm. A healthy inner father is an essential component for developing empathy for the positive aspects of our actual fathers as well.

When it is time to reconcile with our real fathers, we need to pay attention to the opportunities in the relationship. For example, when a father is nearing death, something profound happens with a son or daughter. Both parent and child realize that there may be no more chance to speak the unspeakable. So an impending death can be an incentive to speak from the heart with our fathers or our children.

A Vietnam veteran I interviewed put it this way: "I was estranged from my father before the war. When I became aware that I might not come back, I got his address and initiated an intimate correspondence. When I was discharged, I went to visit him. He died two months later. It was as if he had waited for me to come home."

Robert Bly has helped thousands of men to fully feel their grief from insufficient fathering. At the heart of our inability to mourn lies a denial of our losses. Our grief helps us to clear the way for more generous feelings toward our fathers.

Forgiveness is born in a spirit of generosity. When our cup is full enough, we are able to give something away. At the same time, we receive so much when we offer the gift of giving. There is a circularity to forgiveness.

Forgiving our fathers allows us to stop closing our hearts to them. Ultimately, healing is coming home to feeling fullness and preciousness in our hearts. Giving our offspring what we didn't receive is a wonderful way to heal our own wounds. Caring about and being present with ourselves and our children helps to fill the holes in us that were created by abuse or absent fathers. Fathering a child reconnects us with the pain of our own childhood deprivation, but at the same time allows us another chance to give to someone we love what was unavailable for us.

As my father approaches his final days, I find it important to look at how I hold him in my thoughts and how I regard his limitations and his gifts. Am I open to the transformational energy that surrounds death? Can I ease this transition for him? I am about to fly across the country for what may be my last visit with my father. Rather than the traditional role of the dutiful son role paying homage, I want to honor him by honoring myself, to say what I need to say, to ask what I want to know. I sense that my father deeply fears death, and I intend to ask him about that. I also want to know how it was for him when his father was dying.

Being a very traditional gentleman, my father probably wants to be buried in his blue suit, shoes shined. I'll ask him what he wants. I also want to give him something to be buried with, although it is not yet clear what this gift is—perhaps one of the shells given to me by his mother, who collected them in Key West about the time of his birth.

While death may separate us from bonding with our actual fathers, death is not the final reconciliation with the man who blocked or guided our way. In the absence of dialogue with the living person, we are free to develop further dialogue with the inner images and voices of our fathers.

OVERVIEW

Chapter 29 consists of an inspiring selection from Gabrielle Roth's book *Maps to Ecstasy: Teachings of an Urban Shaman.* She offers some practical exercises, meditations, and insights that facilitate healing the father wound. Roth discusses the father as a sacred teacher whose role is defined by authority, relationship, friendship, protection, loyalty, and fairness.

In an original essay, psychotherapist Alan Javurek deals with four themes of midlife reconciliation with the father: awakening the desire for reconciliation, going home, confronting the creative/destructive father, and entering into dialogue with him. This is a process whereby the son or daughter sees both the positive and negative aspects of the father, and gives up the idealized and longed-for image of the father.

In Chapter 31, social researcher Joseph Pleck reminisces about losing his father; the feelings of loss bring him to understand in greater depth the pain and struggle his father lived with. Pleck reminds us that we need to strike a balance between healing our fathers' wounds and knowing when we cannot. This is an example of the kind of inner work toward reconciliation that other writers call for.

Jungian analyst Linda Schierse Leonard, in an excerpt from *The Wounded Woman,* describes how by rejecting her alcoholic father, she had in actuality refused to claim her own power. Through writing, dreams, and Jungian analysis, Leonard reveals how she was able to see the hidden value her father had to offer and thereby honor her own inner worth.

In Chapter 33, Samuel Osherson, a Harvard research psychologist and psychotherapist, believes nurturing authority, potent mystery, humor, and commitments are required to heal the father relationship. He suggests that the healing process might include: understanding a father's history and connecting the father's plight to our own; recognizing a father's love and shares history; acknowledging our physical yearnings for a father; accepting our existential aloneness; exploring the masculine nurturer and caretaker within; and becoming a parent. His piece was excerpted from his book *Finding Our Fathers.*

Laughter can be the best medicine to heal the soul. Bill Cosby's humorous essay "Look Homeward, Sponger" eases some of the heaviness around the father–child relationship. In this final chapter, excerpted from his bestseller *Fatherhood,* Cosby shares strategies to keep children from moving back into the house after they have "ventured forth."

We are all students of the multifaceted phenomenon called healing. Pain and resistance surrounding our fathers and ourselves challenge us to explore the healing process. Understanding our psychological defenses is one step toward healing. But at the same point we will probably need a willingness to surrender to a largely un-knowable force, our experience of spirit.

At some deep level we know that being with our feelings is the cornerstone of an authentic life. And we know that our relationship with our inner and outer fathers is a key to being fully empowered as a man or a woman. Yes, we may have been victimized, but to re-main so is a form of unnecessary suffering. Men and women who have been able to reconcile themselves with their fathers have crossed an often unacknowledged but significant rite of passage.

Gabrielle Roth

Befriending Your Father

Whether you are wounded or blessed (or most likely some of both) in the first cycle of life, you then move into childhood and need to meet your father as your sacred teacher. He is mother turned inside out, the authority to her permission, the line through her circle, the worldly wise "no" to her cosmic "yes." Through your mother your self-image grows; through your father it becomes defined. In/out, wait for it/go for it, surrender/control, allow/demand, feminine/masculine. Between mother and father you learn to dance the tango of life.

Your mother taught you how to be in your body. Your father teaches you how to express your heart as he initiates you into the world of relationships with others. He teaches the art of how best to relate to another person, because he is the first person outside of yourself that you have to relate to, that is, build a relationship with.

You came out of your mother's body; that relationship is real and immediate. It is a psychic "given." You and your mother are inescapably one. Father is outside of you. He is your first friend and your task (and his teaching) is to connect to him. In the creation of this relationship, you build the foundation for all your future one-to-one relationships; you learn to relate to the world of people through your father. In your later life, you relate to people as your father related to you and you to him. It is from father that we either do or do not receive the ability to instinctively know the answer to the question, "What does this other person truly need from me?" It is from father that we first learn the art of give and take, of giving and receiving, the high commerce of friendship. It is the father's role to pass on the paternal instinct, the instinctive ability to relate appropriately to others, teaching loyalty, companionship, sharing and fairness.

Your father teaches you to draw the line, to feel your own sense of authority, to balance your self-nurturing feeling of boundless permission. "The Child is father of the Man," as Wordsworth puts it. In this whole process you learn to become, to a greater or lesser degree, your own father, your own friend.

Your relationship to your father determines whether you can be yourself and express your heart, or whether you must achieve, perform, charm, seduce, compete, please, demand, negate or destroy to feel recognized. These patterns are created early. In all our one-to-one relationships we tend to do whatever we had to do to get daddy's attention and approval when we were a child. As Robert Frost put it, "You don't have to deserve your mother's love. You have to deserve your father's. He is more particular."[1]

All friends and fathers are in disguise. If your father was there for you, giving you what you need in the moment, responding from his heart to your heart, cheering you on and reining you in, affirming and consoling, cautioning and encouraging, then the world wears a welcome face and you'll know how to be a friend. If he was present for you, you will instinctively know how to be present for others. I remember watching my father taking care of his dying brother. My uncle had a brain tumor, and every day a new piece of his body didn't work. He got to the point where only his face moved, and there was my dad telling him stories, massaging his feet, lighting his damn cigarettes, giving him what he needed. I realized that this was the quality of attention that I had become accustomed to.

To whatever degree your father didn't or doesn't know how to relate to you, he can't know how to relate to others. The distant, absent father is distant and absent in other relationships as well. He tends to relate on the surface and perform, hide his feelings, think and plan, judge and compare. He must analyze his relationships because they're not instinctive to him. He has to decide how and what to feel, making lists of people's good and bad qualities so that he can determine whether to be in relationship to them. He doesn't dare to be spontaneous, because he can't trust himself to respond appropriately. So he develops preplanned and market-tested ways of being with others. Fathers who are wounded are suffering. And they create children who are wounded.

People with a limited paternal instinct develop coping patterns. They become performers, flatterers, deliberators. They hide behind their work or their kids. They worry a lot about titles, credentials, status, wealth, prestige, about who's in and who's out, because they don't trust themselves to be able to respond to another person and be responded to just for who each is. They use money to win control, love, influence. They adopt some pose, some strategy that allows them to get by without really entering into relationships and commitments heart and soul, here and now. I know a kid whose father sent him elaborate presents on his birthday but never showed up himself. When he grew up he gave his dad all kinds of presents—a condominium in Florida, a baby grand piano, a trip to Paris—but he never showed up either. The person without an instinct for relating is, in any encounter with another person or in a social or collaborative situation, ill at ease, in pain, in deceit, and quietly desperate. It's no wonder they act so inappropriately so often.

Children with father wounds are everywhere—surely many of us. They're easy to spot. Without the heart in their day-to-day living, without the color of feelings, life is drab. They can go to all the right parties in all the right clothes and still never have a good time. Pervading their lives is a lack of élan, a theme of melancholy—regret, despair even—that underlies their apparently successful life stories. The spark is missing.

Since many more children now grow up without fathers or with part-time fathers only, whether because of divorce or because many men devote so much of their time to work and other activities rather than to fathering, the number of adult children of absentee fathers is astronomical and growing higher daily. Of course, single mothers and full-time mothers, as well as other parental figures, can and do supply some of the fathering role, and some women have strong paternal instincts to pass on. As we know, some fathers have strong maternal instincts and offer what mothers deficient in nurturing instincts can't offer. But prior to all our social arrangements and penchant for creating structures to fit our worldly goals, there is an elemental and natural power to men playing the paternal role and women playing the maternal role.

The ideal is to have a biological mother who teaches us how to be in a body and trust ourselves, and a biological father who teaches us how to express our hearts. Just having parents doesn't guarantee success. Natural parents can fail their natural children—and adoptive, single, or foster parents can raise their children with instincts intact, as can parents who themselves have been wounded but through awareness and devotion have made the quantum leap into conscious parenting. My dad was one of these.

I've worked a lot with people with father wounds. A physician studied with me who related to everyone as doctor and patient. It was as if he couldn't take off his white coat even for his lovers. He's not alone. Think of the talk show host who can't talk to someone unless there's a microphone between them. Actors who never seem to leave the stage. Executives who run their families like they run their business. Trial lawyers who map out strategies for all their relationships as if they were going to trial. Awareness of this "act" is the beginning of healing this wound.

It seems almost everyone grew up without enough fathering. If mothering has been insufficiently valued in our society, what about fathering? Regarded as a minor sideline, the father's job has been reduced to treasurer and warden. A woman in one of my workshops wrote this poem that captures the experience of so many children:

Daddy lives
behind a newspaper, smoking cigarettes
always reading,
no voice,
no words,
no touch;
just there, behind
the paper wall.

Happily, fathering seems to be making a comeback, but there remain the countless walking wounded who grew up without adequate paternal care by fathers who themselves lacked strong relational instincts.

This father wound, like the mother wound, has reached epidemic proportions. It is everywhere breeding loneliness, distrust, and deceit. We lie to each other about what we think, feel and do, and don't remember how to tell the truth. And we desperately need to hear and speak the truth. We readily see right through others' efforts to hide their pain, shame, disregard. We forget that they also see right through us. They see the fear, anger, sorrow—the real energy we struggle to mask. We pretend to care about each other but end up sharing the worst of ourselves, the stuff that doesn't work. We're as predictable as daily headlines, as spirited as Muzak.

Father wounds take a great toll on our intimate relationships. If we don't know how to talk to each other or to be together without talking, if we don't know how to give and receive, how can we make love? How can we move one another? How can we be touching? How can we be real? We all expect to have wonderful intimate relationships, but how can we be real lovers if we don't know how to be true friends?

Can you remember your last real heart-to-heart conversation, where you really hooked into each other, following every move, every gesture, every wave of emotion, riding the waves together, connected? When did you last partake of such holy communion?

Communion heals the father wound. Communion with friends, lovers, parents, strangers, even enemies. But mostly with friends. Through hard trial and error and working with thousands of people, I've discovered that the heart needs to open up as fully as possible. It is a waste of time to pretend that we can't be hurt. If we're going to be fully alive, we have to be ready to get hurt and even to hurt others. Otherwise, we're dead. Or immobilized in protective armor.

In vulnerability one practices the art of friendship, the art of the heart. It is an essential spiritual practice.

If you don't do it instinctively, you must do it consciously. Stop and focus on your relationships and let them each teach you what you need to know. The more you give to them, the more you will get back. The more attention you pay, the more natural relating will feel, until the impulse to take special care of your relationships becomes internalized and instinctive.

It's interesting to make a list of your friends, then sit and contemplate what each has to teach you. Meditate on each name and ask yourself, "what do I really need from him or her?" Keep asking until answers come.

Who nourishes you? How? Why? Who drains you? How? Why? Who do you avoid? How? Why? Who do you reach out to? How? Why?

Bring your relationships into the moment, including the one with your father. Erase the past, stay out of the future with all its expectations. Let yourself be surprised. Practice "loving the one you're with." Everyone you know is dying for some real attention, someone who really hears what they are saying, sees their visions, cheers them on into the heights and depths of being real.

We need relationships that are alive, vital, changing, moving—relationships that move through all the rhythms. Sometimes they flow, sometimes they pulse, sometimes they erupt, sometimes they lilt along, and sometimes they're very still. It is particularly important to have a moving relationship with one's father, as this relationship is the key to all other friendships.

Here are some exercises to help you discover and befriend your father. With courage and creative reflection often we can forge a very special bond of friendship, regardless of time or distance. Or we can at least learn concretely the truth of our childhood and determine what aspects of fathering we need in order to complete our childhood cycle.

Exercise One. An easy way to begin learning about our childhood cycle is with the mirror opposite of the father/child relationship you may have missed out on. Make friends with a child five, six, or seven. Children at this age are usually spontaneous, warm, enthusiastic, and they don't put up with bullshit. They live here and now. They will be emotionally direct, demand flexibility and patience, and reward your attention with a joy in being that can't be measured.

Exercise Two. Write down your memories of your father before you were five, and what you've been told about him. What was he like? Where was he? Recall his varied guises, smells, habits, the way he talked, sang, cried (or didn't).

Exercise Three. Sit back, relax, and feel yourself moving backwards in time like a movie in reverse. Stop when you get to five years old. Imagine your five-year-old self in a familiar room with your father. How do you feel? Do you make contact? What kind? Are you touching, talking, laughing, cowering, uncomfortable, insecure? Fast forward to about ten years old and see yourself in the same room: how do you relate to your father; how does he relate to you?

Exercise Four. Write a dialogue between your father and yourself at the age of ten. If you can't that will tell you something.

Exercise Five. Who is he? Capture him in an image, a metaphor, a quintessential photo, a characteristic statement, a telling story.

Exercise Six. In your journal, visualize your relationship to your father in an "energy drawing" that clearly conveys the undercurrent as well as the surface waves that flow between you and your father.

Exercise Seven. Write a capsule account of your father's life story, tracing the movement of his life from infancy through childhood and adolescence to adulthood, middle age, and final years. Did he or is he likely to die satisfied, fulfilled, serene?

Exercise Eight. How would your mother tell his story? How would he?

Exercise Nine. How would you speak to your father if you were his friend, not his child? What would you say as his best friend? Somebody has to break the wall of silence: pick up the phone; get on the plane; talk real things out heart to heart. He's probably as lonely as you are. Are you afraid of your father? Afraid for him? Are you angry with him? How does he bring you joy? What's the most compassionate thing you could do for him? Let it all out now. The healing will be wonderful for you both.

Exercise Ten. Since your father was your first friend, you probably treat your friends the way he treated you. Write portraits of three different friends, and your relationship to each. Read them over and over, looking for repetitive patterns, positive as well as negative. Do you run each relationship or do you get pushed around? Do you play hard to get? Are you flirtatious, overbearing, timid? How do you relate? Do you relate at all, or do you perform, plan, seduce, etc.?

Maybe it's easy for you to move heart to heart and easy for you to know what another needs; maybe you come from your heart most of the time. If so, you have your father to thank. If not, forgive him: this is also his pain. You do have something in common.

Life is raw material that cries out to be transformed into art—survival art rooted in truth, carved into poems, into songs, into albums, into communications straight from the heart. You can turn your relationship to your father into art. Think about it, write about it, embrace your childhood, your heart.

Meditating on your father can also be rewarding: Sit back, take a deep breath, settle into a comfortable position.

Father meditation: Imagine your father sitting opposite you: how does he hold himself, how does he look, what is the basic impression he makes on you—weariness, anger, impatience, ebullience, calm?

Think of three things you love about him, three qualities you find endearing. Think of three things that put you off, alienate you. Reflect on how all these qualities are in you as well, on how much alike you are, how intimately connected.

Look your dad in the eye. Let your feelings about him surface, and imagine saying them to him. Empty your heart of all things you might have choked back for years, telling him everything you feel until there's nothing left. Imagine what he would say in response and let him say his piece. Then breathe calmly into the empty space that is left.

Imagine, too, making physical contact with your father, touching him, holding his hand, hugging him, rocking him. Let the blocked affection for him flow and receive in return.

Then let him go back to his place. Look him in the eye again and search your heart for the courage to thank and forgive him, to forgive and thank yourself. Forgive him for his weakness and his failings; thank him for making you who you are and being there for you when he was.

When I have meditated on my dad, I've appreciated his generosity, his loyalty, his serenity. I've acknowledged his stubborn pride, his prejudices, his timidity—all part of me. I've swooped him up in my arms, held him close and rocked him like a baby, wiped the tears from his face and pressed his ear to my heart.

Everyone has a father. Some active and reporting for duty, some missing in action. Some out of step with the beat of their own hearts. Some too busy to relate to the most important charges in their lives. If we haven't found our father outside, we have to find him within, and to reconnect with our father if and when we can. It's a sacred task, a vital undertaking.

As we heal ourselves, we release our parents in some beautiful way to heal themselves. I've seen this pattern repeat itself in many lives. It has inspired and given me hope. We can effect change by changing. And what a gift to be able to heal your parents just by healing yourself. We have the power to give them back the freedom to be who they really are—wounded, human, vulnerable, not giants in a fairy tale or society's police force. But real people—your people.

As we become our own parents, become whole, it lifts a psychic burden off our parents' shoulders; they no longer need to worry about what they did and didn't do for you, and are free to become themselves.

CHAPTER THIRTY

Alan Javurek

Midlife Reconciliation with the Father

Reconciliation with one's father is a significant process during any time of life; however, it is especially meaningful at mid-life, a time of tremendous psychological importance. Midlife reconciliation can facilitate entrance into what Jung called "the second half of life" and change not only the ways we see our father but also the way in which we relate to our inner and outer life. During the course of the father-child reconciliation there is an intensification of emotions needed to bring long-standing inner and outer conflicts to awareness. Resolving these conflicts releases outworn and stuck patterns of the past and opens the way for completing other developmental tasks related to middle age and beyond.

The impetus toward reconciliation with the father unfortunately often begins and ends without achieving much of its potential. The initial urges and desires that lead in the direction of making peace with father are often surpassed by a sense of hopelessness that many people feel about their relationship to dad. Most people who feel estranged or in conflict with their father give up their dreams of connection. This essay offers an alternative. I hope that the experiences described in the following pages will encourage men and women to move through their dark dreams and resistances and explore their inner longings for reconciliation.

I will draw upon anecdotes and examples from two sources: (1) interviews conducted for my doctoral dissertation, which focused on the process of reconciliation with father that men experience during their middle years; and (2) my work with men and women in psychotherapy and through workshops called Making Peace with Your Father, which I have conducted over the past six years.

THE CHALLENGES OF RECONCILIATION

Estrangement between fathers and sons is a cultural phenomenon as well as a personal tragedy. This rift is so common that psychologists have developed terms such as *father hunger* and the *wounded father* in an attempt to describe the psychological and emotional states created by children's experiences of growing into adulthood while living in an emotionally conflicted or deprived relationship with their fathers.[1]

After reviewing an anthology of 100 poems (nine-tenths of which were written since midcentury), author Stanley Kunitz wrote: "The theme of fathers and sons is haunting the imagination of a whole generation of poets." Kunitz suggests that the proliferation of this theme in our country suggests that it is an authentic cultural manifestation. The psychological and physical absence of fathers is, according to Samuel Osherson, one of the great underestimated tragedies of our times. A survey by Shere Hite in the late 1970s revealed that among the 7,239 men of all ages whom she interviewed, almost none reported closeness to their fathers.[2]

The situation for women, although different in some respects, is no less intense. Accounts of women's attachments and wounds in relation to their fathers in the works of psychologists and authors such as Linda Schierse Leonard, Ursula Owen, and Signe Hammer provide moving testimony to the pain of estrangement and the significance of a healed father-daughter relationship.[3]

The healing process, which I call the process of reconciliation with father, involves two challenges. First, there is an outer challenge in which we must come to terms with the conflicts and deprivations we have experienced with the external, physical father. Second, there is an inner challenge in which we must deal with the internalized images and oppressive emotional conflicts that we carry around inside ourselves. These inner images and feelings are related to the original traumas and deprivations with father and are frequently restimulated by situations that are similar in some way to the original experience. Uncovering these wounds and releasing old conflicts is the primary goal of the reconciliation process. This release has a profound influence on a person's abilities to assume appropriate and effective family and occupational roles.

Two additional points should be noted here. First, reconciliation does not end with a single event where both parties "live happily ever after." It is continuous. Although many people report dramatic moments where they experience a significant shift in their feeling and perceptions, the conflicts and struggles as well as potentials for growth never cease.

Secondly, I want to emphasize that successful inner resolution of these struggles does not require the cooperation, or even the physical presence, of the father. In fact, most of the people I have interviewed and worked with had fathers who were dead, unavailable, or who made little change if at all. However, the potential for integrative healing that I am describing here focuses on what is possible for the son or daughter to accomplish in relation to the challenges of his or her own midlife development. Focusing on how to get dad to change is usually the fastest route I know to bringing up a dark dream of hopelessness and despair. It is perhaps the most frequently cited reason (or excuse) for not following one's desires and urges to make peace with father.

THEMES OF MIDLIFE RECONCILIATION

Four themes recur in descriptions of midlife reconciliation experiences: (1) awakening of the desire for reconciliation; (2) returning home; (3) confronting the creative/destructive father; and (4) entering into a dialogue with the father. Although in some people's lives these may occur as sequential stages, they are not usually experienced in a linear, step-by-step fashion.

Awakening of the Desire for Reconciliation

There are many ways in which a person comes to realize that there is something amiss in his or her relationship with father and that it is time to do something about it. This awakening is sometimes described as a very subtle inner longing to reconnect with a father one has felt distanced from in some way. However, in midlife this desire may not emerge subtly. It may erupt dramatically in the form of spontaneous events or emotional outbursts that the son or daughter experiences and associates in some way with the father. These emotional events might occur as an aspect of a specific life crisis, such as divorce, illness, or death of a loved one, or they might be associated with an existential loss of meaning or purpose in life. Reports and studies of midlife development provide numerous illustrations of such disruptions. These crises are usually interpreted psychologically as signaling the occurrence of a necessary breaking down of certain outmoded inner psychological structures of the first half of life to make room for new values and attitudes that will carry one into middle life and beyond.[4]

Such midlife disturbances are often accompanied by a longing for, anger toward, or perhaps even a curiosity about father. The impulse to make contact with the father may be subtle or dramatic but is usually unmistakable. Somehow the message comes through, "It is time to deal with my issues with dad."

One man reported that at age forty, after twenty years of separation from his father, he had "a sudden urge to connect with the old man." Another forty-two-year-old man, when faced with a life-threatening existential crisis that brought him crashing down from the corporate heights, said that the first thing he felt he had to do was to return to his family home and see his father to "find out what was wrong with me." Neither could provide much rational explanation for why he felt these impulses, he only knew he had to do it.

If this sense of inner necessity is not acted on when first felt, the impulse usually comes back—sometimes months or years later. When one does follow these inner calls to focus on dad, some surprising things can happen. The story of the first man mentioned above provides an example. He said that he felt something inside him was telling him to "go home and deal with your father." His immediate reply to the voice was: "But I don't even know where he is, he left home when I was ten!" However, when he gave up his resistance he found that his reconnection was surprisingly easy. Although he had not seen his father for thirty years and did not know where his father lived, he did know the phone number of an uncle. He called the uncle and to his utter amazement, his father happened to be visiting the uncle after a long hiatus in their contact with each other. Within ten minutes of his decision to follow the directive, he had his father on the telephone and was making plans for a visit.

This is not to imply that every reconnection that comes from following an inner impulse for reconciliation will yield such quick and dramatic results. However, when I talk to people about this subject, I find that there are almost always unexpected turns in how the awakening process unfolds.

Going Home

During midlife there are three key issues related to the theme of returning home. Midlife confronts us with the challenge of resolving the polarities of death and rebirth; to begin letting go of the heroic attitudes and fantasies of limitless growth characteristic of youth, and to begin to recognize our own realistic limitations. It is a time when both men and women begin to reappraise their lives more seriously. We often begin to consider the possibility of actualizing some of the unlived potentials that the activities and roles played out in youth have inhibited.

As we awaken to the desire for reconciliation, we begin to consider what it might mean to actually face father and confront the issues that separate us. The theme of "going home" suggests the daughter or son's literal or metaphorical return to the father's home to learn more about him. New information helps us sort out who father is as an individual. The father becomes separated from our own mental versions of him that are largely a product of childhood memories and descriptions by others. This separating and sorting process allows a more up-to-date understanding of father to emerge. Once we see dad more accurately, we can experience our feelings and impressions about him as more real and concrete. We can then respond to conflicts as well as positive feelings and deal with them more consciously.

Some of the men and women with whom I've talked literally went to their family home and spent time with their fathers. Often the most rewarding times were when they just "shut up and listened," as one man put it. Questioning dad about his life and family history occasionally brought surprising results. Fathers who had previously been silent became talkative and seemed to appreciate telling stories about their lives. Although some fathers answered in short, sometimes brusque responses, even little pieces of information were "like gold."

In workshops I have led, people draw lifelines that trace the key events of their fathers' lives. In reviewing memories and letting your imagination enter into his life, you can get a new perspective. As one woman remarked, "It's like walking in his shoes and seeing that he was not so all-powerful. He was full of fear and frustration just like I am. In fact, it seems that I am still carrying his burdens."

People are often bewildered by how disturbed they feel when they start to see their father in new ways. Some attempt to explain their discomfort by thinking that they are just attached to their childhood fantasies or are reluctant to give up habitual ways of thinking about dad. Such explanations are only partially true. Another reason this new information is disturbing is that when we make our father real and acknowledge his material existence, we also become aware of his mortality. To acknowledge that dad was or is a real person brings us closer to our feelings about death and loss. If we have already lost him to death, it reminds us of our grief. If he is still living, it reminds us that he will die. If he who once seemed so powerful and indestructible can die, so can we. In midlife, whether we are ready for it or not, the figure of death lurks in the background and begins to make its presence felt.

Confronting the Creative/Destructive Father

One of the harsh realities that confront people during efforts toward reconciliation is the realization that the father who has created them also can destroy them. While some sons resist the notion that their identity and many of their ways of relating to the world and family life come directly or indirectly from dad, most discover just how much of dad they carry around inside themselves. Although daughters' core identities are more influenced by mother than father, they too are often alarmed at how deeply (or unconsciously) they have internalized a father's abusiveness, neglect, or criticism.

Fathers impact their children by their positive and negative presence as well as by their absence. Absent fathers leave a hole in the child's inner life that is usually filled with childhood demons and dragons as well as longings for a hero to save the day. In other words, children are devoured by their father's negative side. The abandonment, abusiveness, and emotional unresponsiveness they experience from father exists in them as destructive forces they must identify and deal with as adults. The challenge involved in dealing with the creative/destructive father is to release yourself from the father's unconscious and conscious hold. This allows you to enter into a new relationship enabling you to claim both the positive and negative aspects of the father.

One man first identified what he called "a legacy of emotional devastation and emptiness that was the plight of all the men in my family for generations." When he had recognized and understood how his father had been caught by this family legacy, he could then begin to see and feel how he himself had been caught in this same pattern. This awareness helped him accept who his father was (i.e., that dad was human and not an ogre) and begin to release himself from his own emotional devastation and emptiness.

Accepting the father's creative and destructive impact does not imply that the negative behavior is necessarily excused or forgotten. Many sons and daughters, especially in situations of overt physical or sexual abuse, feel a need to directly confront the behavior even if it happened in the distant past. Usually when adult sons or daughters tell the truth of their experience, they are going against strong family taboos about disclosing feelings and secret information. Such confrontations are extremely frightening and painful and can be emotionally, even physically, risky. Most people seek some form of therapeutic support and guidance through this ordeal. Although talking openly to one's father about abuse is not the only way, it is one way in which a daughter or son can begin to break free of the family system and of the unconscious hold the father has had on the child.[5]

Entering into Dialogue with the Father

Entering into dialogue with the father may involve two types of communication. First, there is an inner dialogue in which we observe and comment to ourselves about the many influences we have internalized from father. Secondly, there are the actual conversations that may take place between father and son or daughter.

For example, after a time of working on father issues in therapy or workshops, people often begin to recognize that their father is present in their ways of speaking or acting or thinking. They might say, "I can almost hear my critical father telling me I'm stupid!" Or they might sense the presence of a positive loving father, support-ing or encouraging them ahead. Awareness of this father presence allows them to actually personify it so that they can interact and re-spond to it rather than feel victimized by it. Through a conscious dialogue these internal representations become more tangible and can be transformed.

This type of internal exchange is quite different from the kind of talking to oneself or others that may occur in psychotic or other extreme states where the person doesn't know he's dealing with in-ner representations and may not feel in control of what is happen-ing. Although the inner dialogue may seem a bit unusual and un-comfortable at first, most people recognize that this is merely an extension of the kind of internal commentary we all have going on within us all the time.

One man I worked with found himself in a shouting match with his dead father on the golf course. "I finally told him he was wrong to have been so critical and hard on me all those years, and I yelled at him like I never could as a boy. I told him to get off my back." This man was neither crazy nor psychotic. He was quite aware of what he was doing—consciously talking back to an in-ternal critic that had been undermining his confidence for years. Through such inner dialogues, this man's work with his internal fa-ther resulted in a reduced fear of authority figures in general and a more relaxed attitude toward his work.

The second aspect of this theme of dialogue refers to actual contact between the son or daughter and the father. As pain is re-leased, men and women experience interactions with their fathers differently. Occasionally these interactions change because of changes in the father himself. Illness or retirement can bring an openness that dad did not show in earlier years. (Conversely, he may become harder to reach during these times.) Separation from mother through death or divorce can also change the family pattern, mak-ing dad more available since mother is not around to speak for him.

However, even when a father remains intransigent and con-tinues many of his old behaviors and attitudes, a dialogue may still ensue. Some people have found that the best way to converse with father is to set firm limits on abusive or offensive behavior, calling attention to it and refusing to pursue the conversation if it con-tinues. They can then spend time working together or walking.

"Just doing simple things together provided a wonderful way to be with him and feel him with me," one woman reported. "We would just walk, sometimes talking, sometimes just being silent. He was shocked and complained when I told him I wouldn't see him if he drank, but he agreed and I've actually enjoyed our time together."

Such direct communication can lead to a sense of companionability and mutual respect. In this kind of interaction, differences are not hidden and conflict is seen as a way of celebrating individuality, which brings the parties closer. A forty-five-year-old engineer reports: "We still disagree and fight a lot, but it's a different kind of fighting than before. I don't act like a rebellious adolescent and he doesn't treat me like I'm stupid and don't know anything. I kinda like it. I don't think we could stand it if it got too peaceful between us. He'd never say this (and I don't need him to anymore), but I think he actually respects and admires me."

These types of internal and external communications can be a tremendously powerful and supportive source of comfort after one's father has died. Death will intensify and deepen this dialogue. Those who are able to be with their father near the end of his life are sometimes profoundly moved. At this point if the major conflicts have been resolved and worked through even partially, there is a possibility that both parties may experience a closeness and vulnerability that cannot be duplicated under other circumstances. An excerpt from a letter written by a forty-year-old woman artist who had weathered some intense conflicts with her father describes some of her feelings during his last days. I'll quote it at length because it is a moving description of what many people have felt and many others hope to experience.

> I kept holding his hand, stroking his forehead, my eyes locked to his haggard face in a tender gaze. With all the frustration and pain we'd inflicted on each other through the years, I still adored this man. Sometimes when I squeezed his hand, he squeezed mine in response. He looked old for his 77 years. . . . Sadness and suffering aside, Pop's illness yielded a gift too precious for me to ignore or to waste. It gave me an opportunity to reach out to him while his defenses were down, when he was least likely to reject my overtures. For the past thirty years he's not been an easy person for me to get close to; I'd have been a fool not to take advantage of this.

THE POTENTIALS FOR MIDLIFE RECONCILIATION

Midlife reconciliation is more than a healing process. It is an ordeal and rite of passage through which we can potentially transform our relationship to our unconscious life, moving beyond parental and occupational roles and preparing for eldership and mentorship roles in later life.

As we have seen, conscious communication with father that may begin on an outer level also mirrors an inner relationship. The interchange between our conscious and unconscious life is an essential element of midlife individuation, as well as in later years when physical limitations and developmental urges continue to push us toward developing the inner, as opposed to the outer, life.

In the course of dealing with intense feelings of estrangement and conflict during midlife reconciliation, people often report that something deep and dramatic happens inside of them that makes them feel different and perhaps see things in a new way. If nurtured and consciously followed, this way of feeling and seeing can take us into a deeper experience of our own unconscious life. This experience is often characterized in psychological writings as a meeting with one's own inner wisdom figure.

This dialogue is portrayed in mythological stories where the heroine or hero meets the wise old woman or man after descending to the depths of Hades or the underworld. In this meeting, the wise seer offers some instructions about the hero's special life task that will help carry him or her into the next stage of life. This encounter is not a healing process per se, even though it may be part of a larger movement toward healing and wholeness. It is more like a teaching or transmission of special knowledge between the wise teacher or mentor and the student. Once this meeting has taken place, the person is not the same. He or she may not act directly or consciously on the wisdom gained, but the potential is there to return and pick up the dialogue and act on it in later years. This encounter can happen more easily after midlife reconciliation when negative father images no longer hold the same power to interfere with meeting the inner guide.

On the outer level a similar process also may happen. As we clear some of the conflict with father, the possibility of our finding teachers and mentors in life increases. Many of us reject the learning and wisdom we might gain from older men and women because we are angry or hurt and continue to seek fatherly comfort or support. A mentor's function is different and more specialized than a father's. The mentor is there to help with some specific area or task in life (like professional mastery, or spiritual development) and may not provide the same emotional or survival needs that a father would give us. As Robert Bly has pointed out, we don't need to move in and live with our mentors. We just need to understand what their special teaching may be for us and get it any way we can.

Establishing an inner relationship with our own unconscious wisdom figures and learning to receive teachings from mentors in our outer lives assist us to prepare for our own eldership roles.

CHAPTER THIRTY–ONE

Joseph H. Pleck

Healing the Wounded Father

Recently, I was stunned to learn that long before he died, my father had two heart attacks that he kept secret from his family, including my mother. They both occurred on business trips. He extended the trips, swore his business friends to secrecy and the secret came out only twenty years after he died. He never faced up to how sick he was. To him, sickness was a sign of weakness, something to be denied.

I lived my first five years during what was probably the time of the greatest security and happiness in my father's life. In his early fifties, he was increasingly successful in his work (the law) and his health was still good. In his office he kept a framed set of photographs of his four children. I am about three, sitting, holding an apple; my oldest brother (now over fifty) is a teen. These photos seem to capture a moment in his life that he wanted to keep; he never updated them.

But things did change. I was about five and he was about fifty-five when he had his first heart attack. Though no one told me what happened, I think I knew something had changed. He stopped picking me up to hug me when he came home from work. Perhaps he felt physically weak, or feared the physical exertion of picking me up would bring on another attack. He had a second heart attack at sixty, again a secret he kept to himself. He developed painful calcifications in his shoulders, and later, a golfball–sized cyst on his neck.

During his last several years, he looked so bad that my mother destroyed all the pictures taken of him then. About a year before he died, when I was a high school freshman, I told a teacher that I knew my father would not live to see me graduate. It must have been terribly apparent, though otherwise never openly acknowledged, how physically sick he was.

In this period, he seemed to feel increasingly embittered by how his health, his family, and the world itself were changing around him. He spent his last years on a case involving highly technical engineering matters which he never really understood, something terribly difficult and frustrating to him. He seemed to work all the time. He became chronically irritable and depressed, undergoing what textbooks call the "personality changes of later life." Perhaps he was having small strokes in his hardened arteries toward the end. Those years, especially when I was an adolescent, were hard for the family.

He also began drinking much more. I clearly remember his telling me when I was about eleven (after the second heart attack) that his doctor had said if he stopped drinking he would live another five years. In my eleven-year-old way, I wanted very much to heal him, especially to stop his drinking, but I couldn't. He in fact died suddenly just four years later, when he was sixty-four and I was fifteen.

Recently I've come to understand more deeply some of the hurts and disappointments of his life. Growing up in a small town, German-Irish Catholic culture in the upper Midwest, he went to Chicago and became a partner in a major Chicago law firm in the 1920s. In any organization, before there is the first black, the first woman, the first Jew, there is always the first Catholic. In most of the things he was involved with, that is who he was. It was not easy.

My father worked in his own father's ice cream business until he was eighteen and went to college. I remember him talking about his own father once, describing him as "a good man, but he was a Prussian, he was strict. It wasn't that he refused to give me a vacation from making ice cream every day of my life, it just never occurred to him." His voice expressed not so much resentment as an almost unbearable sadness. He left his family with a strong desire to succeed.

I've also learned more about the losses he had in his family. He had a beloved older brother who died before World War I, of some infection that today would be cured by a dollar's worth of antibiotics. My father had in fact had a premonitory dream, completely accurate in all details, of his family receiving the telegram notifying them of his brother's death. I remember him weeping, nearly five decades later, while reading aloud the poem at the end of Thomas Merton's *The Seven-Storey Mountain* in which Merton says good-bye to his own brother who had died young. Several of his younger siblings died of scarlet fever or rheumatic fever in infancy. My father, as a teen, was usually the one sent to get the doctor, to get the priest, as they died. His mother never really recovered, and he was the one who had to comfort her.

Once when I was about ten, I became very sick, vomiting uncontrollably all night and running a high fever. The next morning he told me he was certain that I was going to die during the night. During acupuncture, I reexperienced this incident, and recognized how concrete this fear must have been for him. He was fatalistically convinced that I, his youngest child, and the one named after him, would die just as his siblings had. The realization of how deeply he must have feared losing me made me weep. Perhaps his fear of losing me (and mine of losing him) was what the tension during my adolescence and the last years was really about.

He was greatly interested in literature and music, and when he was young had aspired to be a college professor. But he felt he couldn't support a family that way. Of his daily ride on the commuter train, he said, "If everyone else is reading a newspaper, you do not read a book." (This was the 1950s.) I remember him spending several years reading *War and Peace,* a few pages a day, secretly.

He and I felt closest around music. He played the piano a bit, and I took after him. My involvement seemed to express a repressed part in himself. When I showed some talent, he wanted to take me to an audition for professional study at a local conservatory. He especially liked to walk around in the backyard in the summer listening to the sounds of my piano practicing coming through the back windows. This seemed to be a way I could give him something he needed.

I am struck by how many men and women describe fathers who are psychologically wounded, often physically disabled. At a cultural level, too, the wounded father is one of the great themes. Think especially of Arthur Miller's *Death of a Salesman.* Feminism, too, has made us aware, not always with sufficient compassion, of the sexism and homophobia which have crippled so many of our fathers. Are these tragic defects part of our fathers' wounded legacy to us?

We all know the mythic pattern in which the father is supposed to do something to bring his children, especially sons, into adulthood. But this relationship takes another form: the child, especially the son, must heal the father's wounds. In one of the central mysteries of the grail myth, the King lies ill, and the kingdom languished, until healed by the virtuous acts of a knight-son who is spiritually pure.

The title of Robert Bly's *New Age* interview asks: "What Do Men Really Want?" At least one answer is clear: the unwounded, healed, whole father. Men—and women—want this not only for what this would mean for their fathers' lives, but also for themselves.

What to do? We have to help heal our fathers' actual wounds, when we can, and to realize honestly when we cannot. We need to heal the so-often destructive and alienated images of masculinity which surround us, the wounded father-images in our culture. And, most important, we have to heal the wounded fathers we carry in our hearts.

CHAPTER THIRTY–TWO

Linda Schierse Leonard

Redeeming the Father

As the protagonist of the play *I Never Sang for My Father* says: "Death ends a life, but it doesn't end a relationship."[1] The relation to the inner father still needs to be transformed. Otherwise the old destructive patterns coming from the impaired relationship will continue. One part of this transformation process entails seeing the destructive patterns and how they have affected one's life. Another aspect entails seeing the value of the father, for if one doesn't relate to the positive side of the father, that aspect of the psyche remains cut off, unintegrated, and potentially destructive to one's life. On the cultural level, redemption of the father also requires seeing both the positive and negative aspects of the father. And it requires changing the cultural ruling principles so that both the feminine and masculine are uniquely valued and equally influential.

Redeeming the father has been for me the central issue of my personal and spiritual development. For the wounded relation to my father disturbed so many important areas in my life—my femininity, my relation to men, play, sexuality, creativity, and a confident way of being in the world. As a therapist, I have seen that finding a new relation to the father is an important issue for any woman with an impaired relation to the father. And culturally, I believe it is an issue for every woman, since the relation to the cultural ruling father needs to be transformed.

In my own life, redeeming the father has been a long process. It started when I went into Jungian analysis. With the help of a kind and supportive woman analyst who provided a warm, protective

container for the emerging energies, I entered into a new realm—
the symbolic world of dreams. There I encountered sides of myself
I never knew existed. I also discovered my father there—the father I
had long ago rejected. There was in myself, I discovered, not only
the personal father I remembered. There were a variety of parental
figures, images of an archetypal Father. This father has more faces
than I ever imagined, and that realization was awesome. It terrified
me and it also gave me hope. My ego-identity, my notions about
who I was, crumbled. There was in me a power stronger than my
consciously acknowledged self. This power rolled over my attempts
to control my life and events around me, as an avalanche changes the
face of a mountain. From then on, my life required that I learn to
relate to this greater power.

In rejecting my father, I had been refusing my power, for the
rejection of my father entailed refusing all of his positive qualities as
well as the negative ones. So, along with the irresponsibility and irrational dimension that I denied, I lost access to my creativity, spontaneity, and feminine feeling. My dreams kept pointing this out.
One dream said that my father was very rich and owned a great pala-
tial Tibetan temple. Another said he was a Spanish king. This con-
tradicted the poor, degraded man I knew as "father." As far as my
own powers went, my dreams showed that I was refusing them too.
In one dream a magic dog gave me the power to make magic opals. I
made the opals and had them in my hand, but then I gave them away
and didn't keep any for myself. In another dream, a meditation
teacher said, "You are beautiful but you don't recognize it." But I
woke up screaming in terror that I didn't want the responsibility.
The irony was that although I criticized and hated my father for
being so irresponsible and letting his potentialities go down the
drain, I was doing the very same thing. I wasn't really valuing myself and what I had to offer. Instead I alternated between the uncon-
fident, fragile pleasing puella and the dutiful, achieving armored
Amazon.

Because of my rejection of my father, my life was split into a
number of unintegrated and conflicting figures, each trying to keep
control. Ultimately this leads to an explosive situation. For a long
time I was unable to accept the death of these individual identities
for the greater unknown unity that could ground my magic—the
mysterious ground of my being, which I later found to be the
source of healing. And so I experienced this powerful ground of my

being in the form of anxiety attacks. Because I would not let go willingly and open up to the greater powers, they overwhelmed me and showed me their threatening face. They struck me suddenly and repeatedly in the core of my being, shocking me out of my clutching hand. Now I knew how little help my defenses really were. Suddenly I was face to face with the void. I wondered if this was what my father had experienced too, and whether his drinking was an attempt to ward this off. Perhaps "the spirits" of alcohol that ruled his being were a substitute for the greater spirits, and perhaps even a defense against them because they were so close. Since I had denied any value to my father after he "drowned" in the irrational Dionysian realm, I needed to learn to value that rejected area by letting go of the need to control. But this required experiencing the negative side, being plunged into the uncontrollable depths where the unknown treasure was hidden. Ultimately, to redeem the father required that I enter the underworld, that I value that rejected area in myself. And that led to honoring the spirits. Jungian analysis led me to this and writing has furthered this process.

Writing has been a way to redeem my father. As a child, I had always wanted to be a writer. Finally taking the risk to put my insights on paper required a lot of assertion and courage. The strength of a written word requires the writer to stand behind it. Writing required me to focus on and commit myself to the relationship with my father. I had really to look at him, to try to understand his side of the story, his aspirations and despair. No longer could I dismiss him from my life as though I could totally escape the past and his influence. Nor could I blame him as the cause of all my troubles. Now, through my writing we were suddenly face to face. Like Orual in *Till We Have Faces,* when I looked in the mirror I saw my father's face. This was incredibly painful because my father had carried the shadow side of my existence, all that was dark, terrifying, and bad. But strangely enough it was a source of light and hope as well, because in all that darkness shone the creative light of the underworld's imaginative powers. And I felt the force of its masculine energy as well. About a year after I started writing and really facing my father, I had the following dream.

> I saw some beautiful poppies, glowing with red, orange, and yellow colors and I wished my mother-analyst were there with me to see them. I went through the field of poppies and crossed a stream. Suddenly I was in the underworld at a banquet table with many men. Red

wine was flowing and I decided to take another glass. As I did, the men raised their wine glasses in salute to my health, and I felt warm and glowing with their affectionate tribute.

The dream marked my initiation into the underworld. I had passed from the bright world of the mother into the realm of the dark father-lover. But there I was saluted as well. This was of course an incestuous situation and yet a necessary one for me. Part of the father's role, according to [Hans] Kohut, is to let himself be idealized by the daughter and then gradually allow her to detect his realistic limitations without withdrawing from her.[2] And of course with the ideal projection goes deep love. In my development the love turned to hate, so that the previous ideals associated with my father were rejected. I had to learn to love my father again so I could reconnect with his positive side. I had to learn to value my father's playful, spontaneous, magic side, but also to see its limits, as well as how the positive aspects could be actualized in my life. Loving the Father-ideal allowed me to love my own ideal and to realize that ideal in myself. This entailed first seeing my father's value and then realizing that that belonged to me. This broke the unconscious incestuous bond and freed me for my own relation to the transcendent powers in my Self.

For wounded daughters who are in poor relation to other sides of the father, the details of the redemption may be different, but the central issue will be the same. To redeem the father requires seeing the hidden value the father has to offer. For example, those daughters who have reacted against a too authoritarian father are likely to have problems accepting their own authority. Such women tend to adapt or react rebelliously. They need to see the value in their own responsibility, in accepting their own power and strength. They need to value limit, go up to it and see the edges, but know when it is too much. They need to know when to say no and when to say yes. This means having realistic ideals and knowing their own limits and the limits of the situation. To put it in Freudian terms, they need to get a positive relation to the "super-ego," the inner voice of valuation and responsible judgment and decision-making. This voice, when it is constructive, is neither too critical and severe nor too indulgent, so that they can see and hear objectively what there is. One woman expressed it this way: "I need to hear the voice of the father inside tell me in a kind way when I'm doing a good job, but also when I'm off the mark." Redemption of this aspect of the father

239

means the transformation of the critical judge, who proclaims one constantly "guilty," and the defense lawyer, who responds with self-justification. Instead will be found a kindly, objective arbiter. It means having one's own sense of inner valuation, rather than looking outside for approval. Instead of falling prey to the cultural collective projections that don't fit, it means knowing who one is and actualizing genuine possibilities. On the cultural level, it means valuing the feminine enough to stand up for it against the collective view of what the feminine is "supposed" to be.

Daughters who have had "too positive" a relation to their father have still another aspect of the father to redeem. If the relation to the father is too positive, the daughters are likely to be bound to the father by overidealizing him and by allowing their own inner father strength to remain projected outward on the father. Quite often their relationships to men are constricted because no man can match the father. In this case they are bound to the father in a similar way to women who are bound to an imaginary "ghostly lover." (Often an idealized relation to the father is built up unconsciously when the father is missing.) The too positive relationship to the father can cut them off from a real relationship to men and quite often from their own professional potentialities. Because the outer father is seen so idealistically, they can't see the value of their own contribution to the world. To redeem the father in themselves, they need to acknowledge his negative side. They need to experience their father as human and not as an idealized figure in order to internalize the father principle in themselves.

In many ways I see the "Beauty and the Beast" fairy tale as telling the story of this kind of redemption. Beauty loved her father so much! Yet in asking for such a simple gift, a rose, which the father had to steal from the beast's garden, Beauty had to go and live with the beast in order to save her father's life. And this was terribly frightening for her. But when she learned to value and love the beast, he was transformed into his original potentiality as Prince, and the father's life was saved.

Ultimately, redeeming the father entails reshaping the masculine within, fathering that side of oneself. Instead of the "perverted old man" and the "angry, rebellious boy," women need to find "the man with heart," the inner man with a good relation to the feminine.

CHAPTER THIRTY-THREE

Samuel Osherson

The Wounded Father Within

The wounded father is the internal sense of masculinity that men carry around with them. It is an inner image of father that we experience as judgmental and angry or, depending on our relationship with father, as needy and vulnerable. When a man says he can't love his children because he wasn't loved well enough, it is the wounded father he is struggling with.

There are three aspects to our image of the wounded father, all linked but separable. The son may remember father as wounded, with father's deep sadness, incompetence or anger dominating his image of the man. He may also remember father as wounding, evoking the loss and needy feelings the son experienced in having been rejected by or disappointing to the father. And thirdly, the son may introject and internalize distorted and idealized images and memories of father as he struggles to synthesize his identity as a man.

What does it mean for sons to heal the wounded father, our internal image of father as wounded or angry, which lies at the core of our own sense of masculinity? Healing the wounded father means "detoxifying" that image so that it is no longer dominated by the resentment, sorrow, and sense of loss or absence that restrict our own identities as men.

There are several avenues by which the process of healing takes place. They include recognizing our fathers' actual wounds, the way they have been wounded by their lives, the complex crosscurrents within our families that led to disconnection, and by exploring and testing out richer, more satisfying male identities as fathers, husbands, and coworkers in our everyday lives.

We are speaking here of a process of grieving. Sadness is involved. Many men have learned to act as if they don't need intimacy, and recontacting their hunger for real intimacy with father can be very uncomfortable. Men learn to drive others away when needy, to act as if they can get along without others. I've been impressed by how many men cry when they come to see what they have not received from their fathers. In trying to understand our fathers, we confront the depths of our neediness and that of our fathers.

Healing a wounded father may not come in actual dialogue with him. There are at times real limits on the degree of rapprochement a man can achieve with his father. Fathers as they age may not see the same importance the son does in "processing things." They may want to feel that everything is "OK," that they can turn things over to the younger, stronger generation—not to open up the past and get into "all that" again.

By the time many men try to work it out with their fathers, having aged into their thirties or forties, they don't get to work it out because the roles are almost reversed; father may be ill, less productive, less energetic. The separation and rapprochement, coming at the end of the father's life cycle, may in such cases be short-circuited. As one forty-year-old man said, ruefully recounting his failed attempt to make peace with the father after a visit home, "age seventy is not the best time for a father to learn new psychological defenses." What's left to many men, then, is to "make it up" to father in some way, to show father that they are a good son, and thus perpetuate the acting-out tradition.[1]

While many men have fathers who are alive and accessible, many do not. A man may not know where his father is, or a parent may have died before there can be reconciliation. The unavailability of fathers when their grown sons search for reunion is likely to become an increasing problem, given the high divorce rate. A recent survey of father-child contact after parental divorce found that by early adolescence 50 percent of the children had no contact with their fathers, while 30 percent had only sporadic contact with him; only 20 percent of the children saw their fathers once a week or more.[2] We may be facing a psychological time bomb within the younger generations of men and women now coming of age.

Healing the wounded father becomes more complex when a father is dead, emotionally inaccessible, or physically unavailable. In such cases one is deprived of the actual emotional healing that comes from reaching common ground with one's father, hearing and seeing a new bond forged between the generations. And the son is deprived too of feeling that he has been able to give to his father, helping to heal his father's emotional wounds.

When a father dies before the son can heal the relationship, the grieving process is likely to continue longer after his death, as the son tries to come to terms with his father and his feelings about him without a sure sense of how to do so. One man told me a year after the sudden death of his father that "a day doesn't go by when I don't think about my father at some point. But my thoughts of him are fleeting, as if I don't want to stay too long with them, like I'm scared to look too closely."

However, it is possible still to engage an absent father in a dialogue of emotional growth. The son may write imaginary dialogues between himself and his father and other family members, or write unmailed letters to a dead or absent father. Such exercises may temper the wounded image of father a man carries in his heart. They allow the son to examine the anger and disappointment in the father-son relationship, often giving way to greater acceptance and understanding. Through imaginary dialogues we can remember the abandonment and betrayal we felt, and it may hurt less; we are no longer prisoners of memories we can't retrieve.

Several men with dead fathers talked of finding letters, journals, or diaries their fathers kept and reading them with a hunger for information about the man's feeling and experiences. Whether the father is available or not, it is important to remember that reconciliation or friendship with father and healing the wounded father are different. It is certainly possible to heal oneself with our reconciliation without reconciliation with father. And it is conversely possible to achieve a surface friendship with father without healing oneself. That is because the essential elements in healing are the internal image of father and the sense of masculinity that the son carries in his heart. The son needs to be able to understand the always poignant reasons why the past was the way it was, thus freeing him from his sense of having been betrayed by father or having been a betrayer of him, and he needs to explore satisfying ways to be male that reflect his own identity. We can recognize that we are our father's son without feeling that we have to accept and love everything about him or all that happened between us.

Ultimately it is the internal image of our fathers that all men must heal. All sons need to heal the wounded fathers within their own hearts, on their own. The process involves exploring not just the past but also the present and the future—ways of being male that reflect a richer, fuller sense of self than the narrow images that dominated the past. In truth that is the task of all men today: to explore the masculine nurturer and caretaker within, to test out and evolve a strong manly sense of oneself as a father, in relation to a wife, children, and peers.

The search to identify what it means to be a male nurturer, to be a father who cares and protects in a fuller, more engaged way than just by imitating a John Wayne tough guy/soldier or a businessman/breadwinner, is the serious quest that underlies the at times seemingly comic male self-exploration of our times. How to be strong and caring? Those are themes that men are struggling with.

Sitting at lunch with a former Harvard administrator who has just turned forty, I hear about his recent week at a men's retreat north of San Francisco. Of all the activities of these days, one incident stands out for him.

"One of the exercises we did was based on those American Indian initiation ceremonies where the brave has to run a gauntlet composed of all the men of the tribe."

The entire group of fifty men lined up in a gauntlet, and each person ran down it, *holding a doll, an infant.*

"The doll was to give us a purpose, we were to shelter it from the blows as we ran."

Enfolding the vulnerable with male strength.

Another image: As I sit at a playground with my son on a pleasant spring Sunday, we are surrounded by other parents and children. It being a weekend, there are many fathers with their kids. Suddenly across the playground I see a familiar scene. An older boy, about seven, goes up to a younger one and punches him on the shoulder. The blow is not particularly savage, and the littler kid seems more shocked than hurt. The older boy seems quite angry and upset; he's clearly working something out. One could easily imagine that boy getting a good spanking from his father. I wonder what I'd do if he comes near *my* boy. As I watch though, the boy's father comes over and gently picks him up. The boy writhes and protests, crying in his father's arms, while the man carries him over to a nearby bench. Despite his son's fighting, the father does this forcefully yet also gently. He sits and rocks the boy in his lap, and then I hear him whispering, almost singing, in his son's ear:

"I'm not going to let you go until you say, 'I am a gentle boy and I do not hit other children.'" As they sit there, the boy sheltered in his arms, the father repeats the refrain: "I am a gentle boy and I do not hit other children." Finally the boy seems soothed, sings along with his father, and runs off to play by himself.

Sheltering with male strength. Is this the old identity or a new one? The underlying wish seems to be to find a way to be a strong male without also being destructive.

Becoming a parent helps. As we have seen, the transition to fatherhood has the potential for creating a vastly changed perspective on one's self and one's father. Yet not all men are parents, and there are other ways to heal the wounded father in our hearts. Creative solutions such as the arts, music, crafts, which allow the exploration of the self, may be very helpful.

One man in a childless marriage, who felt his father left him emotionally at age five, remembered as an adult how much he and his father both loved music. He plays the piano as a hobby today, but recently he realized how much hidden love lay secretly in their shared love of the instrument. "My involvement [in music] seemed to express a repressed part in himself. . . . He especially liked to walk around in the backyard in the summer listening to the sounds of my piano practicing coming through the back windows." This man had completely forgotten for twenty years the pleasure his father took in the son's talent; he spoke now of imagining his father listening happily at the window when he plays the piano, transforming his image of father as a demanding, withdrawn presence into a satisfied, supportive one.

At bottom, healing the wounded father is a process of untangling the myths and fantasies sons learn growing up about self, mother, and father, which we act out every day with bosses, wives, and children. It means constructing a satisfying sense of manhood both from our opportunities in a time of changing sex-roles and by "diving into the wreck" of the past and retrieving a firm, sturdy appreciation of the heroism and failure in our fathers' lives. Wallace Stevens reminds us of "the son who bears upon his back/The father that he loves, and bears him from/The ruins of the past, out of nothing left."[3] Every man needs to identify the good in his father, to feel how we are like them, as well as the ways we are different from them. From that, I believe, comes a fuller, trustworthy sense of masculinity, a way of caring and nurturing, of being strong without being destructive. That way still reflects masculine musculature, our history and our bodies, and our active participation in the future. It is way of sheltering those we love without infantilizing them, of holding them and transmitting the sure, quiet knowledge that men as well as women are lifegiving forces on earth.

CHAPTER THIRTY–FOUR

Bill Cosby

Look Homeward, Sponger

Your reward will be that some day your daughter will come home to you and stay, perhaps at the age of forty-three. More and more children these days are moving back home a decade or two after they have stopped being children because the schools have been making the mistake of teaching Robert Frost, who said, "Home is the place where, when you go there, they have to take you in." Why don't they teach *You Can't Go Home Again* instead?

I recently met a man and woman who had been married for fifty years and they told me a story with enough horror for Brian De-Palma. Their forty-six-year-old son had just moved back in with them, bringing his two kids, one who was twenty-three and one who was twenty-two. All three of them were out of work.

"And that," I told my wife, "is why there is death."

Who wants to be seven hundred years old and look out the window and see your six-hundred-year-old son coming home to live with you? Bringing his two four-hundred-year-old kids.

I have five children and I love them as much as a father possibly could, but I confess that I have an extra bit of appreciation for my nine-year-old.

"Why do you love her so much?" the older kids keep asking me.

And I reply, "Because she's the last one. And I never thought that would occur. If I'm still alive when she leaves at eighteen, my golden age can finally begin."

I find there is almost music to whatever this child does, for, whatever she does, it's the last time I will have to be a witness to that event. She could set the house on fire and I would say, "Well, that's the last time the house will burn down."

She is as bad as the others, this nine-year-old; in fact, she learns faster how to be bad; but I still look at her with that extra bit of appreciation and I also smile a lot because she is the final one.

I sympathize with the older ones for not understanding. They are perplexed because things they did that annoyed me are now adorable when they are done by the nine-year-old. When the older ones took pages from a script I was writing and used them for origami, I was annoyed; but when the last one does it, I feel good all over.

After their last one has grown up, many fathers think that the golden age of solitude has arrived, but it turns out to be fool's gold, for their married children have this habit of getting divorced; and then they drop off the children at your house while they go out and find another spouse.

And sometimes it is not only the children but animals too.

"Dad, I wonder if you could watch our horse while we're away."

"Well, what if your mother and I decide to go someplace?" you say.

"You people are *old*. You don't *go* anywhere."

The only reason we had children was to give them love and wisdom and then freedom. But it's a package deal: the first two have to lead to the third. Freedom—the thing so precious to Thomas Jefferson. He didn't want *his* kids coming back either, especially because he had *six* of them.

In spite of all the scientific knowledge to date, I have to say that the human animal cannot be the most intelligent one on earth because he is the only one who allows his offspring to come back home. Look at anything that gives birth: eventually it will run and hide. After a while, even a mother elephant will run away from its child and hide. And when you consider how hard it is for a mother elephant to hide, you can appreciate the depth of her motivation.

When you and your wife are down to one child and that child is nineteen, when you are in the home stretch of the obstacle course that is leading you to the golden years, *never* buy a bigger house. And if, for reason of insanity, you do buy one, make sure that it's in Samoa or else the children will see it and say, *"Look! They're there!"* Moreover, some of these children have studied biology and know you're going to die, so they express the kind of feeling that is found in the major poets:

"Whoever's in the house when they die, gets it!"

For generations, fathers have been telling sons who are nearing the end of their college days, "Son, your mother and I don't care *what* career you finally decide to pursue because the important thing is that you will be going forth."

The key word here is *forth*. Every time you attend a graduation, you hear a dean or president say, "And so, young men and women, as you go forth . . ."

For years, I had thought that forth meant going out into the world on their own; I had thought that forth meant leaving home. But then I discovered that I was wrong. Every time that they go forth, they come back, so forth must mean home.

My father, however, gave to forth its old traditional meaning. On the day I was graduated from college, he presented me with a Benrus watch and then he said with a smile, "All right, now give me the keys to the house."

"Why, Dad?" I replied.

"Because you are going forth, which is any direction but to this house."

But I got my mother to let me back in.

"He's just a baby," she said.

This baby lived with his parents until he was twenty-four years old. It was a good life: food was free, there was hot and cold running water, and my laundry was done—eventually. It took me a while to have my laundry done because my hamper was the floor of my room. I learned what many young men have learned: if you leave your clothes on the floor of your room long enough, you can wait your mother out. Sooner or later, she will pick them up and wash them for you. The price you pay will merely be her noisy disgust:

"All these stinking, moldy clothes . . . just a disgrace . . . at twenty-four . . . he must think I want to start some kind of *collection* of rotting clothes."

Fathers, however, are a little tougher about such earthy living. My father set my clothes on fire.

"Unfit for man or beast," he said. "Not even fair to the *garbage* men to make 'em handle stuff like that."

After I had been living at home for a while at the age of twenty-four, my mother and father had a meeting about me and they decided to charge me rent. The figure they chose was seven dollars a week; and I considered this figure fair because I was producing forty dollars' worth of laundry.

Once I began paying rent, I had the right to tell my mother that she wasn't doing this laundry well enough for my sartorial style.

"Now look, Mom," I said, "if you want this seven dollars a week, then you've got to improve your work on these collars. If I ever want to *wear* a damp one, I'll tell you."

I really took advantage of those people; but if you can't take advantage of your mother and father, then what do you have them for?

I have known parents who are even harder on adult child boarders than mine were, parents who charge their children as much as eleven or twelve dollars a week. Sometimes this money has to come from the adult child's allowance, thus creating the financial version of a balanced aquarium.

"I'm telling you now, you're gonna pay us rent," the father says. "You're gonna give us twelve dollars a week."

"Don't worry, you can skip the week of your birthday," the mother says.

The best thing about living at home is the way your parents worry about you. Of course, they have *reason* to worry about you. They know you.

Waving Good-Bye
to My Father

My father, folding toward the earth again, plays
his harmonica and waves his white handkerchief
as I drive off over the hills to reclaim my life.

Each time, I am sure it's the last,
but it's been this way now for twenty-five years:
my father waving and playing "Auf Wiedersehen,"
growing thin and blue as a late-summer iris,
while I who have the heart for love but not
the voice for it, disappear into the day, wiping
the salt from my cheeks and thinking of women.
There is no frenzy like the frenzy of his happiness,
and frenzy, I know now, is never happiness:
only the loud, belated cacophony of a lost soul
having its last dance before it sleeps forever.

The truth, which always hurts, hurts now—
I have always wanted another father: *one*
who would sit quietly beneath the moonlight,
and in the clean, quiet emanations of some
essential manhood, speak to me of what,
a kind man myself, I wanted to hear.

But this is not a poem about self-pity:

As I drive off, a deep masculine quiet rises,
of its own accord, from beneath my shoes.
I turn to watch my father's white handkerchief
flutter, like an old Hasid's prayer shawl,
among the dark clouds and the trees. I disappear
into the clean, quiet resonance of my own life.
To live, *dear father,* is to forgive.
And I *forgive.*

MICHAEL BLUMENTHAL

Notes

Chapter 1/Giveans and Robinson

1. D. K. Osborn, *Early Childhood Education in Historical Perspective* (Athens, GA: Education Associates, 1980).

2. T. Parsons and R. F. Bales, *Family Socialization and Interaction Process* (Riverside, NY: Free Press, 1955).

3. J. Nash, "The Father in Contemporary Culture and Current Psychological Literature," *Child Development* (1965), p. 36.

4. D. L. Giveans, "Men in Nuturing Roles," *The Bulletin of NCAEYC* (1978), II, pp. 2, 6.

5. B. Spock, "A Father's Companionship," *Redbook* (October 1974), p. 24.

6. J. Bernard, "The Good Provider Role," *American Psychologist* (1981), p. 36.

7. R. Couchman, "The Fatherhood Revival," *Transition* (June 1982), pp. 11–14.

8. J. H. Pleck and J. Sawyer, *Men and Masculinity* (Englewood Cliffs, NJ: Prentice-Hall, 1974).

9. L. Benson, *Fatherhood: A Sociological Perspective* (New York: Random House, 1968).

10. P. Sexton, "How the American Boy Is Feminized," *Psychology Today* (January 1970), pp. 23–29.

11. R. Sayres, *Fathering: It's Not the Same* (Larkspur, CA: The Nurtury Family School, 1983), p. 11.

12. R. Couchman, "The Fatherhood Revival," p. 12.

13. J. B. Harrison, "Men's Roles and Men's Lives," *Signs, Journals of Women in Culture and Society* (1978), 4(2), pp. 324–36.

14. R. A. Fine, "Research on Fathering: Social Policy and Emergent Perspective," *Journal of Social Issues* (1978), 34(1), pp. 122–35.

15. B. Friedan, "How Men Are Changing," *Redbook* (1980), 155(1), pp. 23, 133–34, 136–37, 139, 140–41.

16. Couvade, the lying-in of the father of a newborn child, is a custom observed in many parts of the world. After the birth of the baby, the father goes to bed and receives all the care that is usually given to the mother. The custom is fairly widespread among South American Indians, certain African tribes, and in parts of Asia. Couvade has been explained as a symbol of the direct physical bond between father and child that makes it necessary for the father to refrain from eating any food or performing any other task that might be injurious to his child.

17. R. Sayres, *Fathering: It's Not the Same*, p. 19.

18. W. Farrell, *The Liberated Man* (New York: Bantam, 1975), p. 124.

19. L. Eichenbaum and S. Orbach, *What Do Women Want: Exploring the Myth of Dependency* (New York: Coward-McCann, 1983), pp. 218–19.

Chapter 3/Stevens

1. C. Waddington, *The Strategy of the Genes: A Discussion of Some Aspects of Theoretical Biology* (London: George Allen & Unwin, 1957), p. 4, para. 744.

2. V. Von der Heydt, "On the Father in Psychotherapy," in *Fathers and Mothers, Five Papers in the Archetypal Background of Family Psychology,* ed. P. Berry (Zurich: Spring Publications, 1973).

Chapter 9/Bly

1. Geoffrey Gorer, *The American People* (New York: W. W. Norton, 1964).

2. Bruno Bettelheim, *Symbolic Wounds* (Glencoe, NY: Free Press, 1954).

3. Alexander Mitscherlich, *Society Without the Father* (London: Tavistock, 1969).

4. D. H. Lawrence, *Apocalypse* (London: Penguin, 1978), p. 21.

5. Marie-Louise von Franz, *Puer Aeternus* (Boston: Sigo Press, 1981).

6. James Hillman, "The Great Mother, Her Son, Her Hero, and the Puer," in *Fathers and Mothers* (Dallas: Spring Publications, 1990).

7. John Layard, "On Psychic Consciousness," in *The Virgin Archetype* (Zurich: Spring Publications, 1972).

Chapter 10/Gustafson

1. Note that Jacob also had to face the consequences of his deception of Esau when, many years later, ten of his sons sold their brother Joseph into slavery—so wounding their father even as he had wounded Isaac.

Chapter 15/Murdock

1. Lynda Schmidt, "How the Father's Daughter Found Her Mother," p. 8.

2. Kathy Mackay, "How Fathers Influence Daughters," pp. 1–2.

3. Ibid.

4. Linda Schierse Leonard, *The Wounded Woman* (Boston: Shambhala, 1982), pp. 113–14.

5. Kathy Mackay, "How Fathers Influence Daughters."

6. Polly Young-Eisendrath and Florence Wiedemann, *Female Authority*, p. 49.

7. Carol Pearson and Katherine Pope, *The Female Hero in American and British Literature* (New York: R. R. Bowker Co., 1981), p. 123.

8. Leonard, *The Wounded Woman*, p. 17.

9. Carol Pearson, *The Hero Within* (San Francisco: Harper & Row, 1986), pp. 125–26.

Chapter 23/Pruett

1. Judith Wallerstein and J. B. Kelly, *Surviving the Breakup: How Children Actually Cope with Divorce* (New York: Basic Books, 1980).

2. E. Mavis Hetherington et al., "The Aftermath of Divorce," in *Mother-Child, Father-Child Relations,* J. H. Stevens and M. Matthews, eds. (Washington, DC: National Association for the Education of Young Children, 1978).

3. Geoffrey Greif, *Single Fathers* (Lexington, MA: Lexington Books, 1985).

4. Hetherington, "The Aftermath of Divorce."

5. A. D'Andrea, "Joint Custody as Related to Paternal Involvement and Paternal Self-Esteem," *Conciliations Courts Review* (1983), 21:2, pp. 41–87.

6. D. Chambers, "Rethinking the Substantive Rules for Custory Disputes in Divorce," *Michigan Law Review* (1984), 83, pp. 477–569.

7. Wallerstein and Kelley, *Surviving the Breakup.*

8. J. Wallerstein and J. B. Kelley, "The Father-Child Relationship: Changes After Divorce," in *Father and Child* (1982).

Chapter 25/Farrell

1. P. Blumstein and P. Schwartz in a lecture given at the department of sociology, University of California at San Diego, May 24, 1984.

2. U.S. Bureau of Census, *Current Population Reports,* ser. P20, no. 389, "Marital Status and Living Arrangements," March 1983, Table 5 (Washington, DC: U.S. Government Printing Office, 1984), p. 32. According to Table 5, 12.7 million children under 18 live with just a mother; 1.2 (or 1.3) million children live with just a father.

Chapter 29/Roth

1. Robert Frost, from interview in George Plimpton (ed.), *Writers at Work* (New York: Viking, 1963).

Chapter 30/Javurek

1. J. Herzog, "On Father Hunger: Father's Role in Modulation of Aggressive Drives and Fantasy," in *Father and Child: Developmental and Clinical Perspectives,* ed. S. Cath et al. (Boston: Little Brown, 1982); S. Osherson, *Finding Our Fathers: The Unfinished Business of Manhood* (New York: Free Press, 1986).

2. S. Hite, *The Hite Report* (New York: Ballantine Books, 1981).

3. S. Hammer, *Passionate Attachments: Fathers and Daughters in America Today* (New York: Rawson Associates, 1982); L. Leonard, *Wounded Woman: Healing the Father-Daughter Relationship* (Boston: Shambhala Publications, 1983); U. Owen, *Fathers: Reflections by Daughters* (New York: Pantheon Press, 1985).

4. D. Levinson, *The Seasons of a Man's Life* (New York: Alfred Knopf, 1978); M. Stein, *Midlife: A Jungian Perspective* (Dallas: Spring Publications, 1983).

5. For more information on confronting childhood sexual abuse issues, see E. Bass and L. Davis, *The Courage to Heal: A Guide for Women Surviving Childhood Sexual Abuse* (New York: Harper & Row, 1988); and E. Gil, *Outgrowing the Pain: A Book for and about Adults Abused as Children* (Walnut Creek, CA: Launch Press, 1983).

Chapter 32/Leonard

1. R. Anderson, *I Never Sang for My Father* in *The Best Plays of 1967–1968* (New York: Dodd, Mead and Co., 1968), p. 281.

2. H. Kohut, *Analysis of the Self* (New York: International University Press, 1971), p. 66.

Chapter 33/Osherson

1. This is not an exclusive problem of sons, of course. A woman in her mid-thirties related how robbed she felt when trying to work things out with a father who was no longer the same person she had fought so bitterly with as an adolescent. "At age twenty-three I went home to do battle with my father and I won. He flipped just like that, a beaten man. . . . What a weird win/lose situation." Her words remind us that many women also grow up with a wounded image of father, feeling abandoned or rejected by the father in whom their sense of masculinity is rooted. Linda Schierse Leonard explores the "father-daughter wound" in her book *The Wounded Woman* and notes how often career and intimacy problems of adult women are linked to a damaged relationship with their fathers, resulting from the father's idealized place in the family. Leonard sees a central task of a woman's adult development to be one of redeeming the internal image of her father: "to understand her father's failed promise and how his fatherhood affected her life." See L. Leonard, *The Wounded Woman* (Boulder, CO: Shambhala, 1983), p. xix.

In my clinical practice, I often encounter women whose self-esteem is crippled by a feeling of emotional rejection or betrayal by their fathers. Often the great rage of such women at men is rooted in the narcissistic wound they have suffered in a household that secretly worshipped father, while mother—their crucial figure for identification—seemed emotionally "dead." What contrasts to the father-son relationship is that often the daughter will retain some avenue for communication and reconciliation with father, which the son is denied by virtue of the male tendency to strive for a false appearance of separation and "independence." Without denying the pain many daughters feel, we can acknowledge that the competitiveness and intensity of the same-sex bond between father and son may add a special complexity to men's task of healing the wounded father.

2. F. F. Furstenberg, J. L. Peterson, C. Nord, and N. Zill, "Life Course of Children of Divorce: Marital Disruption in Parental Contact," *American Sociological Review* (1983), 48, pp. 656–68.

3. W. Stevens, "Recitation After Dinner," in *Opus Posthumous: Poems, Plays, Prose,* S. F. Morse, ed. (New York: Vintage, 1982), p. 87.

Permissions and Copyrights

Chapter 10 is an excerpt from an article by Fred Gustafson in *Betwixt & Between: Patterns of Masculine and Feminine Initiation,* edited by Louise Madi et al. Permission to reprint and copyright © 1987 by Open Court Publishing Company.

Chapter 11 appeared in *A Blue Fire: Selected Writings by James Hillman* (Harper & Row). All rights reserved. Used by permission of James Hillman.

Chapter 12 is an excerpt from "Discovery of a Father" in *Sherwood Anderson's Memoirs.* Copyright © 1939 by The Reader's Digest. Copyright renewed 1966 by Eleanor Copenhaver Anderson. Reprinted by permission of Harold Ober Associates Inc.

Chapter 13 is excerpted from an article that first appeared in an expanded version in *The Sun,* 107 North Roberson Street, Chapel Hill, NC 27516. Copyright © Stephen T. Butterfield. Reprinted by permission of the author.

Chapter 14 is an excerpt from *The Only Dance There Is* by Ram Dass. Copyright © 1970, 1971, 1973 by Transpersonal Institute. Reprinted by permission of Doubleday, a division of Bantam Doubleday Dell Publishing Group, Inc.

Chapter 15 is an excerpt from *The Heroine's Journey.* Copyright © 1990 by Maureen Murdock. Reprinted by permission of Shambhala Publications and the author.

Chapter 16 consists of excerpts from an article by Betty Carter that appeared in *Networker,* which was based on a chapter that subsequently appeared in *The Invisible Web: Gender Patterns in Family Relationships,* published by Guilford Press, 1988. Reprinted by permission of the author.

Chapter 17 is an excerpt from *The Ravaged Bridegroom: Masculinity in Women* by Marion Woodman (Studies in Jungian Psychology by Jungian analysts, no. 41), Inner City Books, Toronto, Canada, 1990.

Chapter 18 is an original article by Connie Zweig. Copyright © by Connie Zweig. Used by permission of the author.

Chapter 19 is an article by Rosalind Warren that first appeared in *A Father's Daughter: Stories by Women,* edited by Irene Zahava. Reprinted by permission of Rosalind Warren.

Chapter 20 consists of an article by Andrew Samuels that appeared in *Psychological Perspectives.* Reprinted by permission from *Psychological Perspectives,* vol. 21 © 1989 by the C. G. Jung Institute of Los Angeles, CA 90064 (10349 W. Pico Blvd., Los Angeles, CA 90064).

Chapter 21 is an original article by Tom Pinkson. Copyright © by Dr. Tom Pinkson. Used by permission of the author.

Chapter 22 is excerpted from an article that originally appeared in *Psychology Today.* Copyright © by Jerrold Lee Shapiro. Reprinted by permission of the author.

Chapter 23 is from *The Nurturing Family.* Copyright © 1987 by Kyle D. Pruett. Reprinted by permission of Warner Books/New York.

Chapter 24 consists of an article by Kip Eastman that appeared in *The Fathers' Book: Shared Experiences,* edited by Carol Kort and Ronnie Friedland. Copyright © 1986 and reprinted by permission of G. K. Hall & Co., Boston.

Contributors

SHERWOOD ANDERSON (1876–1941) was an American poet and short-story writer. His most popular books are *Winesburg, Ohio; A Story Teller's Story;* and *Tar: A Midwest Childhood.*

KAREN HILL ANTON, mother of four, has lived in Japan for the last sixteen years. She writes regular columns for *The Japan Times* Japanese-language newspaper and is a regular contributor to magazines in Japan and the United States. She has recently completed her first novel, based on her teenage years in New York City, her family's life in a Japanese village, and her father's murder at the age of eighty.

MICHAEL BLUMENTHAL, poet born in 1949, is the director of creative writing at Harvard University. He is author of four published volumes of poetry, the most recent of which is *Against Romance.* He has recently completed a new manuscript of poems entitled *The Wages of Goodness* and a novel entitled *Weinstock Among the Dying.*

ROBERTY BLY, an acclaimed poet and translator from Minnesota, is currently writing about men's mythology and is leading workshops for men. His recent book *Iron John* is a national bestseller. He has authored many books, including the National Book Award winner for poetry *The Light Around the Body.*

STEPHEN T. BUTTERFIELD is an English professor at Castleton College in Vermont. This writer and poet is author of the book *Amway: The Cult of Free Enterprise.*

BETTY CARTER is the director of the Family Institute of Westchester, a major training institute in family systems therapy. She is codirector of the Woman's Project in Family Therapy, which gives workshops on methods of dealing with women's dilemmas in families. Betty has received the AFTA Award for Distinguished Contribution to Family Therapy and the Hexter Award for outstanding contribution to social work and theory. She coauthored *The Invisible Web: Gender Patterns in Family Relationships* and the widely used textbook *The Changing Family Life Cycle: A Framework for Family Therapy.*

BILL COSBY is a premier comedian, producer, television personality of the highly rated "Cosby Show," and author of the bestseller *Fatherhood.*

RAM DASS (Dr. Richard Alpert) is a former teacher at Stanford University and Harvard University who researched altered states of consciousness through psychedelics and spiritual disciplines of the East. He is author of *Be Here Now, The Only Dance There Is, Grist for the Mill, Journey of Awakening, Miracle of Love,* and *Can I Help?* He is currently involved with humanitarian service through the Seva Foundation and "Reaching Out," a San Francisco Bay Area TV series.

KIP EASTMAN is a teacher and tour manager. He lives with his wife, daughter, and two stepsons in Watsonville, California.

WARREN FARRELL, Ph.D., is a teacher and lecturer on men's liberation. He authored *The Liberated Man* and *Why Men Are the Way They Are*. He has been described as the Gloria Steinem of men's liberation, appearing on network broadcast shows. He teaches at the School of Medicine, the University of California at San Diego.

PERRY GARFINKEL is a widely published journalist who has worked as an editor at the *Boston Globe Sunday Magazine* and *New Age Journal*. His articles on psychology and social trends have appeared in *Psychology Today, New York, National Geographic, Savvy,* and other publications.

DAVID GIVEANS is an educator, writer, and lecturer on early childhood, nonsexist education, men in nurturing roles, and humanism in parenting. Since 1979 he has published the nationally recognized newsletter, *Nurturing News: A Quarterly Forum for Nurturing Men*.

FRED GUSTAFSON is an ordained Lutheran minister. He is a pastoral counselor and Jungian analyst for the Lutheran Social Services of Wisconsin and Upper Michigan.

JAMES HILLMAN is a Jungian analyst, archetypal psychologist, lecturer, and editor of the journal *Spring*. A prolific author, his books include *Suicide and Soul; The Myth of Analysis; Re-Visioning Psychology; The Dream and the Underworld; Loose Ends; Anima: An Anatomy of a Personified Notion; Healing Fiction; A Blue Fire;* and *Puer Papers* (ed.).

ALAN JAVUREK, Ph.D., is a transpersonal psychotherapist with a Jungian orientation, in private practice in the San Francisco Bay Area.

JACK KORNFIELD, Ph.D., is a psychologist, an ordained Theravada Buddhist monk, and teacher of Insight (Vipassana) Meditation. He is the author of *Living Buddhist Masters* and coauthor of *Seeking the Heart of Wisdom*. He is cofounder of Spirit Rock Meditation Center in Woodacre, California.

LINDA SCHIERSE LEONARD holds a Ph.D. in philosophy and is a Jungian analyst with a private practice in San Francisco. She has authored *The Wounded Woman: Healing the Father/Daughter Relationship; On the Way to the Wedding: Transforming the Love Relationship;* and *Witness to the Fire: Creativity and the Veil of Addiction*.

SARA MAITLAND, Oxford educated, is a writer involved in the woman's movement. She has authored *Daughter of Jerusalem, A Map of the New Country,* and a number of short stories.

ANDREW MERTON is the director of the journalism program at the University of New Hampshire. He has written for the *New York Times* and *Esquire* and has researched a book on fathers.

W. S. MERWIN is a poet born in 1927 in New York City. His published works include *The Carrier of Ladders; Writings to an Unfinished Accompaniment; The First Four Books of Poems; The Compass Flower;* and *Opening the Hand*.

MAUREEN MURDOCK is a family therapist, education consultant, and writer who lives in Venice, California. She is the author of *Spinning Inward: Using Guided Imagery with Children for Learning, Creativity, and Relaxation,* and *The Heroine's Journey*.

SAMUEL OSHERSON is a Harvard research psychologist and psychotherapist in Cambridge, Massachusetts. He is author of *Holding On or Letting Go: Men and Career Changes at Midlife; Finding Our Fathers: The Unfinished Business of Manhood;* and coauthor of *Social Contexts of Health, Illness and Patient Care.*

LOREN PEDERSEN is a Jungian analyst trained at the C. G. Institute in San Francisco, with a private practice in Walnut Creek, California. He is author of *Dark Hearts: The Unconscious Forces that Shape Men's Lives.*

TOM PINKSON, Ph.D., is clinical consultant to the Center for Attitudinal Healing in Tiburon, California, and is a psychologist in private practice in Mill Valley, California. He is the author of *Quest for Vision* and *Do They Celebrate Christmas in Heaven?,* as well as numerous articles on his work with cancer patients, rites of passage, and death and dying.

JOSEPH PLECK is a research associate at the Wellesley College Center for Research on Women. He was founder of the National Organization for Men Against Sexism and is the author of *Men and Masculinity* and *The Myth of Masculinity.*

KYLE PRUETT is a noted child psychiatrist and a clinical professor of psychiatry at Yale University Child Study Center. He is the author of the celebrated American Health Book award winner *The Nurturing Father.*

DAVID RILEY lives in Washington, D.C., with his wife and three children. He has been the director of the National Campaign to Save the ABM Treaty.

MICHAEL ROBINSON is a counselor, teacher, and an associate editor of *Nurturing News.* His major research interests are men's family roles and men's social networks. He has been the primary caregiver for his two young sons.

GABRIELLE ROTH is an international teacher of shamanic healing. A director and producer of plays, concerts, and tapes, she has worked with her own dance/theater/music company, the Mirrors, and recently taught experimental theater in New York. She authored *Maps to Ecstasy: Teachings of an Ubran Shaman.*

ANDREW SAMUELS is a training analyst for the Society of Analytical Psychology, London. He is a Jungian analyst and author of *The Plural Psyche: Personality, Morality, and the Father,* coauthor of *A Critical Dictionary of Jungian Analysis,* and editor of *The Father: Contemporary Jungian Perspectives and Psychopathology.*

JERROLD LEE SHAPIRO, Ph.D., is an associate professor of counseling psychology at the University of Santa Clara. He is also codirector, with his wife, of the Ohana Family Therapy Institute in San Jose, California.

P. GREGORY SPRINGER is the editor of *Men and Wife Newsletter* for gay men and their wives. He lives with his wife and two young children in Urbana, Illinois.

ANTHONY STEVENS, educated at Oxford, practices psychotherapy and psychiatry in London and Devon, England. He is the author of *Archetypes: A Natural History of the Self* and *The Roots of War: A Jungian Perspective.*

WILLIAM F. VAN WERT, single father of three sons, teaches film and creative writing at Temple University. He has authored two film books and two books of short stories, *Tales for Expectant Fathers* and *Missing in Action.*

ROSALIND WARREN is a contributor to *My Father's Daughter* and has published short stories in numerous magazines including *Seventeen* and *Iowa Women*. She edited *Women's Glib: A Collection of Women's Humor* and is working on a sequel called *Women's Glibber.*

MARION WOODMAN is a Jungian analyst who practices in Toronto. Her books include *The Owl Was a Baker's Daughter; Addiction to Perfection; The Pregnant Virgin: A Process of Psychological Transformation; The Still Unravished Bride;* and *The Ravaged Bridegroom: Masculinity in Women.*

CONNIE ZWEIG is freelance writer and executive editor for Jeremy P. Tarcher, Inc. She is editor of the collected volume *To Be a Woman: The Birth of the Conscious Feminine* and coeditor of *Meeting the Shadow: The Hidden Power of the Dark Side of Human Nature.*

ABOUT THE EDITOR

Charles "Sandy" Scull holds a Ph.D. in transpersonal psychology. An author and advocate in the areas of existential and transpersonal healing of post-traumatic stress, he facilitates support groups for fathers and counsels Vietnam veterans and people with AIDS.

He is currently researching a book about the warrior spirit in the world. Scull lives in Northern California with his wife and two children.

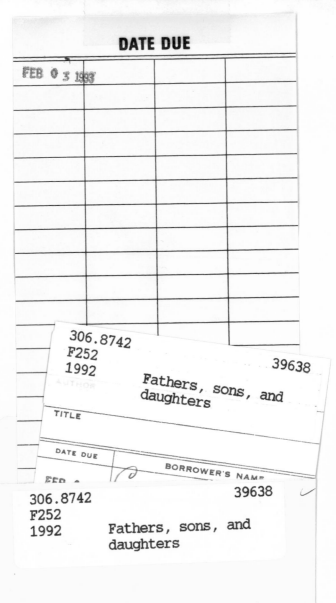